Early
HOMECOMING

Early
HOMECOMING

A Resource for **Early-Returned Missionaries,** their Church Leaders, and Family

KRISTEN REBER

CFI

An imprint of Cedar Fort, Inc.
Springville, Utah

ISBN 13: 978-1-4621-2222-6

Published by CFI, an imprint of Cedar Fort, Inc.
2373 W. 700 S., Springville, UT 84663
Distributed by Cedar Fort, Inc., www.cedarfort.com

LIBRARY OF CONGRESS CATALOGING-IN-PUBLICATION DATA

Names: Reber, Kristen, 1989- author.
Title: Early homecoming : a resource for early-returned missionaries, their
    church leaders, and family / Kristen Reber.
Description: Springville, Utah : CFI, An imprint of Cedar Fort, Inc., [2018]
    | Includes bibliographical references and index.
Identifiers: LCCN 2018025036 (print) | LCCN 2018027662 (ebook) | ISBN
    9781462129256 (epub, pdf, mobi) | ISBN 9781462122226 (perfect bound : alk.
    paper)
Subjects: LCSH: Mormon returned missionaries. | Adjustment
    (Psychology)--Religious aspects--Christianity.
Classification: LCC BX8661 (ebook) | LCC BX8661 .R43 2018 (print) | DDC
    266/.9332--dc23
LC record available at https://lccn.loc.gov/2018025036z

Cover design by Jeff Harvey
Cover design © 2018 Cedar Fort, Inc.
Edited by Justin Greer and Melissa Caldwell
Typeset by Kaitlin Barwick

Printed in the United States of America

10 9 8 7 6 5 4 3 2 1

Printed on acid-free paper

Dedicated to my parents, Jason and Suzie Danner,

for teaching me the gospel and for always
encouraging my writing dreams.

CONTENTS

FOREWORD

By Kristine Doty-Yells, PhD, LCSW

I have been waiting for this book to be written. In fact, I am heaving a sigh of relief. Finally, this topic is hitting the mainstream of Mormon culture! This book validates the phenomenon of returning early from a mission as a legitimate issue that needs and deserves attention.

In 2010, I embarked on what would become the academic passion of my life: studying early-returned missionaries (ERMs). My youngest son had just returned after five months of service, and I struggled to adjust. One would think I would have handled it well because I had been through it before with my oldest son. But I didn't. And to be honest, I would give anything to turn back the clock and get a do-over. A few months later, one of my students at Utah Valley University came to my office and, in the course of our discussion, mentioned that he had returned early from his mission. I asked him some pointed questions about his adjustment experience, and the answers he gave seemed oddly familiar. I had seen similar behavior in my two children. I wondered if this was a "normal" response to an early return. I decided I really wanted to know the answer to this and other questions, so I put together a student research team and we explored the issue. Two years later, I had the answers I was looking for. And my perspective was forever changed. So, I hope, will yours after reading this book.

As I began to present the results of my research publicly, it was apparent many hearts needed to change. The problem had nothing to do with Church doctrine and everything to do with Church culture. I was stunned at the unkind response people had to ERMs. A colleague at the university heard me share the shocking statistic that 72 percent of ERMs had feelings of failure. Her response was sickening: "Your research is flawed, Kris; that percentage should be 100 percent." From that moment, I made it my personal mission to destroy the ugly, negative stigma surrounding an early return.

Since that time, I have conducted four additional studies focusing on ERM issues. I have given numerous presentations and have written several articles on the topic. People started asking me when I was going to write the book. "You need to tell this story!" they said. I pondered the idea, even wrote a few thoughts on the direction such a book could take. But I never felt comfortable actually writing it. I knew the story wasn't mine to tell. It needed to come from someone who had lived it, someone who had actually returned early.

In the fall of 2017, I was waiting for a friend and had a few moments to sit. I mindlessly checked my LinkedIn profile and saw a message from Kristen Reber asking to talk with me about a book she wanted to write on the ERM experience. It was not the first request of this kind. In fact, I have been asked many times to provide research results, statistics, and even an endorsement to a well-meaning author or nonprofit program creator who wanted to help ERMs transition into a successful post-mission life. I admired each of these people; their hearts were in the right place. But most of the efforts never came to fruition.

Moments after reading that message, my phone rang. It was Kristen. "I want to write a book about early-returned missionaries and was hoping I could talk with you about it." We spent a while talking about her ideas, what the message would be, the timeline, and other details. I tried to be blunt and almost discouraging just to give her a "reality check." After all, I had heard this pitch before. But as we talked, she addressed each of my concerns and questions with confidence and clarity. I knew this was it. This was the book that needed to be written, and Kristen was the person to write it.

As she moved through the project, Kristen called me on occasion to get feedback on ideas or ask questions about the research. Honestly, she did not need much help from me. She knew what to do. When she sent me the completed manuscript, I couldn't put it down. It is exactly the book I would want to read if I were an early-returned missionary.

Written with compassion and understanding, it provides beautiful counsel whether you are boarding an airplane to take that long flight home or you have been home for years.

Thank you, Kristen. This book finally tells the story that is long overdue.

INTRODUCTION

My Story

I remember it like it was yesterday: I was home. Home from my mission. I was back in the United States of America, a first-world country, with the comforts I'd known my entire life until twelve weeks earlier. I was again with my family, friends, and ward members who loved me. I had been honorably released but I did not feel so honorable.

I felt guilty, angry, relieved, sad, happy, and depressed all at once. Coming home from a mission early—there is nothing like it. I felt unworthy of the title "returned missionary." My mission had been nothing like I had expected it to be. Nothing. It was the hardest thing that I had ever done—but not in the way that I had expected. Ignoring the physical illness that got me sent home, the trials that I had faced just as a missionary were overwhelming. And because I had to be sent home early, I felt as though I had somehow failed the Lord—as though He could no longer use me as a full-time missionary because I was no longer worthy to be one of them.

How could I have failed the Lord so quickly? Twelve weeks. Only twelve weeks in the field. Ten of those precious days were spent in the hospital. Many more were spent on my bed in the apartment desperately trying to feel better. So much wasted time. Why couldn't I have been stronger?

I remember sitting on my bed the day after I came home and thinking about all that had transpired in the last six months. Every emotion that I mentioned above was coursing through me. My mom found me, and we talked. I told her everything going on in my mind, no matter how angry or sad I sounded. I just didn't care anymore.

"I'm just so angry, Mom," I said. "My trainer and my mission president did not understand me. They made it so hard on me."

"What do you mean?"

"My trainer thought that I was sick and couldn't get better because the Lord could no longer use me."

"That's not true."

"I hope you're right. That's what I keep telling myself, but it's hard to believe." The anger gave way to sadness, and I began to cry. "And my mission president made me make the decision to come home! He wouldn't just send me back! He could see how sick I was and yet he wouldn't send me home! So many missionaries get sick there, so maybe he just didn't want to have another missionary that went home early on his record, but whatever the reason, it was cruel!" I knew he must have had his reasons for having me make the decision; I believed he had been called by God to be my mission president, so he must be a good man, but at the same time, I couldn't help but wonder if it was human weakness that caused him to make me make the horrible decision, instead of relieving me of that burden and subsequent guilt by making it for me.

"I didn't want to go home!" I continued, "But I had to! And I had to make the decision!" The tears came back. My poor mom just did her best to comfort me with hugs and words of affirmation. It helped, but only temporarily. I had my own inner battle to fight now.

Serving a mission hadn't been an easy decision. Thoughts to serve a mission didn't even enter my mind until one day when I was twenty years old and I took a walk trying to clear my head. I felt weighed down by some events that had taken place in the last year. As I walked and thought about the past, a calm, quiet voice entered my mind, and I felt more than heard, "You should not worry about the past. You should think about the future." In an instant I went from feeling sad and anxious to happy and full of energy. I began to think about school and my goals for writing, when just as quickly, the Spirit whispered, "You should think about serving a mission."

A mission? I was taken aback by the thought. I had never thought about serving a mission before. Having been raised in the Church, I knew it was an option, but I'd never given that option much, if any, thought. But now I did, and as I thought about it, I felt a little excited.

I've always loved a good adventure. I also began to feel a desire to serve, to teach others the gospel that I loved so very much. I told the Spirit I'd think about it. It wasn't lost on me what a huge commitment and life change a mission was, and I wanted time to make the decision.

It took me six months to make the decision to serve. And sadly, for most of those six months I felt anxious about the decision rather than calm. I wanted to make the right choice. As I prayed about the decision and talked with others, I really felt like I'd be fine either way. That the Lord did not *expect* me to serve a mission, but rather that it was an option. But why that strong, clear prompting when I went on the walk? Perhaps I just needed to consider all my options. Or maybe I really did need to go? Ugh! I was so stressed out.

I received a blessing at one point that told me the Lord would be pleased no matter what I chose. The decision really was mine. The turning point came when I confided in a roommate that I felt some fear and anxiety about serving a mission. She told me that she had felt some fear before she decided to serve, and even afterward too, but she went ahead with her decision because she knew that the Spirit did not work through doubts or fears. I felt the truth of what she was saying. After our chat, I went to my room and read a letter from a friend serving a mission. For whatever reason, in that letter he encouraged me to read Joshua 1:9. I opened my scriptures and read, "Be strong and of a good courage; be not afraid, neither be thou dismayed: for the Lord thy God is with thee whithersoever thou goest." I felt the Spirit speak to me that I *could* serve a mission; that all would be well. Again, the Lord would be pleased either way, but that if I wanted to serve, I could do so without fear.

I made the decision to serve and didn't look back. When my call arrived and I read that I was going to the Philippines Iloilo Mission, I was ecstatic! I was so excited to teach the gospel! And, admittedly, I was excited to go to a new country and to learn a new language.

A few months later I entered the Provo Missionary Training Center and spent eight weeks there soaking up the Spirit and the Tagalog language. I loved the MTC. I made lifelong friends there. It was wonderful.

I broke my wrist about two weeks before it was time to head to the Philippines and had to stay an extra four weeks. I was frustrated, but I ended up making more friends as a result. I also learned some powerful life lessons that helped me understand others and empathize with those who feel marginalized. I wasn't mistreated for staying longer or anything, but my experiences during this time helped me find empathy for the marginalized.

Anyways, eventually I arrived at my mission, alone, off-schedule, and groggy from the long flight, but I was excited! I was ready to teach the gospel to every person! I had been trained and prepared. In fact, I'd received *extra* training with those four additional weeks in the MTC. I thought I knew what I was getting into. When I arrived in the mission office and saw the sign that read "Welcome—Philippines Iloilo Mission" it hit me how real this was—no turning back now. I felt a little nervous, but I knew that with the Lord's help I would be able to accomplish the work He had for me there. I also noticed the mission's theme on the sign, "Be Strong and of a Good Courage." I smiled. Surely that was no coincidence.

I met with my mission president in his office, where he welcomed me to the mission.

"What kind of mission do you want to have, Sister Danner?" he asked.

"A good one," I replied, still groggy. It was the best answer that I could come up with in the moment.

"Good. And what do you plan to do to make it a good one?"

"I plan to do everything I can to teach the gospel."

"How do you plan to do that?"

"By speaking with everyone! Absolutely everyone."

"Good."

He bore his testimony to me of the truthfulness of missionary work and had me commit to doing the best I could as a missionary, not only to him, but to the Lord and to myself. I happily made the commitment.

I met my trainer the next day and began my work as a missionary. It was exhausting and rather overwhelming, but I loved it all the same and I knew that with time the exhaustion would go away and I wouldn't be so overwhelmed. I worked hard and my trainer and I got along well.

About two weeks later I began to feel "off." I was moody, anxious, fatigued—very much not myself. I couldn't figure out what was wrong with me. I figured it was culture shock. But as symptoms got worse, it became obvious that I was physically ill. My trainer became anxious for me, then impatient, then worried, and then impatient again. It was understandable why my trainer became impatient: I didn't have any obvious outward symptoms—just claims of abdominal pain, nausea, and fatigue. I was also so irritable. She believed that the pain was real but also probably thought I was just having a hard time adjusting to missionary life in a new climate and culture, which is what I thought too, and that I just needed to toughen up. I tried hard to keep working, but it was difficult and my mood and physical pains negatively impacted the work.

Seven weeks later, we discovered that I had two life-threatening parasites in my intestines: *Entamoeba histolytica* and *Entamoeba coli* (which is different from the more commonly known *Escherichia coli*). The doctors gave me powerful medication to kill the parasites, and it worked, but *Entamoeba histolytica* means "tissue dissolver" and that parasite had wreaked havoc on my intestines for nine weeks. I still had a long road of recovery ahead of me. I tried returning to the work after my hospital stay, but it was soon obvious to my trainer (and me) that I could not do the work.

We went to the mission home where my mission president wanted me to rest for a couple of days. In hindsight, seven years later, with all the emotions of my early homecoming resolved, I can see how my mission president mulled over every option to get me to stay. In fact, he decided to emergency transfer me to the area of the mission home so that he would be nearby if I needed him or his wife. I was actually the one who received the prompting that I needed to go home. He acknowledged and respected the prompting and made preparations for me. At the time, I was so shocked that *I* was going home early. I had the perception at the time that only *bad* missionaries go home early, and I couldn't believe that I had actually made the decision to go home, which I thought was even worse than being *sent* home. I felt like I had given up and failed the Lord. I wished my mission president had just made the decision for me so that I didn't have to feel so guilty. At least I could have said, "Well, I had no choice. He made the decision for me." But, no. I had made the choice and I had to own it, and I didn't want to.

Today, I see things differently and am grateful that my mission president tried so hard to let me stay, and grateful too that he let me receive my own revelation that I did need to go home. I likely would have been bitter at him for *sending* me home, especially with the way things turned out (which I'll get to shortly). When the choice was made though, I was upset about the situation and mad about being someone who had to go home early. My emotions were understandable, but my anger was misplaced. In fact, it was rather unwarranted, but I didn't understand that at the time.

Returning to my story, I looked so different on the way home than I had on the way to my mission. On my way to the Philippines, I'd felt perky and happy, and I looked it. When I looked in mirrors on the way home, I didn't recognize myself. The girl staring back at me looked exhausted, defeated, ashamed, and rather sickly. She even looked, if I'm being honest, a little relieved. But, there was no pep her step. She looked like she could use a good night's sleep.

When I arrived at the airport, I was greeted by a great group of family and friends. They held up signs welcoming me home and my mom gave me a big hug. How grateful I am that they were sensitive enough to put aside any judgment of my reason for coming home early and give me a traditional homecoming welcome.

As I hugged my family and friends, it was clear that they were happy to see me, but that they were also concerned. It was a welcome home, but at the same time, a temporary one. My family and friends were so relieved to have me back in the United States where I could receive first-world health care, but they also assumed I'd be heading back out to the field. One of my friends said, "Welcome back—for now," with a twinkle in her eye, and I said, "Yes, for now," but in my heart I already knew that I wasn't going to go back. The option was there once I returned to full health, but I'd never fully adjusted to missionary life or the culture of the Philippines. The last three months had been the hardest of my life. My illness had also heavily tainted my view of missionary work as impossibly hard. I had had enough.

Physically, I healed quickly despite the projected long road of recovery. About four days of some solid rest did wonders for me. Mentally, I was in a world of hurt.

The mental battle a missionary faces when coming home early is easily the worst battle. Coming home from a mission early—there is nothing like it. Terribly unfair thoughts plagued me (for years) about how I was an unsuccessful missionary. I thought about how the Lord had no longer been able to use me. I convinced myself that I'd been unworthy to be a missionary. Why else would He have not miraculously healed me?

I chose to stay home because I was afraid to return to my mission. Again, I never fully adjusted to missionary life or the culture I had been called to serve in, and this lack of adjustment combined with my physical illness, and the subsequent toll on my mental health made missionary work seem extremely difficult and undesirable to me, even if I were reassigned somewhere in the United States. I talk about my decision more in chapter 1.

The Creation of *Early Homecoming*

During the first several months after my early return, I wished desperately for a book by someone who had gone through an early homecoming experience before and come out okay and who could guide me through the healing process. There was no such book though. In 2013, I wrote a book called *My Six-Month Mission*. It was a memoir and I gave a lot of details about the six months that I served. The purpose of it was to let other early-returned missionaries know that they weren't alone. It was also meant to help others know that those who come home early are not *bad* (I still had the perception that most people thought that way). However, it was rejected by the publisher. In a way, I was glad. I was not ready to be known as "the girl who came home early."

The desire to do something stayed, however, and with a professor's encouragement I created a website called earlyhomecoming.com as a resource for early-returned missionaries. But, anxiety caused me to take it down after a year. After that, I moved on with my life. I tried to forget about my mission. I continued my schooling at Brigham Young

University, married a wonderful man that I met while living in Provo, and eventually moved to Washington state where I became a mother. I stayed as involved as I could with publishing and wrote articles for the *Ensign* occasionally. Life was going well.

Every now and then I reflected back on my mission, and finally made peace with it in my mind. It happened. It was a learning experience. When people asked if I'd served a mission, I replied, "Yes, in the Philippines." "Oh, I know someone who served in the Philippines!" and then the dreaded question, "When did you serve?" Sometimes I deflected the question by answering "2010 to 2011." Sometimes I said, "October 2010 to April 2011. I served for six months. I came home early due to some parasites." I never knew why I gave those details, but something in me told me to and I obeyed.

To my surprise, most people were actually pretty kind. Because of cultural notions that returning home early is wrong, and my own shame about returning early, I expected people to feel the same way and be unkind. However, they would usually say something like, "I know someone who came home early due to physical illness" or "That must have been rough. What kind of parasites?" In 2016 I guess I no longer had a pained look on my face, because I began receiving responses like: "Hey, my sister just came home early and she's having a hard time. Maybe you could talk to her? I'll tell her I know someone who came home early and who is doing well now." Those were always my favorites. I slowly began to realize that my experience with coming home early didn't need to be something I hid, but rather something I needed to share.

Thoughts of a book for early-returned missionaries had always been on my mind. Whenever I visited Deseret Book, I always checked the missionary section to see if a book for early-returned missionaries had been written yet. I always hoped it hadn't been. For whatever reason, I wanted to write it, but could never bring myself to dust off *My Six-Month Mission* and re-work it.

In September 2017 I got a job with LDS Publishing and Media Association as the operations manager. During a networking lunch at their 2017 annual conference, I met the acquisitions director, Lorraine Gaufin, from Cedar Fort Publishing and Media. The thoughts about a book for early-returned missionaries had increased in intensity the last several months (I'd even describe them as promptings) and were particularly strong as I talked to Lorraine. Unable to ignore the thoughts, I asked her if Cedar Fort would be interested in a resource book for missionaries who come home early. I couldn't believe I said "resource book." I didn't know that I wanted to write that. But the thoughts came into my head so fast and I just spilled them out to her.

I knew it had to be different than *My Six-Month Mission*. It had to be more than about me and my experience. The chapters began to form in my mind and I knew it needed to be for and about those who came home early for *any* reason, not just my reason. It needed scholarly research, which I was aware of Dr. Kristine Doty-Yells spearheading at the University of Utah for the last few years. It needed quotes from General Authorities. It needed to be for early-returned missionaries, but also their Church leaders, family, and even friends. I could sense the great magnitude of what I wanted the book to be, and for the first time, instead of feeling inadequate, I felt like I could do it.

Lorraine asked me a few questions, and I must have given good answers because she said Cedar Fort would be interested and gave me her business card. She told me to call her, but I never needed to make the call because I received a call from a different acquisitions editor (Esther Raty) the following week, and what followed was a whirlwind of activity as I put myself full-force into making *Early Homecoming* happen. Cedar Fort wanted it, and they wanted the manuscript in six months time.

I dove into the research. I interviewed dozens of people: early-returned missionaries, their parents, Church leaders, friends, significant others, and former companions. I even interviewed missionaries who completed the full eighteen months or two years because I wanted to compare the experiences. I read academic articles on psychology and the work that Dr. Kristine Doty-Yells had published. I read newspaper articles and magazine articles on the subject. I even contacted the Church Missionary Department with my questions and they gave me what they could. I wanted to have a thorough understanding of the early homecoming experience.

Writing this book was difficult. At times I felt daunted by the task and overwhelmed at my inadequacy. I prayed before each interview and writing session. I am convinced that nothing except the power of prayer and revelation made this book happen in the timeline that it did. The unfailing encouragement and support of family and friends also helped immensely.

The Purpose of This Book

This book is for anyone who has been affected by an early homecoming for *any* reason. It is for the missionary who returned early from a missionary training center (MTC) as well as the missionary who returned early from the field. It is for those who came home early for health reasons and family troubles, but also for the missionaries that our culture will barely acknowledge as acceptable: those who came home for reasons related to worthiness and personal choice. It is for family, friends, and Church leaders. Really, it is for anyone who seeks to better understand the experience of someone who comes home early.

All names of those I quote have been changed, with the exception of my parents and my husband, James. I changed names not because of any sort of "shame" in returning early, but rather to protect those they speak about, and in case of any unanticipated backlash from sharing their stories. I am indebted to every person who shared his or her story with me. My understanding of coming home early increased dramatically as a result of the many interviews I did, and I am so grateful. I am also indebted to those who reviewed this manuscript in its early stages and provided valuable feedback. This book would not be what it is today without these individuals.

In 2011 all I wanted was to read someone's story—someone who had come home early from their mission, gone through the pain, made it through, and now lived a good life. Here is that book and more. I hope it will be a valuable resource to many readers. I am so glad that I was given the opportunity to write it. I hope it will bless your life. Wherever you are at in the healing or understanding process, this book is for you.

CHAPTER 1

Physical Health

As you read in the Introduction, physical health was the reason I came home early from my mission. When I came home early, I felt like it was my fault—that if only I'd had more faith or been a better missionary somehow, I would not have gotten sick. I considered myself unworthy to be a missionary, because surely if I were worthy to be one, the Lord would have healed me and I would still be on a mission. I beat myself up horribly with thoughts of failure. I struggled to understand and to accept what had happened. I could not believe that I had come home early; I had not wanted this to be how my mission ended.

If you experienced such feelings, or are still experiencing them, you are not alone. Indeed, out of all the interviews I did in preparing to write this book, missionaries who came home early for physical health reasons beat themselves up the most. Interestingly, when I talked to those who came home early for other reasons, they'd say things like, "Well, it's not like I came home early for something legitimate—like a physical health problem!" or "People can't *see* my illness like they can a physical illness; I wish my problem had been a physical illness! People would have been much more accepting of me" or from someone who came home due to worthiness issues: "I can't really speak for the medical side of coming home early, because that's totally different, but . . ." Yet the number one thing I heard from missionaries who came home early because of a physical illness was that they felt like failures. They were also sometimes treated by others close to them as failures.

This feeling of failure is extremely common among those who return home early (for any reason). Dr. Kristine Doty-Yells in her article *Return with Trauma* reported, "Many young men and women who return early perceive their mission experience as a failed effort. They

11

personalize it and often feel ostracized and unfairly judged by other members of the Church."[1] Also, according to Doty-Yells, 34 percent of early releases are due to physical health reasons. Physical health is the second most-common reason for an early return. The most common reason is mental health at 38 percent.[2]

These feelings of failure can last a long time, especially if there is a lack of support upon returning home. Emma, who was treated poorly by friends and her bishop, struggled to tell me about her experience fifteen years after it happened! You will have a chance to read her story later. My friend Tyler was so hard on himself after he came home, and had others be so hard on him, that he left the church for two and a half years. He has since come back, but he still struggles to feel as though he belongs and avoids talking about his mission, which took place eight years ago! (For more of his story, see chapter 6).

I had plenty of support upon returning home, but it took about two years to get to the point where I acknowledged that my mission happened. Before then, I simply wanted to forget about it and behaved as though it had never happened. It took me another two years to openly tell people in conversations that I had come home early due to some physical health problems, and another year to no longer see myself as a failure, and to look back on my mission and early home-coming as amazing learning experiences. Basically, it took five years for me to stop feeling like a failure.

It's interesting how the adversary works, isn't it? Satan will do anything to make us feel as though we are unworthy in the sight of the Lord and our fellowmen, and I think that's why he works so hard on missionaries who come home early for the most obvious and most accepted reason—and on those they interact with. He does everything he can to keep these missionaries from feeling the support and encouragement of others and amplifies every negative comment. The battle becomes less physical and more mental.

Below are common questions that those who return early because of physical health problems wonder about. They are listed here, in no particular order, to demonstrate how Satan induces mental battles in those who return home early. Many of them were my own questions that I pondered for years.

- Why does no one believe that I really am sick? (Yes, even those who return for physical health reasons deal with this question.)
- Why didn't the Lord heal me on my mission?
- Why did I get sick *on my mission*?
- Could I have pushed through it?
- Was it all in my head?
- Should I stay home or go back out?
- What can I expect if I go back to a mission?
- I'm staying home. How do I move forward?
- How do I forgive those who unfairly judged me?

Let's start with the first question:

Why Does No One Believe That I Really Am Sick?

This disbelief usually starts in the mission field. I heard many stories of companions and even mission presidents not being convinced that the illness was real. People cannot always see an illness, and sometimes doctors cannot even confirm the existence of one. Also, it is not unheard of for missionaries to fake illness or injury to skip out on work for a day or two, or even just to complain about the work itself, lending some credence to the idea that a person might be faking. Missionary work is tiring, and unfortunately, possibly based on other experiences, people who doubted you may not have been assuming laziness without cause. It's unfair, I know, but these may be the reasons why some people did not believe you.

Emma knows what it is like to be called "lazy" because of a physical illness. She told me,

> We got up and went jogging every morning. At first I was fine and could keep up but I was getting slower and slower and walking more. This was strange because I thought I would be getting stronger. My companion gave me a bad time and said I was lazy. I kept trying because she wanted to run, but it was torture. We also rode bikes in our area and it was so hard. I finally got to where I could only bike a block and then was done. She didn't want to let me stay home and rest because she felt fine and I didn't look sick, just lazy. It was the hardest thing in the world.

I finally begged to go to the doctor. This entire time I thought that I was sick because we just were working hard and rode bikes. I told the doctor what was wrong and he ran tests. When they came back he said, "You have mononucleosis." He was very worried about me and didn't want me biking anywhere at all. We called the mission office and they gave us a ride home. Everyone thought I was just lazy (including the mission president and his wife).

The solution that everyone came up with was to give me a couple days to sleep and I needed to get back to work. My companion complained that she was bored so they found a new companion for her and I was left at home and those two went out working. It was torture! They came home telling me about the progress of our investigators, but I was not involved. They were shocked that I didn't get out of bed during the day and just slept. They told everyone that I was SO lazy!

I was getting depressed on top of everything and called my mission president's wife in tears asking to call my parents. I talked to my dad and asked to come home. I told him how depressed I was and that everyone thought that I was lazy. He agreed that I should come home. I called the mission president and he didn't want me to leave because people rarely come back. He wanted me to stay in the apartment and sleep for three weeks. I prayed about it and just decided that listening to my companion was horrible and I decided to go home. Since it was almost transfers they had me wait. They had me do all the farewell missionary things but I didn't want to do anything except sleep. They wouldn't let me stay home and sleep. I kept saying I wanted to return but they didn't believe me. Them not believing me was kinda sad. I didn't look sick so everyone thought I was the missionary that was just giving up and lazy. They wouldn't help me with my bags at the airport, even though I was so weak.

When I arrived home, my parents were waiting for me. They didn't believe I was that sick, so they had planned to go back to work after picking me up, but when they saw my yellow skin and how weak I was, my dad at least called his boss and said he wouldn't be in that day. I wanted to go back but recovery took longer than anticipated. I got calls from the Church wondering why I wasn't back in the field. I said I was still tired and sleeping. The man on the phone commented that at this point it was laziness. I told him that I came home with mono, and he said that the paperwork said, "Bronchitis." It took a bit of work to convince him. He called me every few weeks, and I finally told him there was no way I could go back. It was so hard for me. I loved my mission and had planned to go back, but there was just no way.

Eventually, I returned to a singles ward and the bishop refused to shake my hand because I returned home early. That really stung and I felt like such a failure. I later went to a mission reunion, but everyone treated me like I had the plague because I went home early. I visited my mission with my sister to say hi to people, but shortly after that just stopped doing anything that reminded me of or that had to do with my mission. I chose to move on, and have found peace, but to this day it is still difficult to talk about my mission.

Emma was clearly sick but no one believed her except the doctor. She was told she was lazy, made to feel bad because she needed rest, and actually at one point was refused the care she needed ("They wouldn't let me stay home and sleep"). She suffered some pretty traumatic emotional abuse during her mission, and then again afterward. This was largely due to the cultural attitudes of those around her that missionaries who do not work are lazy rather than really sick.

Tyler told this story:

It was about the two-week mark in the field where I thought, "I don't feel good today. I don't want to eat anything. I'm just not hungry." That happened for a couple of days where I didn't eat anything.

I would try to eat and just couldn't. I didn't throw up or anything like that, but I couldn't eat. I figured I'd let this run its course and I'd be okay. I tried to eat small crackers but I couldn't. They hurt my stomach too much. I began losing weight.

A week later and I was still sick, getting weaker every day. We'd walk maybe 1000 yards a day, and I'd just be exhausted. So we'd only go to see one investigator or we'd walk up to the taxi area and go to church. Even at church I felt like I had to lie down. And then we'd get back and I'd go lie down for the rest of the day because I just didn't feel good.

After a week of that, my companion contacted the mission president's wife and she said, "Okay, come down. We'll meet you at this hospital at this time." So we did that. That was a whole different experience. Third-world hospitals are very different than first-world hospitals.

When I got there, the doctor ran all sorts of tests, blood, X-rays, all that kind of stuff. She said, "There's nothing wrong with you. You're totally fine." I'd lost like fifty pounds. However, the mission president's wife was like, "She said there's nothing wrong, so there's nothing wrong." I ended up going back to our apartment for three or four days. I was super depressed and my companion wasn't helping. Since I couldn't go out, he said I was the worst person in the world.

I chose to go home several days later. I couldn't take the pain anymore. When I told my mission president that I needed to go home, he called me a quitter. I was in so much pain! That hurt worse than anything though. I was very upset. When I got back to the United States, the doctors ran some tests and found lots of a certain type of bacteria in my blood. It was very common in the country I was serving in—everyone there apparently grew up with it, so it was not unusual for the bacteria to show up in blood tests in that country. However, I did not grow up with it, and my doctor back in the United States told me that I would have died within a week if I'd stayed on my mission.

Since doctors are often seen as authority figures in every culture, what they say carries more weight than what you say about yourself. There is a tendency in all of us to believe doctors over patients. However, in Tyler's case this tendency would have been deadly, and it is very good that Tyler listened to his body and insisted that he go home. His companion and mission president were wrong, and he told me that their comments affected him and his self-esteem years after his mission was over. Tyler's story is continued in chapter 6.

If you have people around you telling you that you are not really sick, or don't look sick, or need more faith, or are lazy, a quitter, and on and on, look them in the eye and say, "With all due respect, you're wrong" or at least something to that effect. Do not ever be afraid to stand up for yourself. Physical illness is real and if you came home because of it, it's serious (even if you healed quickly after your return—which I will talk about more in a later section). The normal processes of the body, including disease and infection, don't stop just because you are a missionary.

So, please, tell yourself this instead, "I had enough faith and confidence to do what was right and follow God's command to take care of my body. I am not lazy; I wanted to work. I am not a quitter." Even if others do not respect your decision to take care of yourself, remember that God does, and that He is pleased you are taking care of the body that He gave you. While it may be difficult to have to stand up for yourself constantly, please know you are doing the right thing both by standing up for yourself and for taking care of yourself. God will take care of you and He will help others come to understand your situation in time. He works in mysterious ways, but His work is always for our benefit.

Why Didn't the Lord Heal Me on My Mission?

Because He didn't see fit to do so.

Why not? To answer that I would need to know the mind of God. However, the answer is most likely "No" to the following questions:

- Did I not have enough faith?
- Am I an unworthy missionary?
- Could the Lord no longer use me?
- Was I not meant to be a missionary?

These questions are so heavy with judgment. Can you feel the weight of them? Can you feel how they drag you down?

Elder Holland, in a face-to-face preview for early-returned missionaries, said,

> I don't know that in all eternity, every mission was outlined to be two years or, for the young women, eighteen months. That's kind of a modern invention. I'm sure missions in the scriptures were longer. Some of them were undoubtedly shorter. And a lot of missions currently might be shorter—special missions that are arranged for individual people, including senior couples. . . . And because you were honorable and because you did give your very best service to the degree that you could, please, please do not relive this. Do not rehash it. Do not think you're inadequate or a failure, to use your word. Please just consider yourself a returned missionary who served and was faithful and will continue to serve. And you'll continue to be a great Latter-day Saint.[3]

There are instances where missionaries do not have faith or are unworthy to be serving full-time. Perhaps there are even some who ignored promptings to not serve a full-time mission. However, I wish to tread very carefully here, because the focus of this chapter is physical health, not worthiness. God does not ask that we be perfect before He heals us. If you *strived* to be a good missionary, even if you were not a *perfect* missionary (and, really, no one is a perfect missionary—even the sons of Mosiah struggled from time to time; see Alma 26:27), you were worthy to be healed miraculously. If you were striving to be a good missionary, odds are that you did not lack faith either.

We learn in Ether 12:27 that the Lord gives us (or allows us to have) weakness to humble us and to bring us closer to Him. We also learn in the scriptures that at times He does give us weakness to punish us, as He did to Korihor in Alma 30, but we know that even with Korihor, if Korihor had been willing to humble himself and repent, the Lord would have removed that curse from him (Alma 30:55). I also doubt that your illness was a punishment (more on this in the next question). However, have you sufficiently humbled yourself? This is a personal question, but I'm going to go out on a limb here and say that the very fact you are reading this book seeking to understand what happened shows that you are doing everything you can to be humble. Perhaps there is more you can do, such as see more doctors, but if you feel you have done everything you can to be humble and to try to overcome your illness, then are you ready to accept the Lord's plan for your life?

Paul struggled to embrace the Lord's plan for his life. We read in 2 Corinthians 12 that Paul was unhappy with his infirmity and asked the Lord several times to take it away from Him. But as Paul continued to humble himself and submit his will to the Lord's he began to glory in his infirmity—not of himself but of the Lord and in fact to truly be grateful for his infirmity:

> Of myself I will not glory, but in mine infirmities. For though I would desire to glory, I shall not be a fool; for I will say the truth: but now I forbear, lest any man should think of me above that which he seeth me to be, or that he heareth of me. And lest I should be exalted above measure through the abundance of the revelations, there was given to me a thorn in the flesh, the messenger of Satan to buffet me, lest I should be exalted above measure. For this thing I besought the Lord thrice, that it might depart from me. And he said unto me, My grace is sufficient for thee: for my strength is made perfect in weakness. Most gladly therefore will I rather glory in my infirmities, that the power of Christ may rest upon me. Therefore I take pleasure in infirmities, in reproaches, in necessities, in persecutions, in distresses for Christ's sake: for when I am weak, then am I strong. (2 Corinthians 12:5–10)

You weren't healed from your illness for a wise reason. It may not feel wise to you right now—it certainly didn't feel wise to Paul for a while. But as you humble yourself and seek to know God's plan for you and what He would have you learn from this infirmity, you will understand why it happened.

We have in our minds that it is *wrong* to come home early, but that is a cultural notion, not a doctrinal one. The Lord clearly does not see anything wrong with sending a worthy missionary home early to heal. Missions are hard environments physically, and it can be next to impossible to recover from any illness while also meeting the demands of missionary work. You are not lacking faith, unworthy, or useless if you go home early to heal. Instead, it's quite the opposite: you are being faithful, worthy, and useful by following either the promptings you received in your heart, or by listening to your Church leaders, to go home and heal.

But Why Did I Get Sick on My Mission?

More likely than not, you simply got coughed on, ate bad food, drank bad water, touched something gross and then touched your eyes, nose, or mouth—the usual way any of us get sick. But the question seems to go much deeper than that: the question really is, could I have prevented my illness by being a better person or missionary?

Often in life we expect that as we do good things we will be rewarded. In fact, we have God's promise of being blessed for our righteous actions and thoughts (see 2 Nephi 1–5). So, time and again we are confused when we are doing all the right things, yet we are faced with trials that prevent us from continuing our course of doing those right things. And it seems so contradictory to what God would want, right? Why wouldn't He want you to serve a mission? Why wouldn't He want you to teach His gospel? Why would He allow this affliction that prevents you from doing your very best work on *His* behalf to stay?

And those questions lead to you looking negatively inward: He doesn't want me to serve a mission. Why wouldn't He want me? I must not be good enough. There must be something wrong with *me*.

If you let yourself go down that rabbit hole, you will truly begin to believe that there is something wrong with *you* and not just your body. That there is something about you that God does not like and therefore

He did not want you to do His work.
You are a failure.

that is why He let you get sick. He did not want you to do His work. You are a failure.

That line of thinking is not in line at all with God's thinking. You not being enough for God is simply the wrong conclusion. You are enough for Him. Always. (See Isaiah 49:16.) And He recognizes your hard work and sacrifices to do His work for however long you could. Be wary of asking questions in such a nature that you begin to wonder if God is somehow punishing you with your physical illness. Questions such as "Why did the Lord give this to me instead of someone who doesn't want to serve Him?" "Did I do something wrong in the pre-earth life to deserve this?" or "Am I being punished?" are the wrong kinds of questions to ask. They lead to despair and stunted growth. Instead, reframe the questions to "What does the Lord want me to learn from this? How can I grow?"

Again, we learn in Ether 12:27 that he gives us (or allows us to have) weakness to humble us and to bring us closer to Him. We also learn in the scriptures that at times He does give us weakness to punish us, as He did to Korihor in Alma 30. I think the key to understanding what is happening with Korihor and with you is the situation and circumstances. Did you do something wrong (like Korihor) to deserve a physical illness?

When I first became sick, I thought God was punishing me for a prayer I'd said several weeks back about how tired I was and how I wouldn't mind being sick for a day or two just so I could rest. I was thinking a common cold, not two parasites. But, yes, I asked to be sick. And I was certain God gave me the parasites to teach me a lesson.

Toward the end of my last hospital stay, I confided these thoughts to another sister missionary. She said, "Sister Danner, I don't think that prayer is what has caused your illness. I mean, Heavenly Father is kind, loving, and understanding. He is not a witch. I think He understood your heart when you said that prayer. You were tired and frustrated, and even if you may have meant it at the time, I doubt that this illness you are going through is some sort of punishment for your prayer. I doubt it's some sort of punishment at all. Rather, it's probably a trial that you need to pass through, and when it is all said and done, you are going to be even more amazing than you were before."

She is absolutely right. Heavenly Father is not a witch, and He absolutely understood my heart. I didn't want to go home! I was just exhausted and overwhelmed as any new missionary is when they first arrive! Up to that point, serving a mission was the hardest thing I'd ever done in my life. It was wonderful, but it was also *very hard* and the *work* felt non-stop. Even P-Day was exhausting. I just needed a day to relax. I didn't need to get sick. I've since heard several times missionaries who complete the intended amount of time admit to having privately wished for a sick day so that they could take things a little easier. Expressing those desires to Heavenly Father directly in private prayer was really no different. He knows all the thoughts and intents of our heart (see Alma 12:1–8). I'm sure He was instead glad that I felt I could admit something like that to Him.

My illness was not a punishment and yours wasn't either. Instead, it was caused the usual way physical illnesses are caused, and it would be best for your health (physical and mental) if you simply leave it at that. You did not get sick as a punishment. You got sick because you got sick. If you want to be certain, pray and ask if you did anything beyond the usual to cause your illness. If you don't trust your ability to receive personal revelation, talk to someone who is sensitive to the Spirit that you can trust.

Could I Have Pushed through It?

Gordon B. Hinckley once said, "Good physical and mental health is vital. Parents will say, 'If only we can get Johnny on a mission, then the Lord will bless him with health.' It seems to not work out that way. Rather, whatever ailment or physical or mental shortcoming a missionary has when he comes into the field is only aggravated under the stress of the work."[4]

There is the possibility that you could have toughed it out, but if your mission president advised you to go home or you felt prompted to go home, then it was likely the best decision.

Think back to your mission and how demanding it was. How much more would you have suffered if you had stayed on your mission? How much more would your illness have slowed down the work?

Note that I say *your illness*, not *you*. It is likely best that you are home healing.

You are not less of a person or missionary because you could not push through your illness. You are actually quite amazing because instead of letting your illness slow down the work by selfishly staying on a mission to avoid the cultural shame of coming home early, you let the work continue at its needed pace.

Was It All in My Head?

This question is especially asked if the illness went away as soon as the missionary came home, even if doctors confirmed the physical illness. I certainly wondered if it was much worse in my head than it was in actuality, because I felt much better within a few days of being home.

Also, if you had a physical health issue on your mission, it is likely that you also suffered a bit psychologically. Several missionaries I talked to dealt with depression due to stress and anxiety about not being a good enough missionary. Because being a missionary is part of their identity, they feel like less of a person because they cannot meet the expectations associated with who they are as missionaries. And feeling like less of a person causes all kinds of negative emotions, including depression. These negative feelings can even cycle into major depressive disorder (see chapter 2 for more information).

In Dr. Kristine Doty-Yells's article "Return with Trauma," she reports that "of the 34% who were released due to physical reasons, 72% had a comorbid mental health conditions [*sic*]. The physical issues associated with emotional factors were mostly gastrointestinal tract problems, neurological problems (predominantly headaches), and orthopedic problems with no history of trauma. . . . The most common emotional components of the comorbidity were anxiety, depression, and somatoform illnesses."[5] In other words, if you experienced psychological issues at the same time that you experienced physical issues, you are in good company. Figuring out what caused what, however, can be difficult.

Tiffany, for quite some time, did not know if her issues were physical or mental, but she certainly exhibited symptoms of both. Tiffany told me:

I served in the Philippines. My companion was Filipina and we could barely communicate. Within my first week of being out in the field, I started to have panic attacks, which I'd never had before the mission. For the next week, I also vomited up everything I ate or drank.

The following week I forced myself to go out and teach. I hadn't come on a mission to just sit in bed! I was stumbling around and trying to function. Then I got a call from the mission president's wife telling me I had the opportunity to transfer to an area with an American sister. I immediately said yes and started crying. She said, "I'll see you at the mission home in one hour." I packed up all my stuff and went to the mission home.

With my new companion, things were starting to get better health-wise. I was starting to eat again, and I was keeping things down. We were proselytizing, teaching, and going around talking to people.

One day during a meeting, a sister said something that kind of triggered me. She said, "What happens when you get transferred away from your companion, and you're not with her anymore, and you get sent to a new area?"

My companion was my only solid, the only thing giving me comfort. That question set off a really bad panic attack. I knew she was right—someday, I'd be transferred away from my companion, or she'd be transferred from me. I went into the bathroom, started freaking out and bawling.

Then I got pretty insane diarrhea for the next week. Then there was another meeting, and that same sister said a similar thing that set off another panic attack. I started vomiting insanely for the next week. The week that I was vomiting, I couldn't eat anything.

Although I was trying to get out and work, eventually my companion told the mission president's wife at a zone conference that I was vomiting and didn't want to tell her myself. I was like, "I'm fine. It's okay." We chatted, she brought the mission president over, and I told him what was going on. I didn't want to be a needy missionary. He made arrangements for me to rest and get the medication I needed for my anxiety and depression.

A few days later, I flew to Manila and went to the MRC. Things got worse. The vomiting was still occurring in fluxes. My companion wasn't really responding too much to my texts and neither was my mission president. I chose to room alone because I was crying all the time, so I didn't want to room with two other sisters. That was stupid though because I isolated myself. Eventually, I texted my companion and said, "I noticed you're not really responding. Is everything okay?"

Immediately she responded with, "What did the mission president say?" I said I hadn't heard from him. She replied, "Text me when you get a response from him. When he responds, you can text me." I just kind of snapped inside and started crying my eyes out. She was my only solid in the mission. For the first time in my life, I had suicidal thoughts. I sat there contemplating it for a long time.

One of the sisters at the MRC knocked on my door and I told her what was happening. She said I had to tell the doctor what was going on, so I did. I told him that I had to go home because this wasn't going to get better. He told me that that's what he wanted from the beginning, but he wanted it to be my choice. I flew home two days later.

It was nothing but doctors' appointments for the next ten weeks. Apparently, I'd gotten a parasite pretty early on. I lost 22 pounds in just six weeks. The parasite left bad effects on my digestive system. I got diagnosed with gastroparesis, which causes your digestive tract to not function properly, which makes it so your stomach cannot empty, so of course I was vomiting! I took medications to help clear things up, but I'm still dealing with some of the effects of the parasite more than a year later. I went to therapy to try and get help with the mental stuff. It was all kind of new. Like I said, I'd never had issues before.

Reading that story, you probably initially thought that Tiffany's problems were all psychological. I did too. But, as it turns out, she actually did have a physical problem: a parasite. While Tiffany likely would have struggled with anxiety and possibly depression on her mission, at least for the first bit until the culture shock subsided, it was certainly made much worse by her inability to eat. Her physical condition weakened her and her mental condition also weakened as a result. While she certainly may have ended up going home anyway, due to anxiety or depression, the fact that she'd never faced either before makes me think that she would have been able to overcome them much more easily had the physical health issues not been happening at the same time. In Tiffany's case, her physical health issues were not all in her head, but the co-morbid mental health issues did nothing to help her body.

However, Brad's physical illness *was* all in his head. When I interviewed Brad, he told me,

If you asked anyone why I came home it was because I had a knee problem, which I'd had before my mission. But that's not really true.

I actually came home more because of depression. The depression was brought on by all of the expectations my trainer had for me, and the lofty goals that I felt I couldn't achieve. I'd had knee problems before my mission, so I called my mission president and told him that my knee was still bothering me. Which I felt like it was, but it wasn't, like, really hurt. And so, I got a doctor's appointment. The doctor said that I just needed to keep going because there wasn't anything wrong with my knee. He did all the stress tests and what-not and there was nothing wrong with any of the ligaments or anything. But I felt like it was still hurting and the doctor and my mission president asked me if I wanted to get an MRI or if I just wanted to go home. I was like, "Yep, let's just go home. I can go to my doctor at home." And my mission president said, "Yep, that's fine," and he sent me home. However, as soon as I got home, all the knee problems went away. Apparently, it was all in my head, because as soon as I got home everything was fine. Like I could run and my physical therapist thought I was great. And everything was going really well. I was playing ultimate frisbee that week in fact. Physically, I was fine. I'm sure it was the depression that caused all of that.

Clearly, mental health affects physical health (and vice versa). Brad still did the right thing in coming home as his knee problem was likely not going to go away until he removed himself from the stressful environment. However, Brad did eventually return to the field. We will return to his story momentarily.

If you struggled with mental health issues at the same time that you had physical health issues, you are not alone. What caused what may not be clear, but own both issues. I wish I'd owned my anxiety and depression sooner. It would have made the road to recovery quicker— not my physical recovery, mind you, but my recovery from the grief associated with losing my mission (for more on this, see chapter 4). I didn't want to own up to having anxiety or depression because I didn't want anything to be more "wrong" with me. Not owning it only compounded the psychological issues though, and I spent several years working through my feelings about my mission. For more on mental health, please see chapter 2.

Should I Stay Home or Go Back Out?

Sometimes, it is scary to consider returning to the field after a physical illness. If you have admitted to anyone that you are scared to go back out, most likely they respond with something like, "Well, of course you are! I'd be scared of getting that sick again too!" And while you are certainly afraid of dealing with a physical health issue again, there's likely much more at play than fear of a recurrence of an illness.

If you're like most missionaries who come home early for physical health issues, there's a bit of underlying trauma at play. Trauma of the illness, trauma of people turning against you while on your mission, and trauma just from the *mission*. Did that last suggestion stir any feelings in you? Feelings of revulsion perhaps (how could a mission, something so good and wonderful, be traumatic?), but also feelings of truth?

Missions are hard. Getting sick on a mission just makes them that much harder. Tiffany said, "I did want to go back, but I was also kind of scared. Today, I can say my mission was a traumatic experience. I told everyone I wanted to go back, but I don't think I could have."

Tyler said, "When I came home, *everyone* was asking me when I was going to go back out. I couldn't get away from it. My father pressured me the most, in fact. I needed space and time to heal and think about what had just happened, and because I felt so much pressure to say when I was returning to the field, and I was still trying to figure out what had happened to get me sent home, I became very depressed. I couldn't even think about returning. I finally said, 'I am *never* going back out.' And oddly enough, that is when the healing began."

For me, I was scared to go back out. Scared of the illness, certainly, but more than that I was afraid of the mission. I wanted to teach and share the gospel, but I did not want to deal with other missionaries or judgment if I did struggle with a physical illness again, or if I struggled with anxiety. I also really wanted to go back to the Philippines because I thought it would be so cool to go foreign, but I knew I'd likely get sent stateside and I didn't want to do that. I felt like I was willing to put up with the trials of a mission if I could go somewhere cool, but if I was just going to go stateside, then why bother? So there was definitely a lot of pride going on too. (For the record, I no longer think stateside missions are "uncool.")

If you are struggling with a desire to return and finish your mission, but are scared to do so, this feeling is normal. Now the matter turns to whether or not this scared feeling is something you should listen to—whether it's something deep inside you that you need to acknowledge or something from the adversary. And, if it is deep inside you, once you acknowledge it, you need to decide whether it is a fear you can work to overcome.

This decision is a personal decision between you and God. There is no clear-cut, right answer for everyone. Make sure your physical health issues—and any mental health issues that came along for the ride—are fully taken care of before you return. I'll quote Gordon B. Hinckley again: "Whatever ailment or physical or mental shortcoming a missionary has when he comes into the field is only aggravated under the stress of the work."[6]

I made the decision to stay home after a lot of prayer, reading my scriptures, counseling with my priesthood leaders, and attending the temple. I got the answer that either path was fine with the Lord. I called my stake president afterward and told him I wanted to stay home and go back to school. My stake president told me that he felt good about that decision—very good actually. Everything fell into place for me after that, and I never looked back.

Jessica also prayed, read her scriptures, counseled with priesthood leaders, and attended the temple. She got a different answer. She told me,

> It was basically like eight months of living in limbo. When I'd go look at classes at local colleges, I always felt like I'd make these plans to sign up and start school but it'd always fall through. Nothing was working out the way I wanted it to. I couldn't get a job either. I remember distinctly that there was one day that I got so frustrated that I just turned to the Lord and was like "Fine, you do it. Everything I'm planning is just not working out. Everything I plan just gets shoved back in my face." Ultimately that's when things started working out. Then came the day I went to the temple, and there was like a 45-minute wait to do initiatories. I ended up picking up the scriptures and just started flipping through them. I opened up to D&C 62 and read, "Behold and hearken, O ye elders of my church." I read that and I was like, "Okay,

could you be a little less direct?" I knew then that I needed to return. For me, I needed to learn to finish what I'd started.

Again, this decision is personal and individual. You can counsel with others in your decision, but in the end it is yours to make, and it is between you and the Lord. If you feel in your heart that you have made the right decision, move forward with confidence and trust that everything will be okay.

What Can I Expect If I Go Back to a Mission?

Jessica said,

> Every mission has its struggles. It's not meant to be a smooth path or anything like that. But it's serving the Lord—it's that call and that excitement. There are those hardships and days when you want to punch your companion in the face because you got so frustrated, but there are also the days you find that golden investigator or you find that scripture you've been looking for to help someone understand and seeing that understanding come to people as you teach them. I loved it.

For those who are experiencing comorbid mental health issues, Brad told me,

> At first it was awful. All those insecurities came back. That didn't change. It took a lot of work of forgetting my own problems. Serving others helped me a lot. I had to stop worrying about everything that was going on in me and try to do my best for those people around me instead. And that really changed a lot of my own perspective on some stuff. I wasn't there for myself; I wasn't there to fix me. I was there to fix and help other people and then, by doing that I was fixed. It's unfortunate that it took me ten months into my mission to figure that out. But as soon as I did, my whole mentality completely changed. And I was totally happy.

If you return, there's a good chance it'll be hard. In fact, it sounds like that is a guarantee. But it sounds like there is a lot of joy waiting for you too. Just make sure you take care of yourself first, because if your body and mind are not okay, you will suffer again. Just be honest with yourself, and if you feel you can go, and the Lord tells you to go, then go! Have faith. As Gordon B. Hinckley said, "It will all work out. Put your trust in God, and move forward with faith and confidence in the future. The Lord will not forsake us."[7]

I'm Staying Home. How Do I Move Forward?

However, let's say you've decided that the right thing for you to do is to stay home. How do you move forward? Do you just forget everything that happened and move on?

No, don't forget about it. You may not see it now, but someday, you'll be thankful you served a mission. You may even be thankful that you got sick and came home early. Serving a mission gave you a different perspective of the Church, of life, and of the world, and you are a better person for having that experience, no matter how difficult it was. From coming home early, you've gained empathy and understanding for others who go through difficult things, and also for others who feel judged for things outside of their control. You know what it's like to feel different and you know what it's like to crave to be understood. This experience will be for your benefit if you let it be.

As you move forward, you may feel a sense of loss about your mission, both what it was and what you expected it to be and you may need to grieve. This is okay and normal. For more information on grief and how to work through it, see chapter 4.

Remember that your mission, however long or short, is not what defines you as a person. What defines you as a person is the day-to-day choices you make, and you have a wonderful opportunity to show yourself that you can overcome hard things and stay true to the Lord. So, keep going to church, as hard as it may be sometimes. Keep reading your scriptures, praying, attending the temple, going to institute (if available), and contributing to society (by working, going to school, volunteering, etc). Keep doing those things you love to do. Keep sharing the gospel however you know how—in person or online.

All easier said than done, of course. How do you react to criticism for not returning? How do you not shrink away from conversations about missions when, really, you'd like to talk about anything else? How do you continue to feel at peace with your decision?

It's hard. At least, at first it can be hard. There will be those who criticize your decision to not return to your mission, even if it's only with their eyes. Just forgive them; they haven't yet had the experiences in their life that will teach them to not unfairly judge (at least in this particular situation). Say, "Thank you, but I feel at peace with my decision." What more can they say? A lot, sure, but what more can they say that really *matters*? Nothing. Not a thing.

Try not to shrink away from conversations about missions. It's tempting to do, especially when you really would rather talk about anything else. And sometimes, it might be necessary for you to politely walk away and take a break. Don't force yourself into doing something that causes extreme anxiety. A little anxiety is okay though. We all feel anxiety when we're about to take a risk—and talking about your mission *is* a risk: you're about to relive some memories, potentially tough ones, and you're opening yourself up to possible criticism and judgment. But you're also opening yourself up to acceptance and understanding. By talking about your mission, you'll also be able to remember the wonderful parts of it and see what you learned, experienced, and how you grew as a person. You'll come to see your mission as a blessing, rather than as a failing, and you'll gain deeper spiritual understanding of your experience by talking about it with others. Others will likely also appreciate your stories—the good ones and the difficult ones.

Also, don't be afraid of letting people know you came home early. The only way to make this experience less stigmatized is to talk about it openly and honestly, and without bitterness. Also, as appropriate, share why you didn't return. The more you tell people, the more they'll understand, and the less likely they will be to criticize or judge you.

Finally, how do you continue to feel at peace with your decision? Revisit it from time to time. You don't have to go through the whole decision process again. Just think about it, see how you feel, and say a prayer if needed. Perhaps you'll decide to actually go back out (just make sure that's what you *truly* want to do and not just what you feel you *should* do because of guilt). I thought about it off and on as I finished up school, even dreamed at night about returning to my mission, but it never felt quite right. I felt like I *could*, but I never really felt like I should or that it was what I really wanted to do. Recall also the feelings of peace you had about staying home and moving forward with your life.

My stake president said to me the night I called him, "Kristen, you're the kind of girl where if things don't work out the way you want them to six months down the road, you're going to beat yourself up and tell yourself that you should have gone back. That you're being punished or something. And I have to tell you that that is not the case! You will be blessed either way according to the Lord's timing and you have to let yourself move on and not look back."

There were times when life wasn't easy, and I'm grateful for those words from my stake president, because I could have easily said, "Things are tough because I didn't finish my mission. I'm being punished." Instead, I just attributed those tough times to life's challenges.

I didn't do everything I'm advising you to do now: I avoided talking about my mission for *years* and I internalized the criticism. Doing those things made me bitter toward my mission. It wasn't until I *stopped* doing those things, and brushed off criticism (which wasn't much, but it doesn't take much to destroy a person) and started talking openly about my mission *and* coming home early, that I really began to heal and to see my mission as the blessing it was and continues to be today.

How Do I Forgive Those Who Unfairly Judged Me?

It is so easy to tell someone who is hurting, "Turn the other cheek," "Just brush it off," "Just don't let it bother you," or "Forgive them, for they know not what they do." I'm not going to say any of those things.

Forgiving someone can take time. You have been treated unfairly (to put it lightly, in some cases). As human beings, when someone treats us unfairly, we naturally react negatively. And depending on the nature of the unfairness, we can be hurt (which manifests itself as any number of emotions—usually anger, sadness, and confusion). These are *normal* human emotions, and you have every right to feel them. Even if the person who hurt you was called by God to be your leader.

However, while you may have the right to *be* hurt, you don't have the right to *stay* hurt (see D&C 64:10). When we stay hurt, our feelings go beyond anger, sadness, and confusion and turn into bitterness or resentment. Oddly enough, this feels good for a while, especially when other people agree with us about the injustice. But all that feeling of vindication does is harbor resentment and bitterness, and eventually those feelings are all you have and you become miserable. Trust me, I've been there. And it's much harder to move on from that resentment and bitterness than it is to move on from the hurt.

Why is it so hard to forgive? I adore these words from Heidi Priebe, "The problem with choosing forgiveness is that it feels like the ultimate betrayal of ourselves. We don't want the injustices that have been inflicted upon us to go unpunished. And so anger ignites itself like wildfire inside our systems, pumping toxicity into our blood. We know it's destructive, but we can't let it go. . . . We stay angry because we think that anger has the power to change things. To heal wounds, and reverse the wrongs that have shaped our lives in a way we no longer recognize."[8]

When someone hurts us, it is like they owe us a debt. The amount of the debt depends on how large the hurt was. Some hurts only cost one dollar. Like, when someone tells you they'll take two minutes to grab something, even though they know full well it'll take them five. Kind of annoying, but it's not too hard to forgive. Bigger hurts though can cost hundreds, thousands, millions, and even billions of dollars depending on how much we cherished whatever we lost or whatever price we demand for the wound inflicted on us. Forgiveness demands that we absorb the debt. We take the hit, and it hurts. It is *hard* to forgive a large debt. Forgiveness also lets the other person walk away free—they no longer have to repay the debt. Our normal reaction to this is, "No way! I am not going to hurt myself more and I am *not* going to let them get away without at least repaying me *something*!"

Heidi Priebe continues, "Except the truth about anger is that it's nothing more than misguided hope. Hope that whatever came along and broke us will return to fix the damage that was done. . . . We stay angry because we think it has the power to change the past. But it doesn't. And forgiveness simply means that it's too late to go back." People may be able to repay *something*. That's what an apology is for or service (or even jail) is for—these things are a type of payment for crimes. But a full repayment—making it so the hurt never happened—is impossible for the person who hurt us to do.

She continues with, "Choosing forgiveness means turning your focus toward the future. That as unfair as the storm that tore your world apart was, you still have to live inside its city of ruins. And no amount of anger is going to reconstruct that city. You have to do that yourself. Forgiveness means accepting responsibility—not for causing the destruction, but for cleaning it up. It means putting down the pitchfork and deciding that your peace is finally more important than disrupting someone else's. It means asserting that what happened won't define you any longer. Forgiveness isn't a miracle balm or a magic potion that erases the pain of what happened. It's the window you crawl through to move forward. It's every step you make toward the new future, one that you'll build on a foundation of your own strength, and your own capacity to heal. Forgiveness is not a surrender of your power. Forgiveness is the decision that you're finally ready to take it back."[9]

I love the way she explains the why behind our inclination toward anger, resentment, and bitterness, and the way she explains how forgiveness is actually the ultimate protection of ourselves because it brings us peace. However, I disagree with her on one point: that you have to forgive on your own, that you have to clean up and rebuild on your own strength and capacity. While your own effort is required, Jesus Christ, through the enabling power of the Atonement can assist you. He can lift your burdens, and He can even take away your pain. Priebe is right that forgiveness doesn't erase the pain of what happened; the Atonement does that. By relying on the Savior as you seek to forgive, as you seek to begin that process, you will find the strength that you need to be empowered to move forward, heal, and rebuild the foundation of your life.

Also, Christ can repay the debt. In *The Infinite Atonement* by Tad R. Callister, we learn that the Atonement has the ability to "restore all that was lost, both spiritual and physical."[10] I'm not sure how this works, but I have faith that this is true. Therefore, in this life, it may feel as though we are accepting loss and moving on when we forgive, but through Christ we have lost nothing. Forgiveness is an opportunity to grow, not to lose.

One way to begin to move forward is to contact the person who offended you. In fact, Jesus Christ taught that we should first try to be reconciled with our offender (see Matthew 5:22–25). Let the person know that you were offended and explain what happened from your point of view. Even if the person was a Church leader, such as your mission president. In preparing to write this book, one former mission president told me, "When it comes to relationships, I would hope that whoever I may have offended would reach out to me and tell me. I would feel bad. I would want to resolve things with them. And I would hope anyone who has such feelings will reach out to those who harmed them, if for nothing else than their own healing."

In reaching out, be as objective as possible, but do let them know how their actions or words made you feel. Then, if they respond, listen to what they say, and have an open mind. They may get defensive—try to see past that. Resist the temptation to get defensive back. And whether they get defensive or not, acknowledge their side, and either continue the conversation until you reach understanding, or if needed, end the conversation and walk away. Hopefully, you'll come away with a new understanding of the situation and be able to forgive more easily. If nothing else, you at least gave the other person a chance to explain themselves and to help you resolve things. This is fair and good, and even if you don't feel they deserve it, it is the right thing to do.

However, it may not be possible to contact or talk to the other person. In this case, try your best to see things from their point of view. Were they seeing things through the lens of our Mormon culture? Are they from a different cultural background than you? Did they mean to offend you?

If even after all this, you still feel that the person was in the wrong, and remorseless, then you must be ready to walk your journey of forgiveness. Again, forgiveness can take time. But you must not give up and turn to resentment and bitterness because that will just do more damage to you. There's a famous, anonymous quote that goes, "Holding a grudge is like drinking a poison and expecting the other person to die." That other person is going to move on with his or her life. He or she is still a beloved child of God and entitled to blessings. God will take care of any injustice. Don't try to tell God how to take care of it. He knows the heart of the other person way better than you do. He knows what needs to be done. As Elder Richard G. Scott said, "Don't burden your own life with thoughts of retribution. The Lord's mill of justice grinds slowly, but it grinds exceedingly well. In the Lord's economy, no one will escape the consequences of unresolved violation of His laws. In His time and in His way full payment will be required for unrepented evil acts."[11] You need to focus on forgiving and feel that peace and happiness that comes from forgiving. It's a much better way to move forward with life.

That journey will include praying (and Christ has advised you to "pray for those who despitefully use you and persecute you"—see Luke 6:28), reading your scriptures, talking things out with others (maybe even a therapist), and possibly even journaling. Get to know yourself on a deeper level. Get to know why what happened bothered you so much. Get to know your thought patterns and what exactly is holding you back from forgiving and letting go. And then, as you keep moving forward, and keep trying to forgive and let go, one day, the hurt will begin to lessen and you will feel the healing power of the Atonement. Eventually, you will not feel angry at all anymore. You will have peace. It will be an amazing feeling.

Final Thoughts

There is so much peace and hope waiting for you. Coming home early due to a physical illness is *hard*. There is so much more that goes into it than people realize. I am grateful that I have the opportunity to reassure you that everything will be okay as you stay on the gospel path and move forward with your life—whether that includes returning to your mission or not. There is so much peace and happiness ahead. You are going to be just fine.

Notes

1. Kristine J. Doty-Yells, S. Zachary Bullock, Harmony Packer, Russell T. Warner, James Westwood, Thomas Ash, and Heather Hirsch, "Return with Trauma: Understanding the Experiences of Early Returned Missionaries," *Issues in Religion and Psychotherapy*, vol. 37, no. 1 (2015): 34. Available at http://scholarsarchive.byu.edu/irp/vol37/iss1/9.
2. Ibid., 36.

3. Jeffrey R. Holland, "Elder Holland's Counsel for Early Returned Missionaries," LDS Media Library, March 2016, https://www.lds.org/media-library/video/2016-05-012-elder-hollands-counsel-for-early-returned-missionaries.

4. Gordon B. Hinckley, "Mission Preparation Track 20-1," [worldwide leadership training meeting, LDS media library, January 11, 2003], https://www.lds.org/media-library/video/2012-12-1230-mission-preparation-track-20-1-gordon-b-hinckley.

5. Doty-Yells; et. al, "Return with Trauma," 36.

6. Hinckley, "Mission Preparation Track 20-1."

7. Gordon B. Hinckley, "Put Your Trust in God," *Ensign*, Feb. 2006.

8. "Watch This If There's Someone You Can't Forgive," YouTube Video, 1:55, posted by Sarah Snow, published January 31, 2018, https://www.youtube.com/watch?v=hEyuMRbuOcQ.

9. Ibid.

10. Tad R. Callister, *The Infinite Atonement* (Salt Lake City: Deseret Book, 2000), 59.

11. Richard G. Scott, "Peace of Conscience and Peace of Mind," *Ensign*, Nov. 2004.

CHAPTER 2

Mental Health

My heart goes out to any missionary who has come home early for a mental health reason. Your reason for coming home early is not only difficult, but also in many ways scary. It is scary to not know or understand what is going on in your mind, and to be so overwhelmed by it, or so misunderstood, that you decided to go home (or were sent home against your wishes). It is even scarier when you consider the stigma that society has long had against those who have mental illnesses. While this stigma is improving, it is far from gone, and there is still a fear of being misunderstood, or not taken seriously, or accused of coming home solely by choice, because the illness is not seen.

According to research done by Dr. Kristine Doty-Yells in her article "Return with Trauma," returning for mental health is the most common reason for an early return. "38% of early releases were for mental illness diagnoses alone. However, of the 34% who were released due to physical reasons, 72% had a comorbid mental health conditions [*sic*]."[1] A missionary who comes home for a mental illness may hear phrases like, "Everyone struggles from time to time," "Missions are hard. You just need to push through it," "It was just too much? What do you mean? Nothing is too much with the Lord!" Even worse, some reported being called "quitters" or were sent home without the option of therapy simply because the mission president did not know how to handle mental illness (at least, that was the perception of some of the early-returned missionaries I interviewed, right or wrong).

The questions that a missionary who comes home early for mental health reasons has are actually very similar to those posed by a missionary who comes home early for physical health reasons. Therefore, you will notice a bit of overlap in the questions and perhaps a bit of overlap in the answers. However, I believe there is a difference in the experience of those who come home for physical health and those who come home for mental health, which is why I kept the chapters separate.

The questions often posed by those who come home for mental health reasons are:

1. What happened and why?
2. Why did this happen on my mission?
3. Could I have pushed through the mental illness and stayed?
4. Can I get better?
5. Should I stay home or go back out?
6. How do I forgive those who treated me unfairly?

The answers to each of these questions are as complex as they are individual to each person and each mental illness. However, I will do my best to answer them. I encourage you though to go beyond this book to seek to understand your personal mental illness (even if you feel that the illness went away after your mission—more on this momentarily).

In writing this chapter, I do not seek to make you relive what happened, unless that is ultimately for your healing (sometimes we must relive things to make sense of them, but a constant reliving of something without recovery is detrimental to our health—we must eventually move forward). I only seek to help you understand what happened, so that when the inevitable rehashing comes, or tries to come, you can look at your mission and your mental state within it clearly and move forward with hope and faith for the rest of your life.

Also, for the purposes of this chapter, I will focus primarily on depression, even though there is a wide range of mental health disorders that present themselves on a mission, including eating disorders, schizophrenia, sleeping disorders, bipolar disorders, obsessive-compulsive disorder, anxiety, and more. From the missionaries I interviewed, I found that depression was often comorbid with all disorders mentioned, if not the root cause. I also found that several missionaries only suffered from depression. Again, please consider this book a springboard for you to go beyond and better understand your particular mental illness.

What Happened and Why?

"Why is this happening?" is a question you have either asked throughout your life (if the illness occurred before your mission) or just on your mission. If the illness continued to present itself after your mission, you may still be asking, "Why?" And you are absolutely right to ask. In addition to this question, you might also wonder, "Why did I feel so unmotivated, so scared, and so unhappy while trying to do the Lord's work? Why was it so hard?"

There are two types of depressions: clinical and situational. According to the National Alliance on Mental Health, "'Clinical depression' is a term often used to refer to one or more types of serious depressive disorders that may occur with or without the presence of a specific stressor."[2] On the other hand, situational depression (according to Elements Behavioral Health) "is a short-term form of depression that can occur in the aftermath of various traumatic changes in your normal life."[3] In other words, clinical depression is a disorder of the mind and something you may struggle with the rest of your life. Situational depression is short-lived and disappears once you are removed from the stressful situation and heal from the trauma.

The struggle, of course, is figuring out which type of depression you are suffering from, because the symptoms of situational depression look very much like the symptoms of clinical depression:

- Feeling sad or hopeless
- Tearfulness, frequent crying
- Changes in appetite
- Trouble sleeping
- Increased worry and anxiety
- Headaches and stomachaches
- Low energy or fatigue
- Withdrawal from loved ones or social activities previously enjoyed
- Increased absence from work or school
- Trouble concentrating and making decisions[4]

Therefore, let's take a deeper look at both types of depression. These next two sections will contain information in order to help you determine which type of depression you suffered from, with counsel following in the sections after.

Situational Depression

Again, situational depression "is a short-term form of depression that can occur in the aftermath of various traumatic changes in your normal life." Missions are absolutely a "traumatic change in your normal life." There's a new schedule, new daily clothing style, and another person (who you barely know) around you constantly. Furthermore, there are daily interactions and conversations with strangers about something deeply important and personal, all in a potentially new culture, language, and/or country. There are also the unanticipated expectations of conduct that can come from a companion or mission president, as well as the potential to have to deal with disobedience or apathy from those you've been assigned to work with. Psychologist Dr. Gary Taylor said of missions, "it's a high-stress environment within a high-stress world."[5]

This high-stress environment can be a difficult environment for many missionaries to adapt to, especially if they have never before experienced a dramatic change in their lives or a high-stress situation. Dr. Jeffrey Arnett states that young adults (ages 18–25) are in "a new and distinct developmental stage—emerging adulthood."

> Emerging adulthood is distinguished by relative independence from social roles and from normative expectations. Having left the dependency of childhood and adolescence, and having not yet entered the enduring responsibilities that are normative in adulthood, emerging adults often explore a variety of possible life directions in love, work, and world-views. Emerging adulthood is a time when many life directions exist, when little about the future has been decided, and when the scope of independent exploration of life's possibilities is greater for most people than it will be at any other period of the life course.[6]

At ages 18–25 you are just beginning your journey into adulthood, and there are so many possibilities in front of you. These years are often those where you choose the course for the rest of your life. Of course, you can change your course later, but this is when the most options and opportunities to choose are available to you.

The pressure can be intense, but so can the excitement and a range of other emotions that Christian Smith and Patricia Snell list as "'intense identity exploration, instability, a focus on self, feeling in limbo or in transition or in between, and a sense of possibilities, opportunities and unparalleled hope' on one hand, and 'large doses of transience, confusion, anxiety, self-obsession, melodrama, conflict, disappointment, and sometimes emotional devastation' on the other."[7] To put it lightly, there's a lot going on at this time in your life.

Arnett, however, speculated that "due to cultural beliefs, young Latter-day Saints (LDS) might experience a shortened and highly structured period of emerging adulthood. . . . With that caveat young LDS missionaries still seem to fit the category of emerging adults well. They leave dependency behind as they embark on their missions, and while they are given stewardship and leadership roles and responsibilities that are likely designed to help prepare them for future adult roles, they do not yet take on adult responsibilities, such as careers and families."[8]

Therefore, when you embarked on your mission, you, quite possibly for the first time in your life, took on adult responsibilities, at a time in your life when you were just barely figuring out your place in the world. It was natural and normal for you to feel overwhelmed. If you were fortunate enough to grow up active in the Church with the teachings of the gospel in your home, it is likely that you grew up with a lot of structure and direction for your life, and you had a better chance of adapting to the changes of a mission. However, a mission may still have been just as overwhelming and difficult, simply because your *expectations* of a mission were much rosier than the *realities* of a mission. If you were not so fortunate, a mission and its rigid structure may have been that much more overwhelming for you.

Dr. Gary Taylor said that the number one thing that will "ruin" an LDS mission is unrealistic expectations.[9] And unrealistic expectations seemed to be the main culprit for the early-returned missionaries that I interviewed who came home early for mental health issues, particularly those who suffered from situational depression. Dr. Doty-Yells had similar findings from those she interviewed for her study. She said, "A person's mental health may be affected . . . if preparation for a transition is inadequate, if there is discontinuity between the roles, if there is too much change in too little time, or if those transitioning experience culture shock or role shock service—discrepancies between a person's expectations and the realities of their new environments and responsibilities."[10]

Brad and Karla's mental health was affected because of poor transitioning experiences and unmet expectations. Brad told me,

> My trainer's expectations for me were pretty insane. He expected me to be teaching as well as he was his first transfer, which was crazy because he's a native so he can speak the language. He had expectations due to how his training went and thought that my training should be the same as his. That drove me more into depression.

Brad experienced role shock service when his companion expected him to do more than he was capable, and Brad didn't realize that his trainer's expectations were off. He became upset with himself and wondered why he wasn't measuring up to what he needed to be, and this, combined with his trainer's inflexibility caused his mental health to decline.

Karla told me,

> I hoped that it would be like this amazing experience that everybody seems to make it out to be. You hear people talk about their mission like it was the best thing they've ever done. That it was, you know, the best two years and the happiest time of their life. And growing up in Texas, the missionaries that came to my ward were awesome and everybody loved them and they were so happy. And that was just the image I had. That missionaries were super happy, faithful people.

The reality is that missionaries are actually just people. And yes, they can be super happy and faithful, but they also have bad days. Our thoughts don't necessarily automatically become higher or more spiritual once we become missionaries. Instead, those super happy, faithful missionaries were able to overcome their circumstances and find the joy in the work—and it is work! Adding unrealistic expectations to missionary work (such as being happy *all* the time) will contribute heavily to feelings of disappointment, frustration, and even depression.

Dr. Doty-Yells reported that "the challenges and hardships missionaries face may overwhelm their coping resources and exacerbate the turmoil, anxiety, and crises of emerging adulthood. For example, if missionaries realize that their motivations for serving were more extrinsic than intrinsic, if they can't resolve the conflicts between their expectations or ideals and the reality of missionary work, or if they struggle to adjust to the stresses of new roles and responsibilities in the mission field, a propensity for mental illness may be exacerbated and may affect a missionary's ability to function effectively."[11]

As you've read through this section, does any of what I have described or quoted sound familiar? Were you overwhelmed during your mission? Did you struggle to adjust to your new role and responsibilities? Was this the first time you experienced something so overwhelming? If so, you may have suffered from situational depression.

Some speculate that situational depression can lead to clinical depression, but the research on this is still unclear. Regardless, any form of depression ought to be taken seriously and treatment should be sought. Some missionaries will be able to treat this depression on their mission, but others will need to remove themselves from the situation to get the rest and help that they need. There is no shame in coming home early due to situational depression.

Clinical Depression

Clinical depression, or major depressive disorder, "is a term often used to refer to one or more types of serious depressive disorders that may occur with or without the presence of a specific stressor. Generally speaking, the symptoms associated with depressive disorders are more severe in comparison to situational (reactive) symptoms, and they are more likely to be associated with problems functioning with work, school, etc. They can also have an increased risk of suicide."[12] An individual who is experiencing clinical depression will experience five or more of the symptoms below for at least two weeks:

- "Sleep pattern changes, including early morning wakening;
- Marked diminished pleasure in all, or nearly all, activities every day;
- Observable agitation or slowed movements;
- Feelings of worthlessness, self-loathing or self-hatred;
- Excessive feelings of guilt;
- Suicidal ideation;

- Significant weight loss or gain in a month of 5% or more of body weight."[13]

More internal changes are happening within someone who has clinical depression than with someone who has situational depression. There is not just trouble sleeping, but rather sleep pattern *changes*. There is not just a retreat from previously enjoyed activities, but *marked diminished pleasure* in *all*, or nearly all, activities every day.

Furthermore, it is unlikely that clinical depression would leave you after you come home early. It is normal to feel shame, embarrassment, guilt, or failure upon returning home early from a mission, but if you feel that your symptoms go beyond the usual negative feelings and that you are in fact experiencing any symptoms of clinical depression, I urge you to seek professional help. What is happening in your mind is so serious that Elder Jeffrey R. Holland called it "an affliction so severe that it significantly restricts a person's ability to function fully, a crater in the mind so deep that no one can responsibly suggest it would surely go away if those victims would just square their shoulders and think more positively—though I am a vigorous advocate of square shoulders and positive thinking! No, this dark night of the mind and spirit is more than mere discouragement."[14]

Also, as you try to determine whether you are dealing with clinical or situational depression, keep in mind that "environmental factors and external situations commonly play a role in the onset of major depressive symptoms, even in people with a known chemical or genetic predisposition. Many of these factors and situations . . . are identical to those associated with the onset of situational depression."[15] This means that going on a mission may very well have triggered within you a genetic, chemical predisposition for clinical depression. If you never really dealt with depressive symptoms before serving a mission, but suddenly find yourself experiencing them on your mission and continued to experience them afterward, you may be dealing with clinical depression.

Please though, go beyond this book and learn more about these two types of depression from those clinically certified in their understanding of depression. It is essential that you go beyond this book to learn more and apply what you learn to your own individual circumstances.

Why Did This Happen on My Mission?

Now that we have discussed the possibilities of why situational or clinical depression occurred on your mission, let's discuss the next big question: Why did God allow this to happen? You will notice that these next few pages sound similar to the answers for the "Why did I get sick on my mission?" and "Why didn't the Lord heal me?" questions in the physical health chapter. That's because I've found that the same advice for overcoming physical trials applies to mental trials—with some slight variances, of course. I think you'll still find it worth reading the answer again here.

Anyways, why? Why did God allow this to happen? Whatever your mental affliction and its roots, you were doing, or trying to do, something good by serving a mission. Often in life we expect that as we do good things, we will be rewarded. In fact, we have God's promise of being blessed for our righteous actions and thoughts (see 2 Nephi 1–5). So, time and again we are confused when we are doing all the right things, why we are presented with trials that prevent us from continuing smoothly on our course of doing those right things. And it seems so contradictory to what God would want, right? Why wouldn't He want you to serve a mission? Why wouldn't He want you to teach His gospel? Why would He allow this affliction that prevents you from doing your very best work on *His* behalf to stay?

And those questions lead to you looking negatively inward: He doesn't want me to serve a mission. Why wouldn't He want me? I must not be good enough. There must be something wrong with *me*.

If you let yourself go down that rabbit hole, you will truly begin to believe that there is something wrong with *you* and not just your mind. That there is something about you that God does not like and therefore that is why He is not taking away your affliction. He wants you to go home because He does not want you to do His work. You are a failure.

That line of thinking is not in line at all with God's thinking. You not being enough for God is simply the wrong conclusion. You are enough for Him. Always. (See Isaiah 49:16.) And He recognizes your hard work and sacrifices to do His work for however long you could. Elder Jeffrey R. Holland, in response to a question from a missionary who came home early for mental health reasons said, "I say commendation to you, and the love of the Lord to you, and the blessings of the Church to you for trying to go, for wanting to go, and for the fact that you successfully served. . . . It obviously wasn't a full term, but it was missionary service. It was honest. You were loyally participating and testifying. And I want you to take credit for that. I want you to take the appropriate dignity that you deserve from that and to know that the Lord loves you and the Church loves you for serving."[16]

But the question remains: why did this happen and why was it allowed to continue to the point where you needed to come home early? It is especially useful to ask the "Why did this happen?" if the depression is situational and so can be prevented in the future, especially if you have hopes or plans to return to missionary service. However, if your mental illness runs much deeper, be careful in how you go about answering this question. It is useful to understand the chemical components of clinical depression, the genetic predispositions you may have to it, and what situations or things trigger you to fall deeper into your clinical depression (or other mental illness). Be wary, however, of asking questions in such a nature that you begin to wonder if God is somehow punishing you with your mental illness. Questions such as "Why did the Lord give this to me instead of someone who doesn't want to serve Him?" "Did I do something wrong in the pre-earth life to deserve this?" "Am I being punished?" are the wrong kinds of questions to ask. They lead to despair and stunted growth. Instead, reframe the questions to "What does the Lord want me to learn from this? How can I grow?"

We learn in Ether 12:27 that the Lord gives us (or allows us to have) weakness to humble us and to bring us closer to Him. We also learn in the scriptures that at times He *does* give us weakness to punish us, as He did to Korihor in Alma 30, but we know that even with Korihor, if Korihor had been willing to humble himself and repent, the Lord would have removed that curse from him (Alma 30:55). However, we also know that sometimes the Lord does not remove weakness from us, even after we have humbled ourselves: He didn't remove Paul's weakness even though Paul asked the Lord three times to remove it (2 Corinthians 12:8–9).

I think the key to understanding what is happening in these scriptures and with you is the situation and circumstances: (1) *Did you do something wrong (like Korihor) to deserve a mental illness?* We cannot remember back to our pre-earth life days, but since the only choice we are aware of making in the pre-earth life was to either follow Christ's plan or Satan's plan, and you clearly chose Christ's plan, it is unlikely that you are being punished for a bad choice in the pre-earth life. Perhaps you volunteered to be given this mental illness, perhaps not. We do not know. But volunteering for a trial is much different than doing something to be given the consequence, or punishment, of a trial. Your mental illness was given to you (or allowed) to help you turn to the Lord and let Him show forth His power in you. Let Him strengthen you. With regards to situational depression, did you do anything close to what Korihor did? I seriously doubt it.

(2) *Have you sufficiently humbled yourself?* This is a personal question, but I'm going to go out on a limb here and say that the very fact you are reading this book seeking to understand what is going on inside your mind shows that you are doing everything you can to be humble. Perhaps there *is* more you can do, such as see a professional therapist or talk out your feelings with trusted individuals. Perhaps you do need to read your scriptures more and pray more and give more service. But if you feel you have done everything you can to be humble and try to overcome your mental illness, then (3) *Are you ready to accept the Lord's plan for your life?*

In the scriptures, Paul struggled for quite awhile to accept the Lord's plan to let live him live with an "infirmity." We read in 2 Corinthians 12 that Paul was unhappy with his infirmity and asked the Lord several times to take it away from him. But, as Paul continued to humble himself and submit his will to the Lord's, he began to glory in his infirmity—not of himself but of the Lord and in fact to truly be grateful for his infirmity:

> Of myself I will not glory, but in mine infirmities. For though I would desire to glory, I shall not be a fool; for I will say the truth: but now I forbear, lest any man should think of me above that which he seeth me to be, or that he heareth of me. And lest I should be exalted above measure through the abundance of the revelations, there was given to me a thorn in the flesh, the messenger of Satan to buffet me, lest I

should be exalted above measure. For this thing I besought the Lord thrice, that it might depart from me. And he said unto me, My grace is sufficient for thee: for my strength is made perfect in weakness. Most gladly therefore will I rather glory in my infirmities, that the power of Christ may rest upon me. Therefore I take pleasure in infirmities, in reproaches, in necessities, in persecutions, in distresses for Christ's sake: for when I am weak, then am I strong. (2 Corinthians 12:5–10)

You weren't healed from your mental illness on your mission for a wise reason, and the illness may be persisting now for a wiser reason yet. The illness may not feel wise to you right now—it certainly didn't feel wise to Paul for a while. But as you humble yourself and seek to know God's plan for you and what He would have you learn from this infirmity, you will understand *why* it happened, or continues to happen, in your life.

Could I Have Pushed through the Mental Illness and Stayed?

Some missionaries who struggle with mental illness on their missions do not go home early. Are you weaker than them? Did you give up?

No. You are not weaker than them nor did you give up. Circumstances on their missions allowed them to stay. Consider also that many may have stayed out of fear of being stigmatized, ultimately to their detriment.

My husband, James, wrote out his story in 2013 and has allowed me to share it here:

> By all outsider views, my mission was "successful." I served the full two years; I never had any rule infractions; never sloughed off work; always tried to be a missionary like the greats of the early church days; always tried to talk to every person I saw.
>
> But I still feel like my mission was a failure. I still try not to think about my mission, still feel overwhelmed at the thought of speaking my mission language, still feel anxious and fearful about emailing the one person I taught who joined the Church and remained faithful.
>
> Why do I still struggle with my mission? Why has time not healed all wounds? Since my mission, I have learned that I suffer from anxiety and depression. Looking back, I see that anxiety and depression tinged every moment of my mission. "Just go talk to that person, Elder, and it

will get easier." It never got easier—no matter how many people I contacted on the street, I was always terrified of that next person. "You've been in a slump, Elder; you can work harder. Does your attitude need changing?" At the time, I thought I had a bad attitude. I now see that I was feeling the withdrawal and crushing weight of depression.

I've realized all this in hindsight, but at the time, I had no idea about depression and anxiety. I thought I was being lazy, I thought I was not living up to my calling as a representative of the Church. I thought that if I just lost myself and got to work, I would suddenly be amazing—no more of this pathetic attitude holding me back!

When I came home from my mission, I felt like I had nothing to show for my time. I served a full two years but I don't describe them as my best two years. Even now, I am afraid of interacting with other returned missionaries who spoke my mission language. I could practice my mission language with my sister but I get overwhelmed by the thought. I could email the man I saw baptized but I am scared to do so. I have no idea why I am scared to email a friend from the mission; for some reason, I still can't handle anything related to my mission.

For those of you who have come home early, or who served the full time but still feel like failures, please know that you are not alone. If you struggle to read your mission journal, if you actively avoid thinking about your mission, you are not alone.

James suffers from clinical depression and anxiety. He did not know that this was a struggle of his until a couple years after his mission. He tells me that missionaries who come home early for mental health reasons should be applauded for taking care of themselves and that he wishes he had known what was happening to him so that he could have received the help he needed. He is not sure if he would have been brave enough to come home early, but he absolutely admires everyone who is brave enough to face potential judgment to get the help they need.

Additionally, Abigail struggled with depression due to grief over the loss of a family member. Although she finished the anticipated amount of time of her mission, she said that she still wonders whether she should have continued on as she did or come home. There were certainly blessings and good things she experienced while on her mission, but she also truly did struggle and continued to struggle even after she came home. To you she says,

It's a very admirable thing to put yourself first and to take care of yourself. And I think that if I could go back, that's something that I would have told myself. Your mission your call states that it is anticipated that you will serve for eighteen months or two years, but the Lord knows everyone's heart and He knows the effort that you've put in. Also, if you take care of yourself first, you'll be able to help that many more people.

There is no shame in coming home early to take care of yourself. There may be stigmas against it, but they are wrong. The Lord doesn't see them. He is proud of you for taking care of the mind He has blessed you with and you can continue to expect His help as you seek to understand it.

Can I Get Better?

Yes. Every day need not be a struggle. I have talked about humbling yourself before the Lord, and sometimes that humbling will require you to seek help beyond prayer, the scriptures, and journaling. It may require reaching beyond yourself to trusted friends, family members, and priesthood leaders. Sometimes it may require professional counseling. Elder Holland said, "If things continue to be debilitating, seek the advice of reputable people with certified training, professional skills, and good values. Be honest with them about your history and your struggles. Prayerfully and responsibly consider the counsel they give and the solutions they prescribe. If you had appendicitis, God would expect you to seek a priesthood blessing and get the best medical care available. So too with emotional disorders. Our Father in Heaven expects us to use all of the marvelous gifts He has provided in this glorious dispensation."[17]

It is important to understand that in some cases, there may not be a cure for your particular mental illness. You may only learn coping strategies to confront and better cope with stresses that come up in life, or on a mission. While this can be disheartening to learn initially, it is an essential component about your mental health to realize. Knowing that this illness may manifest itself again and again throughout your life is much better than being blindsided by it repeatedly. This knowledge gives you the upper hand in dealing with it. And being aware that it can come back at any time gives you the heads up you need to constantly be vigilant and prepare yourself for it.

This does not mean that you need to be in a constant state of fight-or-flight. You can continue on to lead a happy life, and if you so choose, a happy mission. You ought to learn and practice coping strategies for things that make you both clinically depressed and situationally depressed. Again, going beyond this book to other resources and even a professional therapist will be incredibly beneficial to you.

Even if this illness is never entirely removed from you, you can continue to find peace and happiness in this life. You can continue to be what Elder Holland calls "appropriately proud." You can "take the dignity and the strength and the faith that came from your [however many days, weeks, or] months and cherish that forever. I don't want you to apologize for coming home. When someone asks you if you've served a mission, you say 'Yes.' You do not need to follow that up with 'But it was only [however long].' Just forget that part and say yes, you served a mission. And be proud of the time that you spent."[18] And, as you move forward with life, you can come to the point that Paul did in praising the Lord for your mental illness.

Really, if you think about it, having this experience of dealing with a mental illness, and even coming home early from a mission, makes you a much more understanding and therefore approachable human being. The Lord does not need more perfect people to tell imperfect people what to do. He already has His Son, our Savior Jesus Christ, filling the role of the perfect example, and even Christ in his Atonement needed to understand what being imperfect felt like, which He did as He suffered in the Garden of Gethsemane. You are going through exactly what God needs you to go through in order to further His work on this Earth. He does not need you to be perfect in mind to use you to accomplish His purposes.

Should I Stay Home or Go Back Out?

Everything I have said regarding the reasons for your mental illness, early return, and coping strategies/treatment plan for the future, leads me back to the inevitable question: should I stay home or should I return to the mission field? For some, the answer to this question will be obvious. For others, it will not be so straightforward. In considering returning to the mission field, again consider why your mental illness either caused you to choose to go home or have someone else make the decision for you. And, if that choice was made for you, was the decision inspired or hastily made? Go back and carefully consider how you felt on your mission, why, and what the circumstances were that led to the decision to send you home.

After you have considered these things, consider your mental state now. If you are not yet at peace, please remember what Gordon B. Hinckley said regarding the importance of physical and mental health while on a mission: "Good physical and mental health is vital. Parents will say, 'If only we can get Johnny on a mission, then the Lord will bless him with health.' It seems to not work out that way. Rather, whatever ailment or physical or mental shortcoming a missionary has when he comes into the field is only aggravated under the stress of the work."[19] Willpower alone to have a better mission (if you return) is not enough. You must have peace of mind and coping strategies in place for the inevitable high-stresses and demands of a mission.

However, if you are at peace, and you can see what happened on your mission clearly, and have good coping strategies in place to appropriately resolve the high-stresses and demands of a mission, *and* you have a strong desire to serve the Lord in this capacity, then I think it is absolutely something that you should counsel with priesthood leaders about. It is a decision to take to the temple and to ponder. It may also be useful to speak to a trained therapist, just to be sure. LDS Family Services is a useful resource the Church offers, and one that many potential missionaries use to be absolutely certain they are ready to embark on or return to a mission. In fact, LDS Family Services offers six free counseling sessions to early-returned missionaries—just ask your stake president or bishop to refer you. Remember to remain humble and listen to the counsel and advice of your priesthood leaders, trained professionals, your parents (as appropriate), and the Spirit.

If you choose to return to your mission, here is what you can potentially expect upon returning, as told by Brad, a missionary who came home early due to extreme anxiety and situational depression:

At first it was awful. All those insecurities came back. That didn't change. It took a lot of work of forgetting my own problems. Serving others helped me a lot. I had to stop worrying about everything that was going on in me and try to do my best for those people around me instead. And that really changed a lot of my own perspective on some stuff. I wasn't there for myself; I wasn't there to fix me. I was there to fix and help other people and then, by doing that I was fixed. It's unfortunate that it took me ten months into my mission to figure that out. But as soon as I did, my whole mentality completely changed. And I was totally happy.

It was not easy to return to the mission, but in the end, for Brad it was completely worth it. He was able to recognize his infirmities—they didn't change—but he was willing to put in the work to forget his own problems and turn his mind and heart toward helping others. He was able to accomplish this on his mission and he experienced the growing opportunities he needed.

Moving Forward with Life

However, many who return home early due to mental health reasons decide that returning to the mission field would be detrimental to their health. There is no shame in admitting that the circumstances and situations of a mission are too much. To a young man who came home early for mental health reasons, Elder Holland said, "Understand, this young man and anybody else out there in the audience who is concerned. There are reasons that people can't serve a mission. There are reasons that people can't go on a mission in the first place. We know that. We understand that. And in this particular reference, the reason was a mental health issue. I love the honesty of that, the candor of that. And I certainly recognize the legitimacy of that. And there would be some in that category who would not be able to serve a mission at all."[20] It is okay to say, "I did my best" and to move forward with your life. The Lord is pleased with what you offered to Him.

Abigail, who I quoted earlier as one who served eighteen months but wonders to this day if she should have, said,

> Mental illness is not something to be taken lightly . . . just because you may struggle with a mental illness, that doesn't mean that you are a bad

person. Your mental illness is a part of you and a part of your life story but it's not who you are. There are a lot of people in the world that are ready to put you down, and a lot of times we're the first to put ourselves down, but, really, we should be especially compassionate in our most vulnerable times. We should be ready to extend compassion to our own selves because if we don't extend that compassion to ourselves, then we're not going to be able to receive that from other people.

So in moving forward with your life, give yourself compassion. And give yourself permission to grieve over the loss of your mission. You lost something precious—something you expected to enjoy and cherish forever. It is only human to feel a sense of loss even as you feel peace about moving forward with your decision to stay home. (To help you understand and work through your grief, please see the section about grief in chapter 4).

Continue to seek treatment options and coping strategies for your mental illness, even if it was situational. The high-stresses of a mission are not just limited to a mission. They are found in many different circumstances throughout life. What a blessing it is, really, to have realized so early on in your life that certain situations trigger a response in you that leads to great anxiety, stress, and even darkness.

In all things, please do as Elder Holland pleads and "never lose faith in your Father in Heaven, who loves you more than you can comprehend. . . . Never, ever doubt that, and never harden your heart. Faithfully pursue the time-tested devotional practices that bring the Spirit of the Lord into your life. Seek the counsel of those who hold keys for your spiritual well-being. Ask for and cherish priesthood blessings. Take the sacrament every week, and hold fast to the perfecting promises of the Atonement of Jesus Christ. Believe in miracles. I have seen so many of them come when every other indication would say that hope was lost. Hope is never lost. If those miracles do not come soon or fully or seemingly at all, remember the Savior's own anguished example: if the bitter cup does not pass, drink it and be strong, trusting in happier days ahead."[21] Do not add to your misery by losing your faith. Hold on, keep trusting in God, and use the resources He has inspired others to create for your benefit.

How Do I Forgive Those Who Treated Me Unfairly?

The last thing I feel we ought to discuss in this chapter is how to forgive others for their lack of sympathy or understanding of what you are going through, and the hurtful comments or actions that can come with that. I have heard and read countless stories of companions, friends, Church leaders (even mission presidents), and parents who say or do damaging things that worsen the mental state of the missionary they have an obligation and call from God to help. To you whose mental state has been worsened because of an unkind comment or action of another, you have every right to your hurt. But here is the catch: you do not have the right to stay hurt (see D&C 64:10). If you do not work through the pain and let these things go, they will fester, grow, and ultimately destroy you.

I cover the doctrine behind forgiveness in the physical health chapter, but I'd like to go one step further here in mental health. First though, please go read what I wrote regarding the doctrine of forgiveness so that we have a good foundation for the next part of this section.

I would like to tell you about a sobering interview I had with siblings whose brother committed suicide that stemmed from unresolved depression due to circumstances on his mission (which he served 2009–2010) beyond his control and things his mission president and mission president's wife said to him. I've already introduced Abigail in this chapter, in fact.

Abigail: Before I left on my mission, my brother told me some things that had deeply impacted him both from serving a mission and from coming home early. These things had contributed to him feeling basically worthless. He expressed having a hard time feeling like he belonged because of that feeling of worthlessness, both from coming home early due to these things, and because of some other things going on in his life at the time when he spoke to me, which was right before his suicide.

It had been a few years since he came home from his mission at this point, but I knew these things he was telling me about still pressed on his mind. He expressed to me his desire that I know that a mission is not going to be "all roses and peachy-keen." One thing that he particularly expressed to me was that he made the decision to come home early because he felt like he, essentially, wasn't able to do what he was called to do, and because he felt a lack of trust from his mission president. He also felt that his mission president was a little abusive in [their] relationship.

William: We all know the rules of the mission to stay away from the opposite sex. And his companion was making out with one of the sister missionaries. In our family, we were kind of the letter-of-the-law kind of people; that's how our parents raised us. I'm sure it was a huge shock to him to have a companion that was disobeying the rules and especially a big rule like that one. He tried to do the right thing and talk to his mission president. And from what I understand his mission president basically said, "You just need to mind your own business." I feel like the mission president basically exercised unrighteous dominion over Alex.

Abigail: The mission president also said, "Elder, this is my mission. You need to let me run my mission." And so my brother, as he was talking to me, expressed that he felt great pressure and great stress because, you know, he was trying to be a diligent missionary and discussing things with his mission president. But he felt that anytime he tried to address concerns with his mission president, his mission president wouldn't take them seriously and would respond in somewhat of an abusive manner. He said the only thing he regretted was not coming home earlier. He said that perhaps he could have avoided going into as deep of a depression as he did. That's what he expressed to me anyway.

Also, something that really stuck with him as he was going home, the mission president's wife basically told him that if he left—if he really was going to go through with leaving early—that he basically he would do nothing but quit in his life. That he would always be a quitter. And so he expressed to me how that really made him feel bad and because of that he felt like he was always going to be looked down upon in the Church.

Before he served, there may have been moments of depression. His best friend died his senior year of high school and he became really somber after that. However, he did work through it, and then he got really focused on going on a mission and really put his whole heart and soul into it. And so, he was actually really looking forward to serving the mission because he was looking forward to sharing his testimony. It's hard to say how much of a depression he was experiencing before his mission, but there was a difference after he returned from his mission early.

Most of the backlash that he received for coming home early was from his mission president and the mission president's wife. He actually never had any complaints about the way the ward treated him. He actually had quite a few people that ended up being a pretty good support for him, and who encouraged him to go on with his life. They helped him feel comfortable. But he was so deeply impacted by what his mission president and the mission president's wife said to him because even years later as he was talking to me right before I went on my mission, he was so deeply hurt by it.

He still didn't seek out professional help. And I think that that is something that I see as a big contributing factor, not only in his lack of forgiveness toward his mission president and his wife, but the course of his life for the next couple of years. And granted I don't necessarily think everyone needs to seek out professional help, because there are some people that are able to talk it out with family and kind of get a resolution. Everyone's story is different. But Alex's mental health got worse as time went on, so it was something that he probably should have seen a professional about. And so that was something that he didn't do: he didn't really give an honest effort to go see a mental health professional.

Forgiving someone for betraying your trust *and* disrespecting your calling as a missionary is no easy task. It is clear too that Alex was suffering from feelings of worthlessness due to what his mission president and mission president's wife said to him, and those feelings of worthlessness contributed to his depression, and that depression caused him to make choices in his life that led to a worsening of the depression and ultimately suicide.

Could all of this have been prevented if Alex had worked to forgive his mission president and mission president's wife? I don't think I can make that assumption, nor do I think I can say, nor can anyone else say, that Alex *didn't* try to forgive his mission president and mission president's wife. But it is apparent in his conversation with his sister that he still harbored some hard feelings against these people, and that he had allowed (by not seeking professional help) what they said to impact him so deeply that he felt worthless. Other circumstances in his life may have contributed to those feelings as well, but the root of his depression stemmed from how he felt about what his mission president and mission president's wife wrongly said to him. And what these people said to him was impactful and hard to forgive, and so I agree with Alex's siblings that professional help should have been sought out to help Alex work through these feelings.

I share this story merely as an extreme example of what *can* happen to you if you allow feelings of hurt to fester, especially due to the danger of a mental illness adding to those feelings of hurt by piling on inappropriate feelings of guilt, shame, and worthlessness that can drive you deeper into depression. If you feel at all that you are struggling to forgive someone, please seek help, and be humble enough to accept professional help if needed.

William said,

> Honestly, I don't know if he would have known that he was that bad off to see a professional. When you're in that state, I don't know if you realize that you're as bad as you are. I think he kind of started to realize that toward the end. When talking to other siblings he did reach out to, he mentioned that maybe he did need professional help, but he didn't have the money for it. He just couldn't afford it and none of us knew that he would make that decision.

Abigail added,

> But he did actually go to a couple of sessions right before his death because there was a couple that had been called on a mission to our home state. And they were professional mental health counselors. Alex had gone to see them but he didn't think that it was of value.

Finding the right counselor that is affordable can be a daunting, and at times overwhelming task. Please seek help from your family, and from your bishop, who can give you access to LDS Family Services. Please just never give up. It is clear from talking to William and Abigail that when Alex took his life, he was not in his right mind. William even shared a spiritual experience he'd had after Alex's death that he felt Alex was okay and that the Lord understood. However, you do not want to get to the point of suicide. Please forgive. Please seek help. Please remember there is always hope.

Final Thoughts

Before I close this chapter, I'd like to share a thought from Lucy who struggled with depression her entire mission and returned after fifteen months of service. She came home due to the depression and a pressing need to have surgery on her hand.

She said to me,

> As I look back on the course of my mission, I see God's hand in every aspect of it. There were things that happened while I was serving that I didn't understand at the time, that I didn't understand until the day I realized I was going home. Everything that happened in my mission happened so that I could come home early and get the help that I needed and that [getting that help] would be okay. Something that's really cool to me [is that] God is so mindful of all of us, that He has a plan for all of us, and it's unique and individual. For me, if I had stayed and finished my mission I wouldn't have had time to have surgery on my hand, and I wouldn't have had time to start antidepressants and get stable before I moved away again. Those are both things that really needed to happen for me to be able to live my life in a normal functional way. And so, as mad as I am about having to come home early, it's okay because God makes it okay.

I hope you will remember as you go forward in life exactly that: God makes it okay. Whether you struggle with mental illness your whole life or just this short time on your mission, God loves you and is aware of you, and He always has your best interests at heart. All that seems unfair about life will be reconciled. God can and will make up the difference as we humble ourselves before Him, seek His guidance and wisdom, and put our life into His hands. There is great purpose in your life. Keep trusting Him. Keep working toward accomplishing that purpose. As Elder Holland said, "If sometimes the harder you try, the harder it gets, take heart. So it has been with the best people who ever lived."[22]

Notes

1. Kristine J. Doty-Yells, S. Zachary Bullock, Harmony Packer, Russell T. Warner, James Westwood, Thomas Ash, and Heather Hirsch, "Return with Trauma: Understanding the Experiences of Early Returned Missionaries," *Issues in Religion and Psychotherapy*, vol. 37, no. 1 (2015): 34. Available at http://scholarsarchive.byu.edu/irp/vol37/iss1/9.

2. Laura Strom, "Situational Symptoms or Serious Depression: What's the Difference?" April 2017, National Alliance on Mental Illness, https://www.nami.org/Blogs/NAMI-Blog/April-2017/Situational-Symptoms-or-Serious-Depression-What-s.

3. Elements Behavorial Health, "What is Situational Depression?" August 2, 2012, https://www.elementsbehavioralhealth.com/mood-disorders/situational-depression.

4. Strom, "Situational Symptoms or Serious Depression."

5. Dan Rascon, "Psychologist warns about top 10 mistakes to ruin an LDS mission," KUTV.com, May 9, 2016, http://kutv.com/news/local/psychologist-warns-about-top-10-mistakes-to-ruin-an-lds-mission.

6. Jeffery Jensen Arnett, "Emerging Adulthood: A Theory of Development from the Late Teens Through the Twenties," May 2000, *American Psychologist*, 469.

7. Doty-Yells; et. al, "Return with Trauma," 35.

8. Ibid.

9. Rascon, "Psychologist warns about top 10 mistakes to ruin an LDS mission."

10. Doty-Yells; et. al, "Return with Trauma," 36.

11. Ibid., 35–36.

12. Strom, "Situational Symptoms or Serious Depression."

13. Ibid.

14. Jeffrey R. Holland, "Like a Broken Vessel," *Ensign*, Nov. 2013.

15. Elements Behavorial Health, "What is Situational Depression?"

16. Jeffrey R. Holland, "Elder Holland's Counsel for Early Returned Missionaries," LDS Media Library, March 2016, https://www.lds.org/media-library/video/2016-05-012-elder-hollands-counsel-for-early-returned-missionaries.

17. Holland, "Like a Broken Vessel."

18. Holland, "Elder Holland's Counsel for Early Returned Missionaries."

19. Ibid.

20. Ibid.

21. Ibid.

22. Jeffrey R. Holland, "The Inconvenient Messiah," *Ensign*, Feb. 1984.

CHAPTER 3

Worthiness

Of all the interviews I did in preparation for writing this book, my favorite interviews were those with missionaries who came home early due to worthiness issues. This was not because I enjoyed the gossip of hearing about what they had done wrong. Not at all; in fact, I rarely learned what sins had been committed. Rather, I enjoyed these interviews because most of these men and women truly understood the Atonement and my testimony was strengthened so much by talking to them. There is absolutely hope and forgiveness for anyone who actively seeks to repent and fix their mistakes with God, themselves, and those they have hurt. The Atonement is a marvelous gift from our Heavenly Father.

There are two types of missionaries who come home early because of worthiness issues: those who come home early because of unresolved transgression prior to the mission, and those who come home early due to transgression committed on the mission. Both are difficult. Those who committed transgression on their mission seemed to feel additional shame, but despite this, the repentance and forgiveness processes were the same. Please take note of that word: processes. You will learn by the end of this chapter that repentance (and forgiveness) is a process, one that can be difficult to go through, but extremely rewarding for those who do.

One story in particular (Michael's) exceptionally illustrated the difficulties and the joys of these processes. I would like to share his story with you now:

Michael came home early due to unresolved transgression. Growing up, Michael struggled to stay on the strait-and-narrow path due to a lack of spiritual guidance in his mother's home, and his own pride when he visited and eventually lived in his father's home (where the gospel was lived and taught). In his own words, Michael said,

> When I was eighteen and graduated from high school, I had done so many things that were contrary to the gospel. I knew I had to make a decision. My dad, who was unaware of my wrongdoings, told me that I was eligible for the Melchizedek Priesthood and I knew I couldn't do both anymore. I told myself, "I've either got to completely go with the Church and the gospel or leave the Church completely. Just excommunicate myself, separate all my ties, and do my own thing."
>
> So, I started doing my own research; I found all the scriptures that I possibly could to overlook or justify my sins. I found countless scriptures of Christ saying, "Thy sins are forgiven thee" and "Go thy way and sin no more." Also, in Doctrine and Covenants it talks about how if you do certain righteous acts that "the testimony of which ye have born is recorded in heaven and thy sins are forgiven thee" (D&C 62:3). So, I was just looking up as many scriptures as I could to try to justify my sins. I confessed in private prayer to God. And I thought to myself, "Look, as long as I never do anything bad again and I just do right, then I'm good. I can get the Melchizedek Priesthood. I can commit to Jesus that I'm going to serve an honorable full-time mission. I'm going to serve him and I'll be just fine."
>
> And so I decided to do that. I stopped cold-turkey doing anything contrary to the Gospel. I never did it again. And then I went off into the MTC. I had committed to myself, to my parents, and to Jesus that I was going to do the very best I could. I was going to be that missionary that spends every waking moment serving the Lord. I was going to be 150 percent obedient. I was not going to take naps. I was going to utilize the time I had. I wanted to be in leadership. I wanted to serve and just have all these great experiences."

Let's pause here real quick and take a look at what is happening so far. First, notice that Michael has actually begun the repentance process: he has recognized his sins, felt bad about his sins, and has even forsaken his sins. He has even confessed his sins to God. However, due to the serious nature of Michael's sins, he needed to confess them to his priesthood leaders, but he stopped short there in the repentance process. Michael justified not confessing his sins because confession is painful and embarrassing. We naturally resist that part of repentance and instead think of all the good we've done, either on our missions or in our lives, and how we will never do those sins again. But that's not true repentance—it's not the "broken heart and contrite spirit" that is required for complete change. Michael addresses this later in his story.

What exactly is true repentance? According to the Gospel Principles Manual,[1] there are seven steps of true repentance:

1. Recognizing sin
2. Feeling sorrow for sin
3. Forsaking sin
4. Confessing sin
5. Making restitution
6. Forgiving others
7. Keeping the commandments of God

Michael stopped at step four. Yes, he confessed to God, but that wasn't enough. In a way, it is easy to confess to God: He already knows. It's more of a formality. What can be even harder, and what can stop us from even confessing to God is confessing to ourselves, which brings us back to step one: recognizing the sin.

I listened to one young man really struggle to accept the fact that he had committed a serious transgression on his mission. He felt he had been wronged and unfairly treated by being sent home early. Sometimes our serious sins can be masked by the more serious sins of others, such as a friend or a companion. Because this young man refused to acknowledge that he had indeed slipped up and fallen into transgression, he felt confused, angry, and bitter. He refused to partake in the process of repentance because he was certain he had done nothing wrong. That denial, pride, and lying to himself cost him dearly in happiness and in his standing with the Church for a while, because his anger led him to commit greater sins.

If you in any way feel that you were wrongly sent home early for worthiness issues, I encourage you to first give yourself an *honest* self-examination and ask yourself if you really, truly did *nothing* wrong, and if the answer is "No, I didn't do anything wrong," I encourage you to talk to a priesthood leader right away to get things straightened out. However, if you did do *something* wrong, ask yourself if it was severe enough to warrant disciplinary action. Were you warned beforehand not to do such a thing, either in the scriptures, by a leader, in the missionary handbook, or even by the Spirit? If so, did you knowingly ignore or disobey that warning? Did a serious transgression result because of that disobedience, either by you or your companion or someone else? If so, acknowledge your fault and begin the repentance process. If not, again, meet with your priesthood leaders and get everything straightened out. If you feel you are not at fault, and you meet with your priesthood leaders, and they insist (for whatever reason) that you are, pray and ask God what His opinion on the matter is, because truly His opinion is the only one that really matters. He will answer you, in His time and in His way. If you are clean in His eyes, you will know it; it will be clear to you.

Back to Michael: he was also confused about step five, restitution, or repairing the damage done. He assumed that he could just make it up to God and others by stopping what he was doing and forsaking it forever. And, in fact, he would take it one step further and be the perfect missionary. That would show the Lord he was truly sorry and his repentance would be made certain. However, this is not how restitution works, which will be discussed in more detail later.

Let's return to Michael's story.

And so the next ten months of my mission were extremely hard. Every day I woke up with the knowledge and the guilt. I could remember all of my sins within seconds—I recollected everything all at once. It was the weirdest thing ever. That was the hardest part for me. Every day I justified it though by saying, "The only reason I'm feeling this way and I remember all of this is because I missed that one person yesterday, or I didn't knock two doors, or my companion wanted to go do this and I didn't really feel like that was obedient, and I didn't do it but he did, and maybe it was because I let him be disobedient that I'm feeling this way." And so, day-to-day I was the missionary that was, "What did I do wrong? How can I do better?" And not only, "How can I do better?" but "I have to do better" because I'm tired of feeling this way and like I need to work off these sins.

And so, in the mission I was actually known as "Rebuking [Last name]." I was a district leader. I trained several missionaries and I was a district leader for eight months of my mission. I never served as zone leader or assistant to the president because for some reason I was just supposed to be a district leader. But, as a whole, missionaries were almost like walking on eggshells around me because I did everything by the books. I mean everything. I didn't want to slip up and have the feelings come back, and so I had memorized the missionary handbook word-for-word, page-for-page. When missionaries were doing something wrong, I could say, "Elder or Sister, look at page such-and-such, this paragraph, this line, and you tell me if that's appropriate." That's how I conducted myself as a district leader. I was very, very staunch. There was no mercy, just 100 percent justice. That was my life. I was feeling guilty every day. I just felt so bad inside.

Here we notice the toll Michael's lack of true repentance took on him, and on other missionaries. He was in a hard place with continued justifications, rationalizations, and "making it up" to Heavenly Father. He had no room in his heart for mercy because he had not allowed mercy to come into his own life. He demanded justice of himself and therefore he demanded justice of others. He appeared to be the perfect, obedient missionary, but internally he was a wreck.

I was training for the third time at month nine and I was super excited. As soon as I saw the name tag, I knew I was training him. On his first day, my new companion was super stoked for the work—just to be there! He was excited to finally be out of the MTC. I took him tracting and we placed several Book of Mormons and just had some really neat experiences.

I don't know what happened in between day one and day two, but day two came and it was like a 180. He didn't want to be there. He didn't want to get up on time. He didn't want to be obedient. He just didn't want to listen to what I had to say. I was like "Man, what happened to yesterday?" And after probably about two weeks, I started noticing just some twitching and some things that just didn't make a lot of sense. Like, I started seeing some things that were relatable to drug withdrawals. No one else seemed to notice something off about him, but I could tell and I knew something was wrong.

For training, I had gotten a giant white board that covered the entire wall. The way I liked to train was before going to bed, I would write down my training which I would give during the additional hour of companionship study the following day. Then in the morning of my personal study, I would pray and go over my own stuff, but also go over the training I had planned. Sometimes, I would get impressions to change everything. Other times I would just get affirmation. One morning, I had the strongest impression when I was praying to confirm what I was training on (I mean, I got just the clearest voice in my head), "You are not to train on this today. Today, you need to talk about repentance."

And I was like, "What the heck?" And so I just said in my prayer, "Okay, Heavenly Father. What about repentance?"

And the only instruction I received in my prayer was, "Follow the Spirit and follow my lead."

And I was like, "All right."

Now, I had questioned several times up to this point, "Should I confess? Do I need to talk to my mission president?" And, obviously, I was teaching repentance and teaching the doctrine of faith. But it was so hard to apply it because I thought everyone was going to be disappointed in me. And how could I let my parents down again? I just thought, "With the stuff that I've done, I'll probably be excommunicated or at least disfellowshipped from the Church and go through disciplinary action." And that really scared me. I had a really hard time thinking about that. And so I kind of went back to the scriptures that I'd found that kind of comforted me and that I used to justify being out on my mission. But then I also thought to myself, "Well, I know I feel the Spirit. If I wasn't worthy, why would I still feel the Spirit?"

I also knew that I'd been called here to this mission by revelation, and so if I really wasn't worthy and the Lord wouldn't accept my repentance through just one-on-one praying to Him, why would He have called me to a mission? And why would I be a district leader? Why would I be training? Why would this be my third time training a missionary? If this was all revelatory and based off of inspiration, wouldn't my leaders suspect or get impressions that I wasn't worthy? So I justified with all those reasonings, and told myself that I didn't need to talk to my leaders. I thought, "The reason I'm feeling this way is because it takes time to become clean. I just need to be patient."

These are all excellent questions that Michael asked himself and questions that deserve answers. Recognizing that I do not know the mind of God, I will first attempt to explain why the leaders of the Church did not feel inspired to keep Michael from serving a mission.

Unfortunately, there are cases of people doing things unworthily almost everywhere. People take the sacrament unworthily, attend the temple unworthily, and give priesthood blessings unworthily. Yet the Lord does not stop them. The Lord also does not inspire others to stop them, except in rare circumstances. Heavenly Father allows us to choose for ourselves whether we will sin, and what we will subsequently do after we sin (in Michael's case, lie and hide).

What He does not allow us to escape are the consequences of our actions. And as we will see, Michael eventually did pay the full price for his sins.

But wouldn't calling Michael as a missionary be potentially damaging to God's other children? I suppose not. As far as I can tell, it was really only damaging to Michael. The Spirit likely made up where Michael lacked on several occasions. We read in the second of Article of Faith, "Men will be punished for their own sins and not for Adam's transgression." The only one who was going to be "punished" for Michael's sins was Michael. Of course, Michael did make things harder on the mission (his area was shut down when he went home) and the missionaries he was over as district leader whom he was unkind to. But the Lord was well aware of why those things happened, and He likely provided the mercy those missionaries needed and eventually reopened the area or saw to it that those who were ready for the gospel received it in some other way.

But why was the mission president inspired to put an unworthy missionary in leadership? God can (and does) use anyone to advance His work and purposes. Michael may have been unworthy to be on a mission, but he was willing to be 150 percent obedient and he was also willing to be bold and demand that others be better. God could use him, and so He did. Being in a leadership position also caused Michael to question more and more his worthiness before the Lord, and ultimately led him to be inspired to give the training that led to his continuation in the repentance process.

I also want to talk about the fear Michael felt about confessing his sins. He worried that everyone would be disappointed in him and that he'd have to go through disciplinary action and maybe even excommunication. Fear is one of Satan's favorite tools and he is very good at using it. Elder R. Lawrence of the Seventy said, "The premortal war was fought with words, ideas, debate, and persuasion (see Revelation 12:7–9, 11). Satan's strategy was to frighten people. He knew that fear is the best way to destroy faith. He may have used arguments like these: 'It's too hard.' 'It's impossible to make it back clean.' 'There's too much risk.' 'How do you know you can trust Jesus Christ?' He was very jealous of the Savior."[2] Fear is natural, but fear can be deceiving and Satan is the master deceiver. He may not know your thoughts, but he can sense your fear and he will use it against you every chance he gets.

On the other hand, Heavenly Father and Jesus Christ want us to feel joy, especially at the opportunity to repent and become clean of our sins. President Russell M. Nelson has taught, "When the focus of our lives is on God's plan of salvation . . . and Jesus Christ and His gospel, we can feel joy regardless of what is happening—or not happening—in our lives. Joy comes from and because of Him. He is the source of all joy."[3] When we focus on where we are going as we repent, and not where we are, we can feel joy and the promise of more joy to come.

Returning to Michael's story:

So my companion said, "Okay, so what are we training on?"

I replied, "I don't really know."

He was like, "What? What do you mean you don't know?"

And I said, "You know, I was praying today and I just got the strongest feeling to talk about repentance."

He was just quiet and said, "Oh? Okay. So what do you want to do?"

I said, "Let's start with the doctrine. Let's look up every scripture on repentance in the Bible Dictionary and the index."

And he goes, "That's going to take hours."

And I said, "Honestly, for some odd reason, we are not going out today. I don't think we need to be outside today. I think we need to do this." And you could just tell something was working on him.

So, we just started reading scriptures together. And a couple hours go by and we're finally getting down the list of scriptures, and talking about them, and we're writing things on the giant whiteboard. We get to a point about putting a lesson about repentance together, and I say, "Okay, Elder. I want you to teach me."

I turned around and I could just see this dark cloud over him. I mean it was so visible to me. I could just tell that he was brooding in his own guilt. I didn't know what he had done, but I knew for a fact that he wasn't worthy to be on a mission. And I knew that, technically, I wasn't worthy to be on a mission either.

And so, I was actually really excited. I thought, "Wow, for the first time, he is really participating. You can tell that the Spirit is piercing his heart." It was just like one of those awesome moments when you know that you're doing something right. I felt like I was being an instrument in the Lord's hands. And it was just such a good moment.

He looked at me and said, "Elder, what would you tell somebody if they needed to confess about something? Would you tell them to go on a mission? What if their confession would stop them from going on a mission? Would you tell them to just wait? What would you tell them?"

It was so hypocritical, but I said, "Elder, it's more important for you to confess and repent the right way the first time. My dad always told me I had to do it the right way. Your mission is not required for salvation, but repentance is."

And he's like, "I think I need to call President."

I said, "That's fine. Call President. You do whatever you need to do."

He called the mission president and because President's schedule is super packed, he only interviewed him for 20 minutes. But because it seemed important, he said, "Tomorrow we will meet at the mission home. We will talk in greater detail there."

So, the next day we went to the mission home after studies. My companion was talking to President and I was in the front room reading my scriptures. While I was sitting there, I was thinking the whole time, "This is awful. This sucks. This is so bad." Here he is talking to the mission president, doing the right thing, and here I am—the one with faith, the one who knows the gospel, the one who knows the scriptures, and has been out ten months—and I can't even do that. So then I was like, "Well, I need to open my scriptures and just read them."

I took my quad out and flipped them open. They opened to 3 Nephi 27. In 3 Nephi 27 it talks about the doctrine of Christ. The first scripture that I read talked about having faith, repenting, confessing sins, being baptized, receiving the Holy Ghost, enduring to the end, and finally being able to stand clean before the Lord at the last day.

My heart sunk. I thought, "I don't want to read my scriptures. I'm not doing this."

So then I was just looking around, fidgety, and bothered. Finally I was like, "Augh, I need to read my scriptures."

So then I randomly opened to Mosiah 4:10, which reads: "And again, believe that ye must repent of your sins and forsake them, and humble yourselves before God; and ask in sincerity of heart that he would forgive you; and now, if you believe all these things see that ye do them."

My heart sunk again. I thought, "I'm not doing this." So I closed my scriptures again. I just thought, "This is so bad. I can't believe I'm finding these scriptures. No."

Here we can see the Lord speaking directly to Michael through the scriptures. Michael recognized his need for further repentance—truly, he'd recognized it all along—and now had the opportunity to confess to his priesthood leader and continue on with his repentance. The Lord wanted this greatly for Michael, just as He wants it for all of us when we sin. Also, note that the Lord didn't have Michael open to scriptures about fire, damnation, and eternal punishments for the unrepentant. He didn't scare Michael, as that wasn't needed. Instead, He inspired Michael to look directly at the scriptures that Michael most needed: not the comforting scriptures that Michael had sought out on his own but, again, not the terrifying scriptures either. The scriptures were simply commands to repent.

Let's continue:

Shortly after I'd shut the scriptures a second time, my companion came out and he was skipping on the clouds—just beaming with happiness and feeling good. He said, "Hey, Elder." And I was like, "What happened in there? You went in with a dark cloud over you and now you're walking out rejoicing." And it had been three or four hours. Our mission president told me that we weren't to proselyte. My companion had to read *The Miracle of Forgiveness* over the next few days.

That night I couldn't sleep. Finally, I got up, went to my desk, turned on my light and thought, "I don't know what to do, but I've got to read something." *The Miracle of Forgiveness* was sitting across from me; I read it in three hours. I'm not a fast reader, by the way. I don't know how I read it that fast and retained everything that I did. But I did, and I made a list of all the things that I needed to confess. I had written a timeline of the details of my sins from start to finish. I looked down at it and I was like, "I can't do this. I'm going to pray about this." I got on my knees and asked Heavenly Father if confessing to my leaders was the right thing to do. And as soon as I said it out loud, I thought, "I can't believe I just asked that question. Of course it's the right thing to do!" And so then, being a very thorough kind of person, I made a list of pros and cons for confessing my sins. I first listed all the cons:

1. I'll probably get excommunicated.
2. I will lose the trust of my current girlfriend.
3. I will lose the trust—forever—from my parents.
4. I will lose the trust of anybody who likes me. I'll just be a big disappointment.
5. I'll get sent home.

So I looked at my list, and I was like, "No, I don't want go through that. You know what I'll do? I will just wait. I'll serve my mission. I will confess after my mission when I'm living on my own. Nobody has to know. I'll get excommunicated, but my parents don't even need to know because I won't be in their home ward."

And I began justifying these thoughts because I had read several stories of people who had waited to confess their sins and been just fine. For example, I read the story of a man who got sealed in the temple at a young age and cheated on his wife with two other women. He felt so bad about it afterward and he never did it again. He and his wife had children together. He served faithfully in the church. Forty-five years go by and he has several kids and grandkids. But this sin has just been eating at him. So he goes and talks to the bishop. He says, "This is when I was like when I was 20-something. I cheated on my wife after we had been sealed in the temple." The bishop told him, "Okay, but look at the life that you've led. You have devoted your life to the Lord and to the gospel. You've made your wrongs right. You're good."

I had also read several other similar ones. So in my mind, I thought, "No, I just need to finish my mission. I can do it. I've only got fourteen more months. I've been doing it for ten months. I can do it for fourteen more months and then I will take care of everything."

But then what began eating at me was the fact that I hadn't made a pros list. So, I started writing the pros:

1. For the first time in my life, actually feel worthy to hold the priesthood.
2. Know that I can be sealed to my family and my future wife for all eternity and be worthy of that.
3. Be able to stand before my Savior after this life and know that I am clean.

And that was all it took. I knew what I needed to do at that point. I got on my knees, and as I prayed, something my father told me when I moved in with him came to my mind:

"Michael, it doesn't matter what other people think of you when you're doing the right thing. You do the right thing because you know it's the right thing to do, and because you're doing right by the Lord. That is the most important thing to do."

After that I started thinking about all the people who would support me. There were several distinct faces that came to my mind. My seminary teacher was one of them. I remembered in that moment a talk that she and I had about me serving a mission and also choosing the right things because they were the right things. There were just moments like that with certain individuals that gave me the courage to do what I was going to do.

Michael is clearly a thorough person. He very much wanted to make sure and know for himself that confession was the right thing to do—that he couldn't just be a very good person for the rest of his life.

I want to point out that each of the "cons" Michael wrote down were *perceptions*. He did not know they were going to happen. Some of them did happen, such as getting sent home, but most actually didn't. Satan often uses our perceptions to scare us from doing the right thing. Even if each of those things had turned out to be a reality, they were still better to face and live with than the awful burden of guilt Michael had been carrying around for months. Trust can also be restored eventually. Also, each of the items on his "pros" list were *realities*. God will only give us realities, and He wants to give us only good things. Repentance exists for our benefit, not for our destruction.

When I woke up the next morning, I sat on my bed and stared at my mission president's phone number for probably half an hour. Finally, I dialed, and as soon as I heard his voice, I hung up. President called me back and he's like, "Hello? [Last name] or [Last name]? . . . Elder, how's your companion doing?" I gave him a brief report. President said, "Well, does he need to talk to me? How is he doing?"

"Actually, President, I need to talk with you."

"Can you be in my office in twenty minutes?"

"Yes, absolutely."

So I went and I confessed everything. I brought my timeline with me and my paper and we talked about everything. He canceled the rest of his appointments that day and we talked for probably a good six or seven hours in his office. It was a very long, detailed talk about things.

He taught me the deeper meaning of confession and repentance that through all of my studies and all of the stories I had heard, I had never looked at confession and repentance quite the way he taught me that day. Going back to that story of the man who cheated on his wife, my mission president said, "You know what's interesting is that you missed that whether he confessed first or confessed last [in the repentance process], he still had to confess. It was required. The one thing you're forgetting too is that when we sin, confession isn't to say, 'See what I did?' or 'Blame me' or 'Burn me at the stake.' It's like making an appointment to see the doctor. When we sin, obviously there's different levels of sin, but sin is sin. And the more severe the sin, the more damage it has on your spirit. Your spiritual body is just like your physical body. Imagine sin like an infection in the bone. You can feel it. You know it's there. It hurts, but you can't see it. You don't know how to fix it. You can Google it. You can ask people, but unless they know how to fix it, they can't fix it. You can take painkillers. You can get drunk, you can go do worse things to lessen the pain, but it never goes away. The only way to get rid of an infection in the bone is to go to the doctor and have surgery. The surgeon cuts you open and then cleans the bones. They scrape out all the infection. That is the role of confession. When we confess we are seeing the spiritual surgeon. The surgeon isn't the one who heals us. But his job is to scrape all the infection out and get rid of it so that the healing process truly can begin."

And that is why prophets and apostles have felt inspired by God to have serious sins be confessed to a priesthood leader. They are often harder to overcome and often also harder to feel forgiven for. It is helpful and useful to have someone with the proper priesthood authority and keys help us repent of and get rid of the sins for good. Leaders help us make sure we haven't overlooked anything and don't damage ourselves during the repentance process (because it is a difficult process!). They also help us *know* that we have been forgiven.

"But why wasn't that husband excommunicated? He had the Melchizedek Priesthood and all these things. Why wasn't he disciplined?"

"Church discipline is different with every individual. Whenever we go through disciplinary action, the Church officials take into account, based upon revelation, what is best for the individual. They consider what is going to cause the person to come closer to the Lord. And sometimes certain sins require disciplinary action to alleviate the covenants so that you're not condemning yourself. You're free of those promises you made, so you can fix whatever you need to fix and then remake those promises and be worthy of them."

Then he said to me, "Another thing you're overlooking in this situation is, what would you rather do? Feel guilty, confess, and go through discipline, or feel guilty every day of your life for forty-five years? Look at the pain that man probably suffered for forty-five years knowing what he knew. You just explained to me that for the last ten months, every day you could feel and see the sins on your shoulders. Could you imagine doing that for forty-five years?"

"I never thought about it like that."

"That's why it's just better to do it quicker and sooner rather than carrying it around with you. The bishop felt that the man had already paid the price. He had suffered and had gone through his repentance process for forty-five years. He felt inspired to say he was good."

"Okay, that's really interesting."

There is absolutely always going to be the temptation to bury our sins and suffer them rather than tell the ones who will be hurt by our actions. We can even pretend that we are being noble by doing so and call it our "penance." But in reality, we are only continuing to hurt ourselves and delaying the hurt of others. In the case of the man who cheated on his wife, in order to make full restitution and repent of his sins, he also needed to confess to his wife. Can you imagine the pain his wife must have felt upon learning about her husband's betrayal *and* forty-five year deception? Can you imagine how many trust issues would result from being lied to for so long? It surely would have been better for the man to confess to his bishop and his wife sooner, and have those feelings worked through and marriage rehabilitated immediately. Forty-five years later they could have both been in a wonderful place. Of course, his wife may have left him, and she may leave him now, but it is better for all parties involved to have a clear picture of what they are dealing with, so that they can make clear choices. The husband chose to live a clean life after his sins, but he also chose to live a lie and let his wife live a lie too.

Returning to Michael's story, he said,

My mission president talked with me about certain doctrines and we read scriptures. He told me that there was a very high likelihood that I would return home, but that he would do all in his power to allow me the opportunity to return to the field. However, he couldn't promise that.

A couple days later, we both met with President again. He informed both of us that we would be sent home in two days. He said that we needed to call our parents and tell them that we were coming home and why we were coming home. He said, "You don't need to go into detail about the sins, but you do need to tell your parents that you have done some things that require you to go home and take care of them. Bear testimony that you know you're doing the right thing."

Before I called my parents, I asked him, "Why? Why do you send missionaries home instead of keeping them here? A couple of my friends have told me stories about missionaries staying out on their missions and repenting."

He said, "You know, for certain sins or certain occasions, I think it's appropriate to keep them here. But some of these things, especially disciplinary sins, you can't take the sacrament. You can't hold priesthood callings or participate in class. What kind of example would it be saying that the Lord's missionary can't take the sacrament? Or can't participate in class? Or be encouraged not to pray publicly because he needs to be praying in secret? That wouldn't be good for anyone because it would draw attention to the mission and would draw attention to you. And then you would have to explain and it would be that much harder to work with the members. It is better for you to go home, take care of these things, and do all that you can to return to the field. And if you return, we will open our arms. We will do all we can to get you back in the swing of things."

So I was like, "All right."

We all have heard at times about missionaries who transgress before or during their missions having the opportunity to stay and work through the repentance process. You might feel that you could have stayed and worked through that process on your mission. You might feel as though your mission president was not as kind and understanding as Michael's mission president. You may feel a lot of shame for coming home early and feel that could have been avoided had you just been allowed to stay in the field. Ask yourself though if it really would have been better to stay. Would you have been able to focus on repentance like you needed to? Even if you didn't need to go through disciplinary action, could you have hindered the work by staying? Could you have truly devoted the time and energy you needed on repenting *and* doing the work?

Coming home early in and of itself is difficult, especially for worthiness issues. In Nathaniel Hawthorne's book *The Scarlet Letter*, Hester Prynne is forced to wear a scarlet "A" on her clothing so that everyone will know she once committed "Adultery." Yet the irony, and hypocrisy, of the situation is that while others were pointing their fingers at her and shunning her from society, or were at least aware of her and what happened, they were committing the same sin, or sins of equal severity. Yet they were not caught in their sins or were able to confess them to their church leaders privately. Hester's sin was much more obvious because she became pregnant while her husband was away at war.

Similarly, coming home early from a mission for worthiness issues can be like wearing a scarlet letter. Everyone sins and many sin severely, but most people are able to keep their sins private. Yet sometimes, such as when missionaries come home early from a mission due to worthiness issues, their sins are much more public and vulnerable to gossip and public consequences. And even if you have supportive family, church leaders, friends, and ward members, that shame is still heaped on in extra doses because other people are *aware* of your sins.

That shame does not have to stay though. You can do as Hester did initially and be ashamed and hide, and even fall away from the Church so that you don't have to face the shame or criticism (perceived or real), or you can own what you did and be humble enough to ask for help.

Let's resume Michael's story:

I got on the phone with my dad and told him that I was coming home to do the right thing and take care of things I should have taken care of before I left. To my surprise, my dad said, "I'm proud of you. I'm happy and I'm sad. I'm sad because for whatever reason this wasn't taken care of before you went out, but I'm happy because you're taking care of it now. That's the most important thing. We're here for you. We will do whatever we need to do for you. You just let us know. All right?"

I got off the phone and our area was shut down. When I got off the airplane two days later, my dad was there to pick me up. Just my dad. My dad paints cars for a living and he took me to work. We just talked. At one point he said, "So I kind of prematurely made this choice for you. I've invited the entire family over for family home evening." I have probably thirty cousins, six or seven uncles on my dad's side, and my grandparents, and my siblings—so there was going to be a lot of people.

And my dad goes, "You're going to tell them why you're home. You don't need to go into detail. You can do it however you want." My dad's been through disciplinary action in his life, and he continued by saying, "One thing I've learned through my experiences is that if you condemn yourself, the world can't condemn you. You have to hold your head high and be proud of what you're doing. Because if you don't condemn yourself by saying 'I did wrong, but I'm here to do it right,' all you're doing is allowing other people to come up to you and say, 'Oh, you came home early' or 'What did you do wrong?' or 'Why are you home?' But if from day one you just say 'Look, I made some bad choices but I'm here to do the right thing,' then nobody can ever say anything. What are they going to say? 'How dare you for using the Atonement? How dare you for using the sacrifice that the Savior made for you?' I'd like to see that."

I said, "Yeah, that's true." So that night I told my family I was home to do the right thing, and they were very supportive. Then I met with my stake president. He submitted my name for disciplinary action and called a high council meeting, and upon their counsel, just due to some of the circumstances of the natures of my sins, they didn't feel that I needed to be disfellowshipped or excommunicated. However, I was put on temporary probation, which is very similar. I couldn't partake in the sacrament and I couldn't pray in church or participate in classes. I couldn't hold a calling. I was asked to not pay tithing. I also couldn't hold a temple recommend and therefore couldn't go to the temple.

An area authority called and discussed with my stake president the nature of the council, and they decided that in six months, I would be re-evaluated regarding my worthiness to return to the mission field. If I was found worthy, I could return. So that was the goal.

And so, for the next six months I met with my bishop every other day and my stake president twice a week. I was encouraged not to leave the state. My bishop encouraged me to stay close to home, and that I needed to keep my eye on the mission, but also that I needed to stay around people that were going to be a strength to me. He said, "If you want to do the right thing, for whatever reason and however it works, Satan's armies have their eyes on you, and you can't protect yourself alone. Doing all the right things such as reading your scriptures and praying— that's not enough. Many missionaries who come home early for worthiness issues are under siege. They are attacked in ways that you will come to find out, and you need other soldiers, so to speak. You need your dad, your mom, your bishop, your stake president. You need all of us. And we need to be there for you. These moments may come when you're on a date, or working, or when you're going to the bathroom. They may come at 2:00 in the morning. You need to have a list of people that you can call and rely upon to protect you. It is my recommendation that you stay close to those people."

Michael was lucky to have such a supportive family. Some are not so lucky. Some of you have had family who have reacted negatively to your early homecoming, which has no doubt added more shame and pain to your situation. If you lack support around you, from leaders, from friends, from anyone, please know that you do have at least two people on your side: Heavenly Father and Jesus Christ. They understand, they know your heart, and they stand by ready to heal you. Ask them to send you someone to be a support to you. It is so crucial to have a good support system at this time.

Also, if you do have a supportive family or leaders, please accept their help and lean on them often. Please, remain humble and ask for help when you need it. Pride is your enemy right now.

It is also important that you follow the advice and counsel of your leaders. It was undoubtedly annoying for Michael at times to have to meet with his bishop and stake president so often, but he did it anyways, and in the end, it helped him tremendously to become clean. You might actually feel like you need to meet with your leaders more often. Don't be afraid to ask for that, and don't begrudge your leaders if they say "No" and let you walk on your own a bit more. Trust that they are inspired, and when you feel you need to lean on someone, but no one seems available, lean on the Lord. He is always there.

Also, trust your leaders' counsel. If you feel that it is too harsh or that it is the "natural man" coming out, talk to them about it. Make sure they are coming from a place of love. If you feel that they are, trust them. They truly have your best interests at heart. If you really feel that unrighteous dominion is being administered, and you pray about it and feel the Lord thinks so too, talk to another priesthood leader about it, or that leader's counselors so that things can get straightened out.

In the next part of Michael's story, he illustrates why a support system is so crucial and why repentance is so difficult:

> I wanted to follow my leaders. However, the next six months were the hardest of my life. I can understand why people go through the repentance process and then leave the Church. I can understand the feelings they have, because I remember a specific day that I could not stop crying. And I could not stop feeling bad. I felt gross, unclean, unworthy—just bad. And there was nothing I could do to stop that feeling. I was working with my dad and I told him about this awful feeling. He put his hand on my shoulder and said, "I know what this is like, but just know you're doing the right thing and that this will pass."

I remembered praying that night, "Heavenly Father, why does it hurt so bad if I'm doing something so good? If I'm doing the right thing? I mean six weeks ago, I came home, and for the first time in my life, I was light. I felt good about what I did. But now I feel like I'm at the low of my lows."

The next day I called my old mission president who had just come home from his mission. He said, "I want you to come to my house. I only live about an hour away." And so I went to his house and I asked him that very question: "Why? I have been home for a month and a half now, almost two months. If I'm doing something so good, why does it hurt so bad?"

And he said, "Because for the first time in your life you're dealing with the pain with no pain killers. You said whenever you would sin, you would do something right. That was like taking pain killers. All you did was numb the pain. It didn't fix it; it didn't go away. But it lessened it. Now, for the first time in your life, you're dealing with it straight on."

He reminded me of a training that we had when Elder Callister came to the mission. It was titled "Becoming a Consecrated Missionary." And in this training, Elder Callister said, "On one occasion a missionary came to me with a belated confession. I asked him what motivated him to come. He responded, 'I finally disclosed to my companion that I had something to confess to the president, but I didn't want to go home. Then my companion said something that struck me to the very core. He said, 'There is something even more important than your mission.' Somewhat surprised, I replied, 'What is that?' Then came his answer: 'Repentance. Repentance is more important than your mission.' The young elder who sat before me said, 'President, I knew he was right. And that is why I'm here. I want to repent.'"

Elder Callister continued with, "Some have honestly asked, 'When should I confess?' When the sin is of such a serious magnitude that it may trigger a disciplinary proceeding or continues to linger in our minds so that we cannot have peace. If we then fail to confess, our spiritual horizons become limited. It is like being surrounded by a circular impenetrable wall. In such a circumstance, we have some limited room in which to move, but we are trapped. We will look in vain for a slit through which we can squeeze, an opening through which we can pass, an end around which we can travel. There are no end runs, no secret openings, no hidden passages. Serving a faithful mission does not obviate confession; months and years of abstinence do not erase its need. One-on-one pleading with the Lord is not a substitute. Somewhere, sometime, somehow one must face the wall, square up, and climb it.

That is confession. When we do this our spiritual horizons become unlimited and we become entitled to the promise of the Lord: 'Though your sins be scarlet they shall be as white as snow' (Isaiah 1:18)."

While I was thinking about that, my former mission president said, "Right now, you're dealing with an extremely limited horizon. But as you become cleaner and cleaner, and feel forgiven, you will have a full horizon, and an open, endless opportunity of the Spirit, the opportunity to move forward and to see the light again."

And that's what kept me going. There were many times when I wanted to give up and I had to remind myself of the reasons I came home, the reasons I was repenting, the people who supported me, the faces of those who were standing behind me. There were several times where I relapsed into some sins that I thought I had completely forsaken. I hadn't been tempted by those sins in years, but Satan knew my weaknesses. And what strengthened me was following the counsel of my leaders and sticking like glue to people who would protect me. Several times my dad caught me doing something or about to do something, and he simply said, "Michael, if you want to do the right thing, you can't do this. If you need to sleep in our room, if you need to go to counseling, if I need to put you in an addiction recovery program, if I need to put locks on everything and anything, if I need to limit things, you tell me what you want me to do, and I will do it." And that was one of my saving graces: I had so many people that protected me like that.

And it was because I started the right way when I got home. I did exactly what my father told me to do. I gave up my pride and I just said, 'I'm here to do the right thing, but I need help.' And people were willing to help me and I was willing to listen to the counsel of my leaders. That's what saved me through those six months. If I didn't have all that, there is no way that I would still be a member of this Church. There's no way I would have slogged through it and made it out. There's just no way. My personality is the type where if something is going to take months to fix, my first thought is "How can I get around it?" or "Forget about it. I don't want to deal with it. I don't want to think about it. Just leave it on the table and move on. It just isn't worth it. It's so hard. I don't feel good."

But every time I met with the stake president, he just kept reiterating to me the doctrine of forgiveness, and of forgiving ourselves. He also taught me that through our true repentance, we would feel the Lord forgive us and that that forgiveness would be a noticeable feeling. That doesn't mean it would be like this crazy, you know, angel coming down to us, but I would know that I had been forgiven.

I remember specifically being really confused about how that works—how I'd just know I'd been forgiven. About five months into being home though, I realized that when I wanted to recall some of the sins or transgressions or things of what happened, I couldn't remember them as much. It was kind of weird. Before I confessed and before I'd taken care of things, I could recall everything. I could recall dates, times, people, outfits, what I was feeling, what I was wearing, and I could recall it all in a moment—everything! And I realized over time that when I couldn't recall everything as easily and was forgetting details, I didn't forget it had happened; I just couldn't remember it as clearly. My mission president told me that it was a sign I was being for-given—that the Lord was forgiving me of my sins. And the scriptures that had comforted me and talked about "Come now let us reason together...though your sins be as scarlet they shall be as white as snow," and "I, the Lord, will remember them no more," made a lot more sense. I realized that forgiveness, like repentance, is a process, even with the Lord. It's not an instantaneous event.

So it took five months for me to feel forgiven. Something else that helped me was my mission president telling me, "You've got to be patient." Patience isn't my strength either. "You've got to remember that you've got years of sins. They don't go away in a month. Confession and doing the right thing doesn't resolve the pain. Justice has to be served. The Lord has got to teach you. And the only way he can teach you is by letting you experience some of the pain. And it hurts and it's hard. Pain is something we don't like. Pain is something that really hurts. He allows us to feel it, so that we say 'I don't ever want to go through that again. I don't ever want to do it again.' It's not like 'an eye for an eye, a tooth for a tooth' where the Lord is going say you did this for five years, now you need to suffer for five years. But He's also not going to say, 'Okay, he did this for five years and in a week's time of doing really well, and confessing, and doing everything he should, it's good. He's just going to be jumping for joy.' No, it's going to take time. And it won't take a long time but it will take longer than what you think it will." And so that's what I had to hold onto. But, naturally, it's not something I'm good at, so I had to work at it.

Here we see justice and mercy taking place in Michael's life. His mission president stated it beautifully: Michael would not have to suffer the same number of years that he was committing serious sin (mercy), but he also would not be absolved of and feel forgiven of those sins in a short amount of time (justice). Thus we see that justice cannot rob mercy, and mercy cannot rob justice (Alma 42:13–25).

We also see him realize one of the great truths of forgiveness: it is a *process*. And just like any process it takes time for it to be completed. But we do not need to fret about that. The Lord will forgive. Enjoy the process and embrace the forgiveness that comes from Him when and as it comes.

I will write more about forgiving yourself and others soon. For now, let's continue with Michael's story and see how he moved into the fifth step of the repentance process, restitution:

While on a run, my dad once said to me, "One thing you've got to remember about repentance is restitution. You don't need to tell me everything, but what have your leaders required of you to make restitution?"

And I told him, "I need this. I need to do that. I need this . . ."

And he goes, "Okay, let me ask you a question. How do you make restitution with the Lord though? Because you didn't just wrong people. You wronged the Lord. So how do you make it right with the Lord?"

And I said, "I've never thought about that."

I knew that I had wronged the Lord, but I thought He just forgave me when He forgave me. Like, it just happened when it happened. But my dad was right: I had wronged the Lord and I needed to make it right with Him.

My dad said, "If you can't go out on a mission, how do you make it right?"

I said, "Well, I move on with life."

He replied, "Absolutely. You don't fall away. You don't become a menace to society. You don't allow yourself to stop going to church and stop following the commandments. You move on. You get involved in church. You get married. You have a family. You continue with life. You don't become suicidal. You don't get depressed. You don't allow yourself to do that. That's how you make it right with the Lord if you if you can't go back out."

Then he said, "What if the option is there to go back out? How do you make it right with the Lord?"

I said, "I go back out and I finish my service."

And he replied, "Absolutely. If you want to make it right with the Lord, if returning to your mission is an option, you need to go back out and finish your commitment to serve a full two-year mission. Obviously,

I'm not Jesus Christ, but I think I would dare say that full restitution is based off of one condition that you finish your service in His name."

That was the other reason why I had the goal always to return to the mission field when I was home: to make things completely right with the Lord. I had several friends come home from a mission early and not one of them planned to return. Not one. And it boggled my mind. I asked them, "Why don't you want to return?" And they said, "Well, I did it. I mean, I was out there for a year, six months, or whatever and so that's good enough." It just didn't sit right with me. I just don't think that that question (how do you make it right with the Lord?) is being talked about enough between parent and child or even bishops and early-returned missionaries, or anybody who is mentoring an early-returned missionary. I can't really speak for the medical side of coming home early, because that's totally different, but for those who return early due to worthiness issues and who have the opportunity to return to the field, this question is not asked enough. Because if you lied in your interview and went to the temple and made it out, you promised to serve for two years. You made promises. It's not just about the time spent, but the fact that you made promises. And you broke those promises. And you need to restore yourself with the Lord. You need to make restitution.

This is how Michael personally felt he needed to make restitution with the Lord. Regarding the "stay home or return to the field" question, I have found that it is a personal question and one that requires a personal answer. I feel strongly that so long as you are right with the Lord, you are right with yourself. But Michael does make a good point that in the case of worthiness, promises were broken, and to walk away from those promises and expect the Lord to say "It's okay, we're good," is deluding yourself. If you can return to your mission, and do not feel it is the right thing for you to do, make sure the Lord feels that way too. Pray, read your scriptures, counsel with leaders, and go to the temple (because if you have the option to return to your mission, you'll also be able to go to the temple with that decision eventually). Then, own your decision and don't look back (either way).

If returning to your mission is not an option, I strongly agree with Michael that the way you make yourself right with the Lord is to continue on with the rest of your life faithfully. Continue going to church and continue to build His kingdom. Help others who struggle. Let the Lord use you for His good.

Also, make sure you also do make restitution with those you have wronged, because part of making things right with the Lord is making things right with those you have hurt. As much as you are able to contact those you've hurt, even if you have to go through a few people to get the contact information, be sure you make a good faith effort to make restitution. If in the end you cannot reach those you've harmed, pray that God will help them to know of the sincere apology in your heart and that they will forgive you and will have peace.

Michael was able to return to his mission and did.

After six and a half months, I returned to the mission. My leaders had resubmitted my application and I was told that I might not return to the same mission, but that there was a chance. My former mission president had personally called my area authority, as well as the current mission president of my old mission. Then I received a call where I was asked about how I would feel about returning to the same mission, and how it would affect the work. I told the person on the phone, "So long as you keep me out of the area I went home in, I should be just fine. I really feel like I was called to serve there, but I will go anywhere that God calls me to go, because I need to serve Him."

And so I received a phone call on a Saturday morning, and the person on the line said, "You're approved to return to [the same mission] and your plane leaves Monday morning." So I packed my bags and got ready again. I was set apart Sunday night, woke up on Monday morning, got on the plane, and went back to my mission.

For the remaining fourteen months, my mission was completely different. It was a night-and-day difference from the first ten months. I can definitely testify and see the truth behind spiritual horizons. I wouldn't say that I didn't feel the Spirit the first part of my mission, because I was definitely guided, and exercised faith, and saw miracles. But the limitations were so much more during that first part in comparison to the second part of my mission. The second part of my mission, I really felt that I wasn't so worried about my sins and comparing myself to other missionaries, and so I was able to focus more on following the example of Christ and helping others to come unto Him, and really study more about His life, and His mission to save souls.

I still stand behind the reasons for what I said to missionaries about being obedient and all that, but the second part of my mission, I was a lot more gentle and Christlike. I was caring toward their needs instead of burning them at the stake. I had a lot of very close intimate opportunities with missionaries to help them experience the role of confession and repentance.

Regarding step six, forgiving others (and I want to add forgiving yourself), Michael told me,

I think when we repent, we are completely clean spiritually. There's not even a scar left. The Lord takes us and makes us completely whole again. But as mortals, part of our mortal experience with repentance is we have to remember certain aspects of sin, and of the repentance process, just so that we learn from it. It's almost like a scar. Spiritually there's no scar, but physically—because we are imperfect and we are in a fallen state—we do remember. We do have a physical scar, so to speak, on our memories so we can recall certain things. So, even though I could remember what the sin was, I started to realize that as I was doing what was right, that I was being forgiven and I didn't question that I could move forward. I didn't really struggle with that. I simply said to myself, "You know what? This is happening. And it's okay to move forward. And I don't need to hold onto it, or rehash, or dig, or try to hold onto this because I have already held onto it for so long in my mind." I embraced the feeling of being forgiven and clean.

However, in the words of Elder Richard G. Scott,

If you are one who cannot forgive yourself for serious past transgressions—even when a judge in Israel has assured that you have properly repented—if you feel compelled to continually condemn yourself and suffer by frequently recalling the details of past errors, I plead with all of my soul that you ponder this statement of the Savior:

"He who has repented of his sins, the same is forgiven, and I, the Lord, remember them no more. By this ye may know if a man repenteth of his sins— . . . he will confess them and forsake them."

To continue to suffer when there has been proper repentance is not prompted by the Savior but the master of deceit, whose goal is to bind and enslave you. Satan will press you to continue to relive the details of past mistakes, knowing that such thoughts make forgiveness seem unattainable. In this way Satan attempts to tie strings to the mind and body so that he can manipulate you like a puppet.

I testify that when a bishop or stake president has confirmed that your repentance is sufficient, know that your obedience has allowed the Atonement of Jesus Christ to satisfy the demands of justice for the laws you have broken. Therefore you are now free. Please believe it. To continually suffer the distressing effects of sin after adequate repentance, while not intended, is to deny the efficacy of the Savior's Atonement in your behalf.[4]

Michael had this to say regarding forgiving others:

As far as forgiving others, to this day there are certain scenarios I've played in my head such as conversations that might take place if I ever ran into somebody. I've thought about asking that person, "Why did we do this?" or "Why did you persuade me to act this way or participate in this action?" And I'll recall a training I gave on justice and mercy during the second part of my mission where I said, "We have a tendency to try to take justice upon ourselves. We've been wronged, and we want to become the judge. We want the person to suffer exactly as we suffered, if not worse. We want to set the terms for how they suffer. And so we take the role of the judge for justice. Which is wrong because that is the role of the Savior, and that is something we can give to Him knowing that He has not only experienced our pain so that He can give us succor, but He also knows exactly what the person who wronged us is feeling and He knows how to give justice in a perfect way." I think forgiveness falls into the enabling power of the Atonement. While the redeeming power is what saves us and takes us from an imperfect sinner to a clean person, the enabling power is what we rely upon when we want to forgive someone who has wronged us. Because it can be hard to forgive someone, yet the Atonement enables us to forgive.

That enabling power helped me realize that other people will go through what they need to go through. I know that I am clean and worthy before the Lord, and that's all that matters. If those people who wronged me have taken care of things, great! If they haven't, they will be accountable for that and Heavenly Father and Jesus Christ will take care of it. I don't need to worry about that.

Really, I can't say it better myself. Embrace forgiveness if you haven't yet, for yourself and for others, and if you are struggling, learn more about the enabling power of the Atonement. Research it through scriptures, general conference talks, prayer, journal writing—anything you feel inspired to do! It will provide the healing and peace that you seek (although not instantly! Remember, forgiveness is a process).

Michael completed the repentance process, and not only did he make it out with his testimony still in place, he came out with it stronger. He was also a much happier person. He truly repented fully of his sins and experienced that "mighty change of heart" that Alma talks about (see Alma 5:14). He completed his mission successfully and with honor. That's not to say that the rest of his mission looked picture-perfect. He didn't get along as well with his second mission president, and he struggled with a companion or two, but the difference in how he felt just being on a mission was striking. He has also lived the rest of his life so far in a way that embraces the commandments of God. He seeks to do good and to teach others. He married in the temple and has a happy family life today. He is so grateful that he came home early and repented fully.

Michael's advice to anyone beginning or struggling through the repentance process is this:

> If you do the right thing, you can make it through it. Don't give up. Keep your head up high. Focus on one thing: the Savior. If you focus on following Him and doing the right thing, you'll be okay.

I want to add my testimony that the Savior loves you. He knows you personally and He is intimately aware of your struggles. He wants you to come to Him so that He can scrape out those sins and make you clean again. It will not be a painless process and it's not meant to be. But from pain we can know joy, comfort, and peace, and that is what He promises to all who come unto Him and repent.

Notes

1. See "Chapter 19: Repentance," *Gospel Principles* (2011), 107–13, https://www.lds.org/manual/gospel-principles/chapter-19-repentance.
2. Larry R. Lawrence, "The War Goes On," *Ensign*, Apr. 2017.
3. Russell M. Nelson, "Joy and Spiritual Survival," *Ensign*, Nov. 2016.
4. Richard G. Scott, "Peace of Conscience and Peace of Mind," *Ensign*, Nov. 2004.

CHAPTER 4

Family Troubles

Coming home due to family troubles is like receiving a double helping of grief. First, you lose a family member and/or family structure and stability. That loss can come packaged in any number of forms: severe illness, death, divorce, apostasy, and so on. Second, you lose the mission. The grief that results from these losses can be intense. My heart goes out to you. You have a heavy burden to carry.

You are not alone in having walked this path. Heavenly Father and Jesus Christ understand *your* road exactly and will send you the help you need exactly when you need it. Continue to rely on them, talk to them, and listen to the promptings and comforts of the Holy Ghost, and you will have the strength you need to move through the grieving process. Also, while your path may look different from others' (because no two paths are exactly the same), there are many others who understand this road of loss.

In this chapter, I will first share some stories of those who know this road. Then, I will walk you through the grieving process, keeping you and the stories in mind. It is vital that you understand the grieving process so that you know what is going on in your mind and how you are currently processing information. Understanding the grieving process will also help you understand the stories below and why each person made the decisions he or she did as they moved through this process themselves.

Ava's Story: A Desire to Help Her Mother Grieve

I'm a convert to the Church, and the only member in my family. I left for my mission about a year and a half after joining the Church. While my parents were okay with my desire to serve a mission, they didn't really understand it. However, they were kind and wrote me letters frequently.

I was out for two months, and just beginning to enjoy the work and fall in love with the people, when my mom told me my aunt's terminal cancer had gotten worse. I felt guilty for not being at home with my family. I was not close to my aunt, but my mom and I were close and I felt bad for not being able to be there for her. My dad was having health troubles as well and that added to my guilt. I felt very torn about whether or not I should go home. I loved my mission and wanted to be there, but I also really wanted to be at home helping my family. I kept going back and forth. I prayed a lot and eventually I decided that it was time for me to come home.

My companion and mission president were supportive. My mission president was just making sure that this is what I wanted to do. And he was aware of my family situation. I'm sure he talked to my family much more than he let on. And so he was aware of what was going on which made me feel very loved.

My mom actually came and picked me up from my mission. We drove to my aunt's home, and I saw my aunt for the last time. Then we flew home.

I didn't get home until late Sunday night, so I didn't have a big homecoming. I didn't tell anybody I was coming home either because, you know, it was also shameful to come home early. I kind of hid at home for a while. I didn't tell too many people, although I think a month or so later people kind of found out on their own.

I talked to my stake president and he was loving and supportive. He still talks to me all the time today. I talked to my bishop. He said, "How are you doing?" And I was like, "Well, I'm trying to get through." As far as ward members go, there was an awkward time where they were like, "Are you going to go back out?" and I was like, "I don't know yet. Probably not." But yeah, just a lot of, "Why are you here?" and "Are you going to go back out?" I'm sure they didn't do it purposefully.

As far as I know, there wasn't an option for me to return to my mission. None of my leaders ever approached me about it, and I didn't think to ask. Today, I think about that often. Looking back, a year and a half later, I think I would have gone back out. But, at the same time, I'm okay that I didn't. I'm at a good place in my life now. I was able to help my mom grieve. In fact, a year after I came home, my grandmother died, and I was able to help my mom grieve again. My relationship with my mom hasn't always been strong, but it is stronger than ever now, and I credit my mission—or rather my coming home early from a mission—for that.

However, I did grieve the loss of my mission. I went to the temple a lot. I did that quite a bit. I kept going to church, as hard as it was. And I went to institute. If that's available, I say go to that, because it helped me greatly. And I hung on to the friends that I knew would love and support me. I kept doing the things that made me happy. And I prayed a lot and I cried all the time. I just spent months crying. I think you have to go through that grieving process to be able to accept the life that God has planned for you.

In the end, you can't dwell on how much you would have liked to finish your mission. You can't think that you failed. You have to think that you served the amount of time that God needed you. It's not any fault of your own that you couldn't finish a mission—or rather, the intended amount of time you'd set aside to serve a mission. The fact that you went out and you were willing to sacrifice your time, talent, and efforts in serving the Lord is admirable and that's what you should put your focus on. If you want to go back out that's wonderful, but if you don't go back out, there will be many more opportunities for you to be able to share the gospel at home.

Ava's situation was unique in that she was a recent convert to the Church and was not as familiar with some of the cultural expectations surrounding missions, such as not leaving a mission even if a family member passes away. She felt torn and guilty, and in the end decided to go home, which she does not regret. She would have likely appreciated the option to return to her mission, but she is okay with the way her life turned out, even though she did grieve the loss of the mission and gave some sound advice for anyone else struggling with that loss. Ava's situation is a difficult one to understand completely, as it is a path that not many walk, but I love how much peace Ava feels with her life, and the fact that she stayed faithful after losing her mission even when it was sometimes hard. I will discuss Ava's story more shortly.

Olivia's Story: Inability to Grieve Her Mother's Death and Homesickness

After I had graduated from high school, my mom passed away unexpectedly. All through high school we talked about if I was going to go on a mission. Most of the time I was hesitant, like "I don't really want to go," but she really wanted me to go. And so when she passed away, I felt like it was a way for me to honor my mom. It also felt right, so I went.

My mom passed away in July and I left in April. My family situation was very crazy after my mom passed away. My dad moved away and left the Church, so it was just me and my siblings. We were all pretty grown, but not enough to know what to do. We had to hurry and move out of our house and into a family friend's home. There were a lot of crazy changes and it was all very quick and I didn't have a lot of time to process everything. I didn't really let myself think about my mother either. When my siblings and I packed up her things, we didn't really go through them or look at them. We just put them in boxes in our hurry to get into the family friend's home.

After I'd moved into the family friend's home, it was time for me to get ready to go on a mission. Then I left. When I got to my first (and only) area, I started to feel really anxious and homesick. I tried to tell myself that this is normal and everyone feels like this. I was a little standoffish and shy with my companion, and when she'd go take a shower or something, I'd just cry. I was so sad. I wanted to go home. I missed my family. I really felt like I was never going to see them ever again. My time processing abilities were off; the end of the day seemed so far away. I was just like, "I need to get home."

That was the first couple of days. By the middle of the week, I remember asking my companion, 'When did you get over this homesickness feeling?' And she was like, "Oh, well, it never really goes away." She didn't really know what I was going through. She didn't know that I was thinking about going home. So all I could think was, "Oh my gosh. I don't want to feel like this my whole mission!"

Mother's Day came, and as we were sitting in Sunday School, I leaned over and asked my companion if I could have the phone. She slowly handed it to me and I stood up and left the room. I called my brother's phone. When he answered, I was just crying and like, 'I'm coming home.' He was completely shocked. My crying was so intense;

I just wanted to get home so bad. My homesickness was at a whole new level.

All day on Mother's Day, the mission president gave my family permission to call me because I was feeling horrible. I told my family, "I'm going to buy my own plane ticket right now because I want to get home so bad." I was very determined to get home that day.

My companion was really sweet about it. She came and found me when I was on the phone with my brother at church. She just sat there and didn't try to tell me to get off the phone. She just rubbed my back while I cried and talked to my family. When I hung up, she asked me if I wanted to go home. I said I did. Well, she was still a missionary, and she was like "I think we need to go do service," so that Sunday we went to a home for the elderly and sang to some mothers that were there. She just kept doing her work and trying to comfort me and let me know it was fine that I wanted to go home.

My mission president was awesome. He said the same thing and added, "Sisters aren't even required to go, and for you to come out here with all of your family problems and complications and still have the courage to come out here—you're amazing!"

I wanted to go home that day, but my mission president said it would take a week to get home. It was my decision to go home. I personally feel like I came home because I didn't have time to come to terms with my mom being gone, and I missed my family.

I didn't even think that my family would be there to welcome me home. I was thinking the worst. As I was in the airport, I wanted to take off my tag, but multiple people had told me that I needed to keep my name tag on because I was still a missionary. I was like, "I don't want anyone to know I'm a missionary. I don't want them to ask me anything." And sure enough, multiple people, as I was waiting for the flight, came up and thanked me for serving. I thought, "I was only out for a month. This is embarrassing. They don't even know I'm going home only after a month. I just kind of played it off like, "Yeah, thank you!"

I was very scared to get off the plane. Surprisingly my entire family was there waiting for me. They embraced me, and it was nice and very comforting.

My stake president was interesting. I didn't really get a feeling of comfort when I talked with him. It was very cold and awkward. He released me and we talked for a very short time and then I was on my way.

I was so happy to be home, to be back in Utah. I never felt regret or sad that I came home. Sometimes I felt scared to see people because I didn't want to hear their reaction or their surprise at me being home. Other than that though, I just felt so happy and relieved to be back home. I'd never been away from my family for a long period of time before, and I was happy to be back.

I was also able to finally grieve my mother's death fully. I was able to think about her and go through her things that had been so hurriedly boxed up. I didn't have such a fast-pace of life anymore, now that I was no longer in the field and things had settled down at home.

Olivia suffered from homesickness, which was made worse by her inability to grieve her mother's death. I cover the homesickness side of Olivia's story in chapter 5. It is extremely difficult to grieve the loss of someone if we don't allow ourselves time to grieve. Olivia did not allow herself this time and she paid a large price for it: she lost her confidence and her mission. Some might look down on her for leaving her mission over an inability to grieve, thinking she should have put behind all her cares, but working through grief is so important for our mental health. I will discuss this more after the next story.

Mason's Story: Divorce

I would like to put a quick caveat in here and tell readers upfront that Mason did not actually come home from his mission, but was *very, very* close to doing so. I include his story because Mason provides excellent insight and understanding into why one would choose to go home early after learning that one's family is breaking apart—about what happens in our minds and bodies as we handle such tragic, and traumatizing, news. Mason decided to go home and would have followed through on that decision except for circumstances that made it possible for him to stay: he had a mission president who was willing to talk to him frequently, and while he didn't have a good companion at first, eventually he had a good companion to talk to, and was able to even speak to a mission therapist in the field.

If you came home early due to divorce, apostasy, or anything else that caused the family structure you loved to disintegrate, I do not want you to read Mason's story and think, "Well, he didn't come home early, so I should have been able to stick it out." Each person's road is different, and therefore every person's thought processes and circumstances are different. Mason did not necessarily have clearer thought processes than you or even better circumstances. Rather, things simply worked out differently for Mason, and he was able to complete the intended amount of time. This was not done by his own strength though; he had extra help. For whatever reason, the Lord saw fit to keep Mason on the mission. The Lord saw fit to let you go home. There is no shame in returning early because of an inability to cope with family troubles, and you must not think you are worse of a person or missionary than Mason because you returned home early. That thought is simply untrue, and you must accept that before you read his story. You must not read his story looking for the differences; rather, you need to look for the similarities. You need to read his story through the eyes of someone who understands the road you are on. His road looked different, but the grieving process that he went through, and that you must go through, are very similar if not the same.

> My family structure had been falling apart for quite some time, but I was too naive to see it. I thought everything was okay. I left for my mission, but while I was in the MTC, I had an email conversation with my sister where I realized that things weren't actually okay. I struggled a little with worry but was mostly able to focus on preparing to go to the field. Things were going all right.
>
> About four months later, I was in the field, and found out that Mom and Dad were getting divorced. And it was an ugly divorce. There was so much going on back at home. I couldn't believe what was happening. There were several times that my companion and I went back to our apartment early, and I just cried on the bed. I just felt like I was falling.
>
> However, I was in a busy area and was able to keep busy and distracted for about six months. In those six months, there had been a lot of communication about money, and how a trust had been set up in my name, and one of my parents had taken my mission money with the promise to pay it back. Things were getting crazy. We later learned that one of my parents had a mental illness. But, again, I was in a busy area, and so when I wasn't trying to sort out family and money stuff, I was able to work and forget about things for a while.
>
> It wasn't until about six months later, when I was in a much slower area, that it really started hitting me. Like everything kind of settled out emotionally, and it finally hit me what had happened to my family.

I was with a missionary who was extremely sarcastic. I couldn't trust him at all. I couldn't open up and be real about anything. He made fun of me with anything he could. I was struggling to work. I mean, I struggled to even make it out the door. And there were a couple times where I was just like, "I need to go home." My companion would get upset and he would get mad. Or, worse, he would just sit there and stare at me until I looked at him, and then he'd simply say "What?"

I remember going into my room one day, shutting the door, and climbing up to the top bunk of our bunk bed, and as I was climbing up the rungs of the ladder, it hit me like a train that I couldn't do it anymore. I couldn't. It was too much. Maybe I should go home.

Admitting that to myself felt like contemplating suicide. Being a missionary was just such a part of my identity; I felt like I was giving up everything that I was. And while I wasn't thinking about suicide in and of itself, the thought of going home felt poignant enough that especially looking back, suicide was probably only a short throw away. I was at a really low point.

Fortunately, I had a good mission president. I called him up and said, "I need to go home." He and I had talked about it before, but I'd always said, "No, I don't want to go home. I'll keep on going." But this time I said, "I need to go home." And we talked for like half an hour on the phone. At the end of our conversation, he said, "Mason, I'm thinking that it's probably not wise for you to go home. You're probably actually better off being away from the family drama that's going on there. It's probably better that you're here. Can you hold out to the end of the week and then come to my office? And if you still feel that way, then we'll talk about it."

I agreed. I remember those four or five days passing by and I truly didn't know if I was going to stay on my mission or not. I really did not know. Each day, each missionary experience, I was wondering if I would be having those experiences the following week. I wondered what my life would even look like the following week. But I also weighed through in my mind what my mission president had said about it being better for me to be on my mission, away from the family drama, than at home in the middle of it. And over the course of a week, that really sunk in. That the mission actually was good for me. It really was, in a way, saving me.

So, in a week, we went to the mission president's home. Because I could not confide in my companion at all, he had no idea why we were there. He just knew that I was just chatting with the president about something.

My mission president asked if I still felt like I needed to go home, and I replied "No. I'll keep on going. I'll keep on working. I'll keep on trying." I asked him for a priesthood blessing. He asked me if I wanted my companion to join me, and I said, "Heck no." Because I did not want him in there. I couldn't trust him at all.

So my mission president gave me a blessing by himself. And I remember that blessing because it was a very profound blessing. It really carried me through for months. Toward the end of my mission I reflected on it and just how remarkable that blessing was, and how accurate. It was just very spiritually powerful. And also, not just the blessing but the spirit of the mission. I developed the testimony that a mission was really something more than just me—and I think that's the biggest reason why I stayed on my mission. That ultimately, I was convinced that this was something that was about more than just me. It was something of God because otherwise, there ain't nothing that would have kept me on my mission. It was much too difficult, just a mission in and of itself, but especially with the family drama.

So, anyways, I had that experience with the blessing, which carried me through as I developed my own testimony of the importance of missions, specifically my mission. The depression still lasted. It didn't just go away. And it wasn't until I was able to work through with a therapist that I was finally able to make it through the depression. But it took about a year.

So by no means was that conversation with my mission president the end. The struggle continued. I had monthly chats with him on the phone. I always wondered if I would make it through to the end of the mission. I always wanted to stay on the mission, but I just didn't know if I would.

The hardest part of being on a mission and having family troubles going on back home is that you have very few ways to cope, especially if you feel you have no one to talk to. And my mission president actually highlighted that. In his own words, he said, "When you were at home, you could go watch movies and play games. You could hang out with friends and just relax. You could do whatever you needed to do to get through hard things that happen in life. But on a mission, you don't have your usual coping mechanisms to fall back on. So when life hits you in the face, you struggle much more, and despair much more easily."

When faced with grief, it can be incredibly hard to fulfill responsibilities as vast and as consuming as a mission's and also work through grief. Mason was lucky to have such a kind, understanding mission president who helped him work through his grief and fears and also helped him get the professional help that he needed. If you came home due to a divorce, or similar fracturing in your family, please know that your feelings of despair are real and valid. We are going to talk about how to work through them healthily next.

Working through Grief

One of the best books I've read on the subject of grief is *Good Grief* by Granger E. Westberg. It is also one of the shortest books I've read on the subject. At sixty-three pages long, it gives just enough information to help give a basic, yet adequate, understanding of what we experience when we feel grief, and I recommend you get yourself a copy of it if you can. Westberg breaks the grief cycle into ten stages:

1. We are in a state of shock.
2. We express emotion.
3. We feel depressed and very lonely.
4. We may experience physical symptoms of distress.
5. We may become panicky.
6. We feel a sense of guilt about the loss.
7. We are filled with anger and resentment.
8. We resist returning.
9. Gradually hope comes through.
10. We struggle to affirm reality.

Westberg says in the introduction to his book that it is important to "remember that every person does not necessarily go through all these stages, nor in this order. Moreover, it is impossible to differentiate clearly between each of these stages, for a person never moves neatly from one stage to the other."[1]

So as to do no disservice to Westberg and his hard work that created his book, I will summarize each stage and apply them to the coming home early experience. For a more thorough understanding of his ten stages of grief, I again recommend that readers purchase and read his book. It is excellent.

We Are in a State of Shock

When we first encounter something that causes us grief, we may feel temporarily numb to the feelings of pain and sorrow. In a way, this state of shock is something to be grateful for as it keeps us from feeling everything all at once. This stage can last anywhere from a few hours to a few days. If it goes on for a few weeks, the grief is not being worked through healthily and professional help needs to be sought.

Olivia and Mason stayed in the shock phase for too long. Olivia likely would have taken the time to grieve her mother's death, but she had to hurry and pack up her mother's things and move into a family friend's home after her dad left. After things settled down a bit, it was time for her to leave on a mission. She stayed numb and didn't let herself feel the emotions of losing her mother.

Mason stayed busy for the first year of his mission, although grief did break through his tough exterior occasionally when he would come home and cry. Because Mason stayed busy, he did not have to fully face the reality of what was happening at home. He knew what was happening, but he didn't stop and think about it too often. When he finally didn't have enough to distract him, the feelings that had been suppressed for so long welled up, and Mason did not have a healthy way to cope. He was unable to be distracted. He had to finally face what was happening back at home.

Ava stayed numb for about a week before she began to grieve the loss of her mission. This was healthy, and although Ava cried for several months, she went through this stage of grief healthily and was able to move forward with her life even as she grieved, whereas Olivia and Mason were unable to take on new challenges (a mission or a sarcastic companion).

Where are you at in regards to this stage? Did you visit it? How long did you stay in it? Are you still in it? If so, are you afraid of leaving it?

If you are still in this stage and are afraid of leaving it, you are letting your brain trick you into thinking that staying in grief is better than moving through it and on to a new life. Grief does hurt and does require work and that's why it is so scary to all of us. We'd rather just not feel it. But it is absolutely necessary to feel what we need to feel in order to make sense of our situation, come to know ourselves better, and move forward healthily with our lives.

We Express Emotion

The emotion comes when we realize how terrible our loss is, and sometimes it comes without warning. We feel an uncontrollable urge to express our grief, and Westberg encourages his readers to do so. It is so important to express what we feel—to *feel* what we feel. Ignoring the feelings only makes them go into storage, and as a therapist once told me, "They come back later with interest." The sooner we can express our emotions, the better our mental health and the better we move through the grieving process.

When Olivia reached her first area, she cried a lot. By coming on a mission, she had lost her family and therefore the support system she had always known. More than that, though, the family she knew and had grown up with was gone and she'd never given herself the chance to come to terms with that. She'd stayed numb for far too long. Now, on a mission, her usual coping strategies were gone and she was in a completely new situation. Of course the emotions welled up and she wondered what on earth she was doing there! Any of us would wonder the same thing if we were in her situation.

Ava cried for months over her lost mission. She allowed herself to fully feel the emotions of the loss and let them come at a healthy pace.

Mason let the emotions hit him here and there, but didn't allow them to fully come until a year into his mission when things slowed down. All of the suppressed emotions rose to the surface and Mason was forced to feel the full weight of them. They nearly crushed him. He felt a lot of sadness and despair.

The sadness Olivia and Mason suppressed, and that Mason could not express openly to his companion, came to a head finally and blocked their progress because they were forced to deal with it all at once instead of slowly letting themselves feel it. Ava cried for months, but she also dealt with the grief more healthily because she allowed herself to do this and to go places where she could seek counsel and comfort.

Where are you at? Have you allowed yourself to feel the emotions of your grief? You may wonder if these emotions will ever go away. They will, but you must allow yourself to feel the emotions of your loss in order to ever come to terms with what happened. You must not correct your emotions so as to feel happy or hopeful. You must allow your body and mind to feel what it feels. Be kind and do not judge yourself. It is okay to feel strong emotions.

We Feel Depressed and Very Lonely

Eventually, we may come to feel isolated and depressed. We feel distanced from God, and we may even feel as though He does not care about our suffering. We are certain we are alone in our feelings of grief, that no one understands us, that no one has ever grieved as we are now grieving. And although it may be true that no two people face the same kind of loss the same way, and grief is an individual experience, being completely alone is a "universal phenomenon."[2] While in our lowest points of despair it is helpful to remember that despair "is to be expected following any significant loss and that such depression is normal and a part of good healthy grief."[3]

Olivia felt like the homesickness would never go away. Mason felt like the feelings of sadness, despair, and utter helplessness would never go away. Both felt like they could not continue on in their missions and needed to go home. Neither felt like they had people around them who really cared about them. Olivia was "standoffish and shy" toward her companion and so isolated herself that way, and Mason felt as though he could not trust his companion and so felt forced into isolation. Ava hid from others for a time. While it can be embarrassing and hard to let others know we are grieving or did something potentially shameful (or perceived as shameful), it is much, much better to simply own the grief or shame, rather than to isolate ourselves. Isolation is where depression lives.

It is *normal* to feel depressed when we suffer a great loss. And, as we can see in the case of Mason, having someone he could talk to and trust (his mission president) was essential for his healing. Ava made herself get out of the house and go to the temple, be at institute around others her age, go to church, and continue to do things that made her happy. Olivia worked through her grief by looking at her mother's things and processing the memories and events of the last several months. She allowed herself to go slowly and take her time and by so doing found peace and happiness again.

Where are you at? Are you still hiding? Have you given up praying to God? Do you feel like He is no longer listening to you or that He even cares? Such feelings are normal, but they can lead us down a road we do not wish to go down, so it is important that you find someone you can trust to talk to—this can be a family member, friend, Church leader, or professional therapist—and help you come out of your depression and isolation and continue working through your grief.

Also, remember that God does not forget you and He never stops caring about you. In Isaiah 49:15–16 we read, "Yea, they may forget, yet will I not forget thee. Behold, I have graven thee upon the palms of my hands; thy walls are continually before me." Take a look at your hand. See how close you are to God's face? He cannot forget you and He does not want to.

We May Experience Physical Symptoms of Distress

Westberg has worked as a clergyman in a medical center for many years. He realized in the course of his work that many of the patients he saw were ill because of unresolved grief. Although the patients would go to the doctor with a physical complaint, many would tell Westberg about a substantial loss they had experienced in the recent past. These experiences led him to conclude that there is a correlation between our physical health and the way we handle loss, and that until we work through our grief, nothing will take away our physical symptoms.

In the course of our conversation, Mason told me that he lost a lot of weight as he went through his grief process on his mission, especially before he started talking to a therapist. It can be difficult to take care of ourselves when we go through grief. So often, we simply want to disappear. Self-care takes great effort when we are stuck in grief, and especially when we are depressed and see no way out of it.

Common physical manifestations of grief are

- general tiredness and extreme fatigue at times
- random pains and aches, such as headaches and rib, neck, or back pain
- an inability to sit still, restlessness
- gastric distress, such as an ulcer, inflammation of the esophagitis, or colitis
- shortness of breath
- heart palpitations
- loss of appetite or it's opposite: comfort eating
- insomnia
- finding it hard to sleep or fear of sleeping
- muscle weakness
- increased blood pressure, risk of heart attack and blood clots
- anxiety attacks
- suppressed immune system[4]

It is always wise to see a physician if any of these symptoms are prolonged. However, consider seeing a therapist to help you work through your grief, if a medical doctor is unable to help you. LDS Family Services "provides short-term professional counseling for individuals, couples, and families. Services need to be authorized by a bishop, stake president, or mission president."[5]

We May Become Panicky

When we can think of nothing except our loss, we may find ourselves becoming panicky. We begin to question our mental health, we stop producing the work that we are capable of, and when people ask us questions we often have to ask them to repeat themselves. Others may begin to worry about us too, which naturally only incites more panic within us. However, this inability to concentrate is natural, and that "It would be stranger still if we could easily put aside our grief for routine matters. When something has been terribly important to us for a long time and it is taken from us, we cannot help but be constantly drawn to the lost object."[6]

Olivia and Mason could not focus on the mission due to their lost family structures. Mason felt at times like he was falling. Both wondered what their lives would look like in the future and neither felt as though it would get better. They became ineffective as missionaries. Ava cried for months and could think of little else except her mission. While it was good that Ava processed her emotions, they may have at times been taken to an unhealthy level, especially if she ever felt panicky or like she had really done wrong by the Lord in coming home early and that He was displeased or unhappy with her.

Westberg strongly recommends during this time when we can think of nothing except our loss that we be open to new and different human relationships, even though new things are undoubtedly the last thing we wish to do. We'd prefer to stay home and "be gloomy rather than go out and be forced to be nice to people and think new thoughts. Such an attitude is natural; it is to be expected. We must not, however, wallow in our gloom, for it will only prolong our grief work. And to work through grief is very hard work!"[7]

Ava got back out into society and made sure she stayed involved in the Church. She did not let herself leave the Church and stayed where her support system was. She really enjoyed institute and highly recommended it to anyone else struggling to move through grief.

Mason developed a good relationship with his mission president. He was humble enough to recognize that he needed to call him every month and chat about the problem. He also saw a therapist, and that's when things really started turning around for him. Soon, he was able to get out of his gloom, and subsequent anxiety attacks, and formed relationships with others on his mission. Through persistent effort (over the course of eight months) he was able to stay away from the panic that made him feel he could no longer be a missionary.

Have you panicked? Have you decided to leave the Church, or avoid people, or sit and be gloomy? Have you made any rash or extreme decisions? Was leaving your mission a rash decision? What can you do today to start moving forward instead of backward into panic?

We Feel a Sense of Guilt about the Loss

It is important to note the difference between "normal" guilt and "neurotic" guilt. Normal guilt is what we feel when "we have done something, or neglected to do something, for which we ought, by the standards or our society, to feel guilty. Neurotic guilt is feeling guilty all out of proportion to our own real involvement in a particular problem...it is often intertwined with real guilt."[8]

Ava told me that she felt a lot of guilt about being on a mission while her mother was dealing with the loss of a sister. Ava felt guilty that she could not be there to help her mother, which is normal guilt. However, the part that I'm concerned became neurotic is where she felt like her mother would not be able to cope without her. Whether or not this is true is between God, Ava, and Ava's mother. Ava's mother well may have been able to cope on her own, but undoubtedly it was made easier by Ava coming home.

Ava also likewise felt guilty about leaving her mission. It is normal to feel guilty about breaking a commitment, especially a commitment to the Lord. However, Ava's guilt would have become neurotic if she felt like the Lord would not accept her offering of a mission unless she returned and finished her mission, which as far as she knew was not an option. Therefore, Ava did the next best thing she could: she stayed faithful to the Lord and carried on with her life in a healthy, spiritual way.

Did you or are you now experiencing any sort of neurotic guilt? Remember it can be intertwined with normal guilt, so look deep within yourself and ask yourself if the guilt is in its proper proportions. If not, ask God to help you to keep the guilt in is proper proportions and to resolve the guilt. Be open to the idea of talking to a trusted friend or therapist to help you overcome any neurotic guilt.

We Are Filled with Anger and Resentment

While no one would encourage you to stay angry or resentful, it would be wrong not to acknowledge that anger and resentment are normal feelings as we move through grief. "When we have something precious taken from us, we inevitably go through a stage when we are very critical of everything and everyone who was related to the loss. We spare no one in our systematic scrutiny of the event, attempting to understand exactly why this thing happened, and who is to blame."[9]

When Olivia arrived in the mission field, and no longer had the security of family or the MTC (which can feel a lot like family), she felt as though something precious had been taken away from her: her familiar environment and security. She was "standoffish" toward her companion likely because her companion was related to the new environment, which was related to her loss of the old environment.

When I lost my mission, I blamed my trainer for her lack of understanding and my mission president for "forcing" me to make a decision I didn't want to make. I thought that if my trainer had just been more understanding or if my mission president had just listened harder to the Spirit (and therefore would've *known* I'd quickly heal—as though the Spirit works like a crystal ball), I would still be on my mission. I even went through a phase where I blamed my leaders, parents, and friends who had served missions for not preparing me enough for the realities of a mission. I blamed the Church for only publishing pictures of happy missionaries. No one was exempt from my scrutiny as I tried to make sense of losing my mission.

This is normal, and the emotions are necessary to feel if they are there. However, they must not stay. Anger turns into resentment and bitterness, which leads to nothing except misery. If you are struggling to forgive someone, including yourself, for injustices or unfair expectations, please read the sections I've written regarding forgiveness in chapters 1–3.

We Resist Returning

When we suffer a loss, our world has changed, and it feels strange to get back to life as usual, even though that is also what we long for. It is strange to watch other people carry on with their lives as though nothing tragic has happened to us. Indeed, as a society, we are rather ineffective at helping others work through their grief, and we ought to do better at "bearing one another's burdens" (Mosiah 18:8) so that no one is made to feel that they must keep the memory of their loss alive. Furthermore, when we try to move back into life as usual, it can be painful, and we would rather stay in our grief than try to cope with new situations from our new worldview. We find our new world to be unpredictable, and the grief has become familiar—even comfortable.

In my course of chatting with Mason, he opened up to me about how hard it was for him to accept even after his mission was over that his parents were divorced. He felt a lot of anger over how things had played out and was confused. Most of his siblings had moved on, but he felt like everything still needed to be discussed. Several years later, he was able to move on and is in a much happier place with life, but for a while, he needed to talk and felt the need to keep the memory of the previous family structure alive. He simply couldn't accept the change immediately.

For me, in moving on from my mission, I felt like I couldn't let people forget that I came home early. It was a long time before I realized I could just say "I served a mission" without the added "but I came home early." It's not necessarily that I wanted people to know I'd come home early so that I could have sympathy—in fact, I didn't want their sympathy. Rather, it was that I resisted returning to the idea that I was okay in the eyes of God. I resisted the idea that my mission was just as valid and good as someone who had served the full eighteen months or two years. I resisted the idea that my offering was acceptable to the Lord. I had suffered a great loss in losing my mission, and I wasn't quite ready to let go of that loss for several years.

Of course, I didn't grieve openly because that would have been out of place in society. I definitely stayed silent about my grief. Eventually the questions stopped. Everyone in my life knew I wasn't going back out. We all went back to business as usual. Except for me. I continued to grieve in silence. Returning to college was strange. I wasn't supposed to be there. "Look at all these normal people" I thought. "I shouldn't be seeing any of this. I should be looking at dirt roads, traveling in a jeepney, teaching the gospel. I shouldn't be going out on the weekends with friends or working late at night on a homework assignment." I appeared to be moving on, but I continued to grieve silently. Only my closest friends knew what I was really going through.

It is important to find someone that you can talk to and share your burdens with. I know full well how hard it is to talk to people about your problems—I often talk about my problems with someone by first apologizing for bringing them up and reassuring the person that I don't wish to burden them. But, more often than not, people are more than willing to lend a listening ear and help you however you need to be helped. We all have burdens that we carry, so we all understand how heavy they can be, and we all likewise know the relief of just sharing them with another person. Just the fact that someone else knows, and you have someone else you can talk to if needed, brings a feeling of relief.

Sometimes, though, I'll talk to someone about my problems and then never talk to them about my problems again. I'll feel embarrassed about bringing them up in the first place. I'll even avoid that person. Often, out of consideration, others don't ask how things are going because they don't want to bring up bad memories, especially if things appear to be going well. I (and you) might often have to reach out several times for help before a friend will feel comfortable checking in occasionally. We might even have to ask that they check in with us every so often and see if we need a listening ear or a chance to get out and do something.

Talking about coming home early to close friends was the best thing I ever did. And then eventually, chiming in to the "RM conversations" where returned missionaries share their mission stories was another wonderful thing. I was able to remember the good parts of my mission and those things that I'd learned and come away with. I realized that I'd truly become a better person thanks to my mission.

If you are the type that likes to work things out in silence, then that is okay too. Just do not think that you have to. If you find yourself repeating the same things over and over to yourself, try talking them out with someone. You may find that it helps you move to the next step, which is what we all want: hope.

Gradually Hope Comes Through

"Now and then we get a little glimpse of hope in one experience or another. This cloud that had been so dark begins to break up, and rays of light come through. We may be in deep grief anywhere from a few weeks to many months. We are never quite sure how long grief is going to last. We must remember that no two people are the same, nor are any two grief situations identical."[10] But the little rays of hope tell us that it will not last forever.

Ava felt hope as she attended the temple, went to institute, prayed, read her scriptures, and continued to do what she loved. Olivia felt hope as she talked to priesthood leaders and trusted family members. Mason felt hope as he counseled with his mission president, good companions, and a therapist. After his mission, Mason felt hope as he talked through his family situation with trusted family members and close friends. All of these things helped to keep things in perspective for Ava, Olivia, and Mason and that perspective is what allowed hope to come through. I felt hope as I began to participate in conversations about missions and saw people respond positively to my comments and stories.

We Struggle to Affirm Reality

I love what Westberg says regarding this final stage of grief: "Please note that we do not say that the final stage is 'We become our old selves again.' When we go through any significant grief experience, we come out of it as different people. Depending upon the way we respond to this event, we are either stronger people than we were before, or weaker; either healthier in spirit, or sicker."[11]

Furthermore, he has found that those who are mature in their religious faith tend to weather the grief process much better than those with immature faith because they were better able to rely on God and know that they would not face this trial or the future alone. People mature in their religious faith still grieve deeply, but they come out of it with a better understanding of why the loss happened and that although life will never be the same, there is still "much in life that can be affirmed."[12] Westberg encourages everyone to continue to exercise their faith, much the same way an athlete exercises his or her muscles, so that we can always be prepared for whatever may come. As Elder Joseph B. Wirthlin said, "If we approach adversities wisely, our hardest times can be times of greatest growth, which in turn can lead toward times of greatest happiness."[13]

You will come out of this a new person (a better person if you move through it healthily). Grief changes us, and I believe that's exactly what God intended it to do. We are not meant to stay the same person as we go through life, so it would be completely wasted effort to move through grief and come out of it exactly the same as we were before.

Should I Stay Home or Go Back Out?

God cares about you and your situation. You may have felt that you should go home because God knew that was the best place for you to grieve. Or perhaps you needed to go home to realize that the mission was truly your best option, and that allows you to make the decision to go back out without any "What ifs?"

The decision to stay home or go back out is extremely personal and what may be right for one person may not be right for another. I encourage you to pray about your decision, seek counsel from your priesthood leaders, visit a therapist if needed to make sure you are thinking and processing things clearly, talk to family and friends, and finally take your decision to the temple and ask God to confirm your decision or make it clear that His will is the opposite of whatever you've decided. Then, have faith, and follow through with whatever promptings you receive. If you feel it is right to go back out, do all you can to be ready to leave again and dedicate that time to the Lord. If you feel it is right to stay, move forward with life knowing that you are right with the Lord. Continue to dedicate your life to Him—He'll make so much of it if you do. If you feel that either choice is right with the Lord, then go with what you feel in your heart is what you truly want to do. Go serve that mission, or go back to school, or take that job. Whatever you do, stay faithful, and know that He will stay faithful to you.

Final Thoughts

Finally, know that your family will be blessed for your service. In Mormon culture, we sometimes hear that a family would have been blessed more if a missionary had just stayed on his or her mission. However, the Lord is fully aware of your circumstances, and your offering is acceptable before Him. Just as we have a responsibility to share His gospel, we also have a responsibility to take care of our family and ourselves (and you cannot help others if you do not help yourself). As

Ava said, "You can't think that you failed. You have to think that you served at the time that God needed you for it. It's not any fault of your own that you couldn't finish a mission. The fact that you went out and you were willing to sacrifice your time, talent, and efforts in serving the Lord is what you should put your focus on. You have to know that it's ultimately best for your family and they will still continually be blessed because you did go out and serve a mission. It doesn't matter how long you served the mission. It's the fact that you went out and you did serve a mission."

Notes

1. Granger E. Westberg, *Good Grief* (Minneapolis: Fortress Press, 1971), 19.
2. Ibid., 29.
3. Ibid., 30.
4. "Physical Grief Symptoms," Obit Tree, retrieved April 28, 2018, https://obittree .com/funeral-advice/grief-articles/physical-grief-symptoms.php.
5. "Counseling Services," LDS Family Services, retrieved April 28, 2018, https:// providentliving.lds.org/lds-family-services/counseling-services.
6. Westberg, *Good Grief*, 40.
7. Ibid., 41.
8. Ibid., 44.
9. Ibid., 47.
10. Ibid., 53.
11. Ibid., 57.
12. Westberg, *Good Grief*, 59
13. Joseph B. Wirthlin, "Come What May and Love it," *Ensign*, Nov. 2008.

CHAPTER 5

Personal Reasons

I still remember arriving at my apartment in the Philippines for the first time. I had arrived three weeks late due to a wrist injury, so my trainer was waiting for me in the apartment with the companionship that shared it with us. She was so excited to meet me, and I was excited to meet her! She welcomed me into the apartment and introduced me to everyone. One sister was sitting over at the kitchen table smiling politely. The other sister was right next to my trainer gushing about how happy she was to finally meet me.

"We've been waiting for you, Sister Danner! We hope you had a good trip!"

I told them it had been a good, albeit long, trip and I was glad to finally be there.

The sister continued to smile and then she lowered her voice. "We are also hoping you can help us. My companion—she wants to go home. We've tried everything we can to get her to stay, but she is determined. We are hoping you will be the one to help her."

Talk about pressure. I looked over at the sister at the kitchen table, who was now looking out the window and seemed more pensive. I looked at my trainer. She nodded and said, "You may not be able to help her, and we recognize that. But we are hoping you will be able to say *something* to her that perhaps we haven't thought of. We are also hoping that she will see your excitement for the work and become excited again too."

"How long has she been on a mission?" I asked.

"Three weeks," they replied. "She arrived in the same batch as you. Or the batch you would have arrived in."

Three weeks? And she'd already lost that excitement?

I turned to go say hi and strike up a conversation with this sister, but they cautioned me saying, "She hardly speaks English, and she doesn't speak Tagalog or Ilonggo."

I was surprised! How was I supposed to communicate with her then? "What language does she speak?" I asked.

"Um, we're not sure what it's called. She's from Pakistan though."

Pakistan? There are members of the Church in *Pakistan*? I let that information hit me and realized how little I knew about the spread of the Church throughout the world. I also felt a little nervous for some reason. I'd never spoken to anyone from Pakistan before, and the media in the United States had not painted a good picture of Pakistanis for the last ten years (it was 2011).

"What have you said to her so far?" I asked.

"Just the usual about trying and forgetting yourself and praying. We're really not sure how much she understands."

I nodded and then took a deep breath. The girl seemed a little more sinister to me now: Pakistani and wanting to go home early—two things that I'd been culturally taught were bad. I approached her carefully, not wanting to spook her for some reason.

"Hello," I said.

She looked at me and I noticed how dark, yet how pretty, her eyes were. "Hello," she replied.

"How are you?" I asked.

She smiled politely. "Today I want to go home. I do not want to be here anymore." She watched me, waiting for my response.

I was truly at a loss for what to say. I had never imagined encountering a missionary who wanted to go home. Plus, I was still a little caught up in the fact that an American and Pakistani were speaking to each other on an LDS mission in the Philippines. Thoughts swirled in my head. Finally, I simply said, "Why?"

She replied, "Do you speak Urdu?"

"What?"

"Urdu."

"I don't understand."

She nodded sadly, then looked out the window.

"Sister, what is your name?" I asked, changing tack.

She told me her name. My eyes flew open. It was the other name on a card I was given when I arrived at the MTC that told me who my companion would be! I'd originally been assigned to be in a threesome, but was told one of the girls couldn't come due to visa issues. She'd been trying to come for three months apparently.

"Sister, you were supposed to be my companion in the MTC!"

She regarded me. "What?" she asked.

I explained the card to her as best I could. I hadn't kept it unfortunately. I was finally able to communicate to her through a lot of charades and pointing that she and I were originally assigned to be together for nine weeks in the MTC along with another young woman.

"We were so sad when we learned that your visa was delayed! How did you finally get here?"

She told me in broken English about how her visa had never been approved to go to the United States, but how she still wanted to serve a mission. So they decided to try to get her visa approved for the Philippines, and it was, so they sent her to the MTC in the Philippines. She had culture shock the moment she arrived. Her home in Pakistan was beautiful and clean. She felt like the Philippines was very dirty. She did not like the food and had developed some physical health problems. She could not understand the people and no one could understand her. Furthermore, her skin was dark and she felt like no one wanted to talk to her (Filipinos are rather partial to white skin). She wished to go home and serve a mission in Pakistan.

I remember feeling sorry for her physical illness and her distaste for the food, but not having a lot of sympathy for her negative attitude toward the Philippines and especially not for what I considered a lack of faith regarding her assignment to the Philippines. I tried to explain to her that she didn't get to choose where she served, but she just looked at me, shook her head, and said that she would have preferred to have served in Pakistan.

Looking back in hindsight and with more maturity, I can understand the nuances of her confusion in this regard: As a first-generation member of the Church, and having converted recently no less, she was confused about how she was assigned to the Philippines. She did not understand that she would not get to choose to serve in Pakistan instead upon returning. At the time, I simply assumed that she understood this concept and didn't have the necessary faith in God that He'd assigned her where she was meant to serve.

Three weeks later this sister had had enough and called our mission president and asked to be sent home. The other sisters and I tried very hard to convince her to stay, but her mind was made up: she did not want to be in the Philippines anymore. She wanted to go home, get her physical health issues resolved, and then serve a mission in Pakistan. She felt a great error had been made and that once she was healthy again, she would take the steps needed to correct this error and get called to the right mission. At least, that is what I understood through our broken-English conversations.

I remember watching her enter the airport and feeling sorry for her and how she just didn't understand the importance of a mission. I remember wishing she would stay and "tough it out." I remember wanting her to have "more faith" in regards to the language. I remember wishing she and I could speak plainly to each other, so that I could really understand her concerns and convince her to stay. But she left, and I just felt sorry for her. I'm sorry to say that I put her out of my mind until I came home early myself. I tried to email her and get in touch and see how she was doing, hoping maybe she'd have some tips for me to cope with the feelings of failure that I was now feeling, but she never replied. To this day, I don't know how she is doing, but I hope very much that she is well and that she learned whatever she needed to learn and recovered from her physical health problems.

That was my first encounter with someone who had chosen to go home early. One thing that surprised me about the experience was how nuanced it was: this sister had a desire to serve a mission, but not this particular mission. I always had thought that choosing to go home was a little more black and white, in particular that the missionary just loses his or her testimony and goes home. This experience taught me otherwise. This sister was a good person, but she had several things going against her. Could she have "toughed it out?" Was "more faith" all that was required? Perhaps. And if so, then I trust that God helped His daughter learn those things when she got home and could speak openly to her family and priesthood leaders. But perhaps there was more, and if I'd been able to dig beneath the surface a bit, perhaps I'd have been able to understand.

Since then I have found that there are six reasons for why missionaries *choose* to go home early, although there certainly may be more. Also, these reasons may at times be attached to any of the other four reasons that I discuss in this book, but they are the *main* reason why a missionary goes home early:

1. Lack of desire or strong testimony
2. Loss of desire
3. Homesickness
4. The Spirit told the missionary to go home
5. Inability to continue due to the wickedness of others
6. Loss of testimony

Do any of those reasons bother you? I'd be surprised if number four didn't. If I hadn't heard the stories myself and talked to the faithful young women who told them to me, I wouldn't have believed that the Spirit would actually do that. We will get to this reason momentarily. First, let's start with lack of desire or strong testimony.

Lack of Desire or Strong Testimony

As I was writing this book, a young man named Logan who knew of my project sent me his story:

> I grew up in a small town in the western United States, working on farms, cherry orchards, and ranches. It was about as perfect a way to grow up as there is, and I wouldn't trade any of it for the world.
>
> Like a lot of kids, though, I went through a rebellious stage where everything I wanted to do was the height of coolness and everything my parents wanted me to do was "stupid." That included church on Sundays, Boy Scouts on Wednesdays, and family home evening on Mondays. I figured my time was better spent hunting and fishing in the rolling foothills of the Rocky Mountains than inside some church building.
>
> And just like a lot of kids do, I came back around. I realized my parents knew what they were talking about, and I slowly found myself gaining a testimony. It wasn't much, but as Alma famously taught, you just need to plant the seed.
>
> I think it was the October conference of my junior year of high school when President Thomas S. Monson announced the age change for missionaries. Immediately, my friends decided they'd leave as soon

as they could after graduation. When asked about my plans, I'd shrug and mumble something about a mission.

The truth is that I wasn't certain about a mission. My testimony wasn't to the point where I felt a burning desire to share the knowledge of Christ's gospel with others. As the famous missionary scripture reads, "If ye have desires to serve God ye are called to the work" (D&C 4:3).

Senior year came too soon, and it was suddenly February and my best friend pulled me out of class one morning to go home and watch him open his mission call. I was genuinely happy for him, but I had a sinking feeling in my stomach. I didn't really want to go, but now that my best friend had his call, I'd be expected to go too, right?

Honestly, that's a large part of why I went. I went because everyone else was going, because my dad wanted me to, and because I have two younger brothers for whom I knew I needed to try to be an example. I've failed more often than not in that regard, but I knew I had to try a mission at the least.

So I put my papers in and waited. I hoped the post office would somehow lose the envelope with my call in it, but I grew up in a really small town. Small enough that when the giant white envelope showed up at the post office, the mail lady called my mom to let her know it was there.

I skipped school the day my call came and went fishing instead. I didn't want to open that letter. I didn't want to go. I wanted to stay home, pursue my writing career, and find a job in the sports writing world. A mission got in the way of those plans.

Rain eventually pushed me off the river, and I got home about a half-hour late for my own mission call opening extravaganza. Aunts, uncles, grandparents, cousins, friends, and neighbors crammed into my tiny kitchen and waited with bated breath while I opened the call.

"Whichever of the Quorum of the Twelve Apostles who assigned this call must've made a mistake," I thought. Because they'd called me to the New York New York South mission.

A country guy, more comfortable in boots and Wranglers than a shirt and tie, was supposed to head to New York City and teach people about a gospel he didn't even completely believe in?

I truly didn't want to go on my mission now. I'd been hoping for Alaska, or New Zealand, or England. Not New York.

Yet a few months later, I stood in the Provo MTC, shuffling through a line as I was handed my nametag, a few books, and a bag. There weren't even refreshments set out.

I'd been called to teach the gospel in Spanish, so I had a six-week stay in the MTC in front of me. Those six weeks were the longest six weeks of my life. I got so anxious and depressed that I stopped eating. I lost something like twenty pounds in the MTC. I didn't have twenty pounds to lose, either.

My depression and anxiety got bad enough that I couldn't sleep. I lived on Mountain Dew smuggled through MTC security, and the occasional muffin or cookie I'd eat when my companion got on my case. I was in a bad place, headed quickly for an even worse spot.

Then we flew out to New York City and I thought maybe, just maybe, things would be different in the field. There couldn't be a place as stressful and annoying as the MTC, right?

The field was different, and I certainly had more freedoms, but I still didn't feel right being there. I had no desire to serve, and each morning as we'd read scriptures, my companion would ask how I was doing with the language. I answered the same each day—"I'm working on it"—and then thought about how I didn't want to be on a mission. I wanted to go home.

Those thoughts didn't stop, and the homesickness combined with my depression and anxiety came to a head one night. I had a pretty close brush with suicide, and luckily retained enough presence of mind to realize that I needed to go home and get help.

My mission president wasn't supportive of the decision. He thought I could get the treatment I needed in the field, instead of going home. My parents weren't thrilled either, but I was done. Mentally, spiritually, and physically, I was spent. I had nothing left in the tank.

There are many things happening in this story: (1) A testimony of the gospel was alive in this young man, but just barely. (2) He had no desire to serve a mission. (3) He'd gone only because it was expected of him and he was afraid of what people would say if he took more time to mentally prepare himself for a mission. And (4) there were mental health issues that arose while he was on his mission due to that lack of desire to serve. When we try to force ourselves to do something that we really don't want to do, there is naturally going to be a physical and/or mental reaction in our bodies to try to keep us from doing the thing we don't like.

Many people would probably read this young man's story and think, "He needed to toughen up" or "He just needed to exercise faith." I'm going to make the argument that he tried hard to do both. He went even though he didn't want to, hoping that it would get better. He continued to study his scriptures and pray, but physically and mentally his body rebelled. He held onto his testimony, but he could not force that desire to go out and teach the gospel every day. He wanted to have that desire, but it wasn't there, and nothing he did could force it to be there. He was not ready or prepared to serve a mission. He needed to come home. In my opinion, he made the right choice.

Logan continued his story by telling me,

I returned home just under three months after I'd left. To a small town where news spreads faster than folks can update Facebook about it.

Coming home wasn't easy, nor enjoyable. At the end of the day, though, the fact remained that I'd made the choice to leave and it's hard not to second-guess a decision as big as coming home from a two-year commitment to the Lord. Also, after I came home early from my mission I let my choice to come home early define me, rather than teach me. I was the missionary who came home early. I was a one-dimensional person at the time because of this.

In the midst of this, someone said to me, "Your mission is in the past. You can't keep harping on about it and whining about it. You have to either buck up and deal with it or go back out to the field." This person had never been known for having tact, and for a long time after that brief conversation, I held a grudge against him. Who was he to say anything like that to me, much less in that brusque a manner? He probably could've been nicer with his words, but they wouldn't have stuck in my mind otherwise. I heard plenty of words of encouragement and a fair amount of snide remarks and stony silences. I hadn't heard outright, no-holds-barred criticism of how I was handling the consequences of my decision.

I'm sorry to say that I left the Church as a result of this person's words, which I take full responsibility for. I eventually worked my way back and can look back on that exchange with better clarity. I think he was getting at the same point shared by President James E. Faust during the 2004 priesthood session of general conference:

"The choices we make, however, determine to a large extent our happiness or our unhappiness, because we have to live with the consequences of our choices," President Faust said. "Making perfect choices all the time is not possible. It just doesn't happen. But it is possible to make good choices we can live with and grow from."[1]

I know I did the right thing in coming back. I was treated for my depression and anxiety. While I still fight them to this day, I have much better coping skills at my disposal.

And, interestingly enough, I have the strongest testimony of our Savior that I've ever had. He helped me through so much of this challenging time that I came to know Him in a way that felt like He was truly the older brother I never had.

Logan made it through this difficult time, and although the choices he made upon coming home were not perfect, they were in many respects understandable. He had just returned home from a traumatic experience—he had nearly taken his life which meant the depression, anxiety, and pain that he was feeling were so all-consuming that he saw no alternative to escape them than ending his life. He fell prey to the notion that he would never amount to anything more in his life than an "early-returned missionary" despite encouraging words from those around him. He was overly sensitive and critical of himself and others. Those feelings of failure are strong, but they do not come from the Lord. Satan really works on early-returned missionaries.

Logan tried to move forward with his life in a positive way. He likely wanted nothing to do with missionary work or even the Church for the time, but admiringly, he still went to church, at least until he became offended and fell away. Even if he only went to church because it was a small town and expected of him, he still went and tried. The comment he received was unfortunately tactless, and he did choose to take it in such a way that caused him to grow further from Heavenly Father. But he eventually came back and lives a good life now.

Regarding President Faust's quote about the choices we make determining our happiness—that's absolutely true. The choices we make do determine our path and happiness in this life. We often view those choices in terms of life-altering decisions such as where to go to school, what career path we will choose, who we will marry, if we will serve a mission (or return early from one), and so on. What we often forget is that we also choose how we will respond to the *consequences* of these choices.

The consequences of Logan coming home early was that his small town found out rapidly about it and he chose to perceive being viewed a certain way. While some people may have silently viewed him as only an "early-returned missionary," the man's tactless comment shows that the only person who really cared that Logan was an early-returned missionary was Logan. He had received encouragement for moving forward with his life or figuring things out and returning to the field. But he did not choose to internalize that encouragement and move forward with life. Instead he chose to look inward and wallow in self-pity, creating fertile ground for offense to be taken and to move himself further from the love and guidance of Heavenly Father.

Logan could have instead chosen to work through his feelings of failure. It is likely that he was unaware of *how* to do this, though, and it may be the case that you likely are at a loss too. Let me offer some suggestions, based largely on what Logan told me helped him:

1. Write daily in your journal about your trials. Even if you feel like you are making no progress, you'll be surprised as you look back and see how much you've grown. Journaling will also give you the self-awareness and spiritual strength you need at this time and will give you a place to work through your innermost thoughts and feelings.

2. Serve. Missions are not the only ways you can serve and lift others. Perhaps there is another missionary who came home early that you can help, even if the reason is different from yours. Also, service is one of the quickest ways God has given us to get outside of ourselves and stop negative thought patterns that stem from self-pitying. If you are thinking about yourself only as an "early-returned missionary," it's time to find a new role in your life. Ask for a calling or get involved in the community and show up and serve faithfully. By doing this, you will again find purpose and come to know and understand yourself better and see that you are not at all a failure.

3. Remember that you are not the only one to pass through this trial. You are not the only one to have felt so overwhelmed or so lacking in desire to be out in the field that you went home. Often in Mormon culture we dismiss these real feelings of not wanting to be on a mission with the famous line to President Gordon B. Hinckley from his father, "Forget yourself and go to work."[2] It is important to note though that even President Hinckley, at one point, for many weeks, did not desire to be on a mission and in

fact felt like he was wasting his time and his father's money.[3] It is also important to note that that famous line was written *for* President Hinckley. It has been a line that has motivated many missionaries to lose their selfish desires and get to work, but it has also been taken to the extreme of a "one-line-fix-all" and has caused a lack of understanding for those who really are not ready to be on missions and need more time to get that desire before they go out and serve. Share your story so that others may better understand that a lack of desire does not always equal a lack of faith; sometimes it simply means that you need more time.

4. Stay prayerful, keep reading your scriptures, and go to the temple. You don't have to continue reading your scriptures as much as you did as a missionary, of course, but please don't ever stop reading them. Even a verse a day and a prayer a day will give you added strength to overcome the overwhelming feelings of failure (and if one verse and one prayer will give you strength, then imagine how much more strength you will receive by diligently studying the scriptures and praying several times a day). The temple can also be a refuge and a safe place for you to ponder and think in a quiet, spiritual environment and receive the peace that you may need or the spiritual answers that you seek.

5. Learn more about the grief cycle and how you respond to loss. The grief cycle is discussed in detail in chapter 4.

As you do these things, be mindful of the Spirit and the gentle promptings you receive. The question about whether or not to try again and go back on a mission will likely weigh heavily on your mind for some time. You'll likely feel pressure to get that desire and go complete your mission (especially if you are young man). Staying close to the Lord will give you added strength and resolve when you make a decision about whether or not to stay home or return to the field. If returning is the right thing to do, He will guide you as you work (and it will be *work*) to gain that testimony and desire to serve a mission. Be certain you have that testimony and desire before you go out and serve again. If returning to your mission is not the right thing to do, you will feel in your heart that this is okay with the Lord and that He accepts your sacrifice and will help you as you move forward with life.

God's love for you is unfailing, and He will be with you as you seek His will. He will put people in your life that will help you and prompt you to avoid those people who might drag you down and cause you to doubt yourself and your standing with Him. Keep in mind that either path may be okay with Him, and if so, that is a great opportunity for you to recognize that you are right with the Lord and He trusts you. He will help you to have a good life no matter which path you choose.

Loss of Desire

What if you had great desires to serve a mission and then lost them once you got to the field? Or what if you just want to serve somewhere else, like the sister from Pakistan?

Missions are difficult and unfulfilled expectations are often at the root of why missionaries develop mental illnesses or choose to come home early.[4] However, there is a difference between being unable to continue due to a mental illness caused by unmet expectations (we often call this situational depression or anxiety) and choosing to come home because you simply no longer want to be there. If you left your mission because it was too much work or not up to your standards of what a mission should be, take this time to do some deep introspection and work through things with the Lord (see Isaiah 1:18). Reneging on a commitment to serve the Lord isn't something that should be done lightly. Take a deeper look at yourself and ask if there was anything more you could have done to have made your situation better. Ask the Lord to help you see yourself clearly. Even ask Him if you have cause to repent—if leaving the mission was purely selfish and if by leaving you forfeited opportunities for spiritual growth for yourself and others.

If you find that you do have cause to repent, take heart. You are not the only one to have acted selfishly—not by a long shot. With regards to missionary work, it is normal to not want to be on a mission from time to time. I have met plenty of people who finished the intended amount of time who admitted that there were plenty of days when they would rather have been home, and you can find countless anecdotes on the internet where people talk about the difficult days on their missions when they wished for home. But there are also countless stories of people putting aside their own desires, focusing on the people they were serving, and finding absolute joy in the work.

There are of course ways to combat selfishness and avoidance of hard things. Some of those things are listed in the "Lack of Desire" section: journal, serve in your community, stay close to the Lord through scripture study, prayer, and temple attendance, and remember that you are not the only one to struggle this way.

If you choose to return to your mission, keep in mind these words from Elder Holland:

> Anyone who does any kind of missionary work will have occasion to ask, Why is this so hard? Why doesn't it go better? Why can't our success be more rapid? Why aren't there more people joining the Church? It is the truth. We believe in angels. We trust in miracles. Why don't people just flock to the font? Why isn't the only risk in missionary work that of pneumonia from being soaking wet all day and all night in the baptismal font?
>
> You will have occasion to ask those questions. I have thought about this a great deal. I offer this as my personal feeling. I am convinced that missionary work is not easy because *salvation is not a cheap experience.* Salvation *never* was easy. We are The Church of Jesus Christ, this is the truth, and He is our Great Eternal Head. How could we believe it would be easy for us when it was never, ever easy for Him? . . .
>
> The Atonement will carry the missionaries perhaps even more importantly than it will carry the investigators. When you struggle, when you are rejected, when you are spit upon and cast out and made a hiss and a byword, you are standing with the best life this world has ever known, the only pure and perfect life ever lived. You have reason to stand tall and be grateful that the Living Son of the Living God knows all about your sorrows and afflictions. The only way to salvation is through Gethsemane and on to Calvary. The only way to eternity is through Him—the Way, the Truth, and the Life.[5]

There is joy to be had in missionary work, but that joy is not meant to come easily or even constantly. Missions are meant to test you and to try you so that you can come closer to Christ, and so that you can help others do the same.

Whatever you choose—to stay home or go back out—make sure you choose it prayerfully. If you need to repent, make sure you have repented fully before you make your decision. Weigh things carefully in your mind, ask yourself if you are truly ready to give your all to the Lord if you return to your mission. Ask yourself what you want your life to look like as you move forward and be sure you are willing to face adversity and work hard to get the life that you want.

Joy does not come without work—very little in life comes without work, in fact. Even desire doesn't always come without work, and it certainly cannot stay without it. As Elder Holland said, "And so I ask you to be patient in things of the spirit. Perhaps your life has been different from mine, but I doubt it. I have had to struggle to know my standing before God. As a teenager I found it hard to pray and harder to fast. My mission was not easy. I struggled as a student only to find that I had to struggle afterwards, too. In this present assignment I have wept and ached for guidance. It seems no worthy accomplishment has ever come easily for me, and maybe it won't for you—but I'm living long enough to be grateful for that."[6]

If you lost the desire to serve a mission due to physical health problems, mental health challenges, worthiness issues, or family troubles, please read the corresponding chapters in this book. These are separate issues.

Homesickness

In chapter 4, I shared Olivia's story about her inability to grieve her mother's death due to various circumstances. Olivia also suffered greatly from homesickness on her mission. She felt "really anxious" and "sad" and even felt like she would never see her family again. She longed for the security of home and eventually did return home early. I'd like to share the rest of her story in this chapter:

> When I moved away to college, I again found myself in a new situation with no friends. I felt alone and didn't have a good way to cope. I remember looking at some other people who were breaking the Word of Wisdom, and they looked like they were having a great time, and I wanted to be happy too. I made some mistakes, but eventually repented and got back on the right track.
>
> Eventually, I received a prompting to return to my mission, and after a lot of consideration and counseling with my Church leaders, as well as talking with family and a counselor from LDS Family Services,

I felt like it was the right thing to do. By the time I got my mission call, I was excited to go.

However, after just two days of being in the field again, I felt overwhelmed with homesickness. My heart was racing and I couldn't catch my breath. I was having anxiety attacks, and it was hard to handle. I talked to my family, my companion, and my mission president and they kept pushing me to keep trying. I talked to a therapist too. But about two weeks in, I just decided that I wanted to go home and I couldn't do the mission.

This time, when I arrived home, I felt like a failure. I felt horrible and I think for the first two weeks home, I felt really bad. I started questioning my testimony and if I even got the prompting to go out. On top of that, no one knew I'd come home. I'd posted on social media that I was leaving, but when I came back it was Christmas time, so I wasn't in a hurry to post that I'd come home again. So it felt like I was in hiding. Whenever people knocked on the door to drop off a Christmas treat, I'd just run away from the door and hide in the house. I didn't want to see anybody.

However, about a month after that, now, today, I'm beginning to feel more at peace with my decision. I recognize that I have anxiety and that's something I need help with. I'm planning to talk to a therapist, and get help with that and build up my confidence. I posted on social media so that people knew I was home. I still hide from people, but you know, I'm working on it.

Homesickness is a normal response that everyone feels at times throughout their lives. In her book *Beating Homesickness: Understanding Homesickness and Learn How to Overcome It*, Amy Hartfield writes, "It's crucial to realize that homesickness is a normal process. It's a time of change and a natural response to loss and adjustment. It doesn't in any event mean that we are inadequate or immature. As a matter of fact, it may be viewed as a positive emotion as it suggests that we're connected to a familiar and comforting place, to acquaintances and loved ones."[7]

In his talk "A Yearning For Home," Elder Marvin J. Ashton said,

It's natural to miss the people you are closest to. It's normal to long to be where you feel secure, where those you love have your best interests at heart. It's understandable to want to return to the place where you learned how to walk and talk, where you felt loved even when friends turned away, and where you were accepted, regardless of the situation. There's no place on earth that can take the place of a home where love has been given and received. . . . We let ourselves become homesick for love, acceptance, security, understanding, and guidance that generally are taught and shared there. Home should be the place in which a person can unburden his soul and find renewed strength to face the world, where there is comfort, joy, and understanding, where best friends live, and where we can learn to be our best selves.[8]

It is very understandable then that you feel a range of emotions upon leaving what is familiar and comfortable, and where you feel most secure and loved. The range of emotions you feel might include "feeling sad, lonesome, insecure (or as if [you] don't belong), crying, feeling remarkably anxious or upset about matters, being unable to get into a comfy routine, often thinking of individuals at home, wanting to leave and return home, feeling broadly depressed or anxious, [and] minor physical ailments."[9]

These emotions are absolutely difficult to get through and it is understandable that you came home early due to them. A mission is a huge change from the familiar! Even if you grew up with the gospel, a mission is hardly like speaking in church or even teaching a Sunday School class. You are surrounded by new people, new settings, new situations, and possibly even a new language. It is normal that you would feel homesick. In fact, it'd be odd if you didn't.

So, you may think, "If it is so normal, and if every missionary experiences it, how come I couldn't push past it?" You might feel like a complete failure. Olivia sure did. Olivia had only been home for a couple of months when I talked to her, so she was still working through her emotions of coming home early, but she had at least started to recognize that she struggles when she is away from home: she gets anxiety and that's something she needs help with. Admitting this to herself is a huge first step toward growth and healing. Admitting to yourself that you have a tendency to succumb to the negative emotions of homesickness will be a huge step toward your own growth and healing too.

There are many things you can do to combat homesickness whether you choose to return to your mission or to move forward with life. Here are a few general tips:

1. Recognize your love for home and embrace this as a good thing. It means you are rooted in something, that you have a place where you feel secure and loved.

2. Realize that there are negative emotions that come with homesickness but that they *can* be worked through with time and patience. There may always be a bit of a longing for home, which is what I think Olivia's companion meant when she told Olivia that the feeling of homesickness "never really goes away" (see chapter 4). As Elder Marvin J. Ashton once counseled a homesick missionary, "the right kind of homesickness [can] be desirable, but it must be kept under control."[10]

3. Be open to new things. Amy Hartfield says, "The more open you are to new things, the less you might miss the past things. Be open to exploring fresh situations, opportunities, individuals, classes, and choices. Try to prevent comparing your new environment to home; they're dissimilar. It may be scary to face so many new things, but they'll provide new opportunities to meet new acquaintances." She also adds that, "Studies indicate we fear an unknown outcome more than a recognized bad one. . . . Attempting something new opens up the possibility for you to savor something new. Entire vocations, entire life paths are carved out by individuals dipping their toes into little ponds and suddenly finding a love for something they had no clue would capture their imaginations."[11] Be brave and be ready for new experiences to expand your mind and give new purpose to your life.

4. Take care of your body. Eat good food and exercise. Amy Hartfield says, "One of the keys to having a happier living and a healthy lifestyle is to know how to take care of your body. . . . Likewise, being active can help in improving your moods and lessen your chances of suffering from depression."[12]

If you choose to return to your mission, also keep these tips from the "Adjusting to Missionary Life" booklet in mind:

1. "Keep busy. Homesickness is common, especially if you haven't been away from home much. Let yourself feel sad for a few minutes, but then get up and get busy. The best way to combat it is to distract yourself from worry or self-pity by keeping busy and serving others.

2. "Unpack and settle in. Don't live out of your suitcase. Set up your personal space. Put up a picture that helps you feel the Spirit and

remember why you want to serve the Lord. Clean out old trash, and make your apartment 'yours.' Make foods you enjoy.

3. "Make a long list of things that have not changed about you. Think of your relationships, your strengths, and other things that are still the same, even though a lot has changed. Examples: 'I have a sense of humor; my parents love me; I want to serve.' Add things you would still have to do if you were home: 'I would still have to make decisions; I would still have to get along with others; I would still have to work hard.'

4. "Review your reasons for coming on a mission. Consciously offer your mission as a gift of thanks to the Savior, and list your blessings. Remind yourself of what supportive leaders or loved ones at home would tell you about your service.

5. "Ask for a priesthood blessing.

6. "Remove distracting photos. Put away any photos or pictures that distract you from feeling the Spirit or that stir homesickness. You may choose to bring some of them out again once you are more adjusted. Encourage your family to write only once a week so you, like Jesus's disciples of old, can leave your 'nets' behind (see Matthew 4:18–22) and focus on the work.

7. "Be patient. It generally takes about six weeks to begin to adapt to a new environment. Put off making any decisions, and give yourself time to adjust. Take one day at a time."[13]

Again, homesickness can be a good thing, so long as it is kept under control. I hope you can move forward now with your mission or with your life (or both) with some extra tools to help you get through those negative feelings that would halt your opportunities for growth. It is okay to love home and to miss loved ones and our familiar environments, but it is also good and okay to embrace new environments and to make new acquaintances who can also become loved ones.

The Spirit Told You to Go Home

I will admit that the first time I heard someone tell me that the Spirit told her to come home from her mission, I worried that this person had misunderstood a prompting or had been deceived by the adversary. Then another woman told me that this was her experience. I have not been able to find any comments from General Authorities regarding the Spirit telling someone to go home from a mission, but I have found talks that discuss the difference between the Spirit and the adversary. My findings are at the end of this section. First, I would like to share AJ's story:

> From the minute I got my call and I opened my letter, I had the impression that I wouldn't serve a full 18 months. When I got to the MTC my return date was on a card that they gave us. It felt like a lie when I would say it. I kind of tried to write it off, but the feeling only intensified once I got to the field. I distinctly remember sitting in my first apartment with my trainer and we were talking about things that would be happening way off in the future. I think we were talking about getting to your year mark and knowing that you only have six months left. I just remember feeling like, "I'm not going to get there." And not because I was so discouraged or anything. I mean, the beginning of the mission is hard, but I didn't want to leave. I just felt like that was a point in my mission that I would not reach. And it kind of faded a little bit the longer I was out, but it was still kind of always there in the back of my mind. But I kept it to myself because I didn't want my companions to think that I wasn't committing myself to the mission or that I was doing everything with the intention to quit because that was not the case. It was just something that I felt for a while. It was just kind of there and I knew it was there, but I just ignored it because I was like, "It's not time yet. I'm happy here. I'm enjoying the work even though it's really hard. It's not now. Why think about it now?"
>
> Then, it was my sixth transfer and I was in a ward filled with Pacific Islanders. I loved that ward, but I also kind of hit a little hint of seasonal depression, which is something that I've struggled with for a while. It's kind of something that I muddle through and then I'm good. And it usually only lasts for like a week or two. So I didn't really think anything of it.
>
> This happened right around the April general conference. I had a really hard time during the Saturday session. I talked to my mission president's wife afterward, and I told her that every warning or admonition from the speakers felt intensely directed at me. I didn't find any comfort in general conference. I just felt very suddenly over the course of a couple of days, very, very off—more so than I can remember ever feeling before. I wasn't quite in tune with anything and that was really hard for me because it was terrifying. And I was really scared for myself because I couldn't feel the Spirit anymore. I was really concerned

because I couldn't be a missionary if I couldn't feel the Spirit. I mean, you have to spend every minute of your day in tune with Heavenly Father so that you can do His work the way He wants it done. And so I was extremely concerned.

I talked to my mission president's wife and she suggested that I pray for healing and that I let Heavenly Father know just everything that I had told her. In fact, I had found that my prayers had become rather routine and weren't very genuine throughout the day, simply because of how often I prayed as a missionary. And so she said, "At night, especially when you're having your personal prayer, you should really just talk. Don't think about the structure of the prayer or anything, just talk to Heavenly Father." I was also given the opportunity to see a family services counselor.

So I saw a family services counselor and I mentioned to her that I had contemplated going home early a few times. She told me that that was something I should ask Heavenly Father about. So that night I said my prayers and I made sure that it was very personal and that it was what I really needed. Not just another thing to check off like, "Okay, I did my nighttime prayer." It was really sitting down and talking to Heavenly Father.

The next morning I woke up and the thought was just there clear as day like, "You're going home at transfers in a week." We were in week five of the transfer and there was no question in my mind when I woke up the next day. I was immediately shifted from "What do I do?" into "This is what I'm doing." And I went through my morning very quietly thinking about it. Finally, I told my companion who was doing her makeup in the hallway, "Hey, so I've prayed really hard and I think I'm going home next week." And she just kind of looked up at me and said, "You know, that actually makes sense." She had been privy to all of my struggles the past couple of weeks with feeling so out of touch, and when she said that I realized that I didn't feel that way anymore; that overnight I had shifted back into feeling like I was perfectly in tune with Heavenly Father. And it was my decision to go home that had put me back in communication with Him.

She said to me, "Obviously I don't want you to go. But as you say it, I can see that it's what you need, that it's what's right for you." And it was nice to kind of have that confirmation that I'm not crazy. It truly felt like the right decision. And I must have prayed about that decision at least five more times that morning. I just kept asking Heavenly Father, "Is this really what I'm supposed to be doing, or is this a trick of the adversary to get me out of the field? Or is it me being lazy and trying to project that onto a spiritual moment so that no one will question me?" And every single time I prayed about it, I just felt like it was what I needed to do. That it was from the Lord, and not from anybody else.

AJ did return home to a supportive family that understood this wasn't a decision she made lightly. AJ was able to look back on her mission too and see how much she had grown and changed as a person because of what she had experienced in the mission field. Her family could see it too. She did beat herself up a bit when the reason for her early return didn't immediately appear. She called herself a quitter and a failure. She learned to stop that line of thinking though by turning her trust to the Lord. Regarding why she felt prompted to go home, she said, "It's just not something that has been revealed to me yet, if it is going to be. And if it's not, if I don't find out in this lifetime, I trust that on the other side of the veil I'll know, and that I'll finally get to understand. And I'm fine with that. I'm fine with waiting."

Sometimes the Lord absolutely does ask us to do things that seem contrary to what He would normally want, or even contrary to what He originally asked us to do. For example, He commanded Nephi to kill Laban in order to "bring forth his righteous purposes" (1 Nephi 4:13), which meant He was commanding Nephi to murder Laban, even though He had also commanded "Thou shalt not kill" (Deuteronomy 5:17). Likewise, AJ felt that He commanded her to go home even though a letter was sent to her from the prophet saying that it was anticipated that she would serve for eighteen months. AJ does not know why she felt commanded to go home, but she obeyed that prompting and has remained faithful to the Lord despite not receiving an answer to her question of "Why?" I think the Lord knows her heart and is grateful for her willingness to be obedient to the Spirit's promptings, even when they do not logically make sense.

I would like to share what Don Norton, a former professor of English at Brigham Young University, wrote in the 1978 *Ensign* about how to discern between feelings of the Spirit and deceptions of the adversary. He said: "Here's the list of the kinds of things young people say they feel when the Spirit is with them, and what they feel when Satan tries to take over—making them unhappy or tricking them with counterfeits. Do these feelings match your experience?"[14]

When you have the Spirit:

1. You feel happy, calm, and clear-minded.
2. You feel generous.
3. Nobody can offend you.
4. You wouldn't mind everybody seeing what you're doing.
5. You are eager to be with people and want to make them happy.
6. You are glad when others succeed.
7. You are glad to attend your meetings and participate in church activities.
8. You feel like praying.
9. You wish you could keep all the Lord's commandments.
10. You feel in control—you don't overeat or sleep too much; you don't feel uncontrollably drawn to sensational entertainment, lose your temper, or feel uncontrollable passions or desires.
11. You think about the Savior often and lovingly; you want to know him better.
12. You feel confident and are glad to be alive.

When you don't have the Spirit:

1. You feel unhappy, depressed, confused, and frustrated.
2. You feel possessive, self-centered, or resentful of demands made on you.
3. You are easily offended.
4. You become secretive and evasive.
5. You avoid people, especially members of your family; and you are critical of family members and Church authorities.
6. You envy or resent the successes of others.
7. You don't want to go to church, go home teaching, or take the sacrament. You wish you had another church job or no job at all.
8. You don't want to pray.
9. You find the commandments bothersome, restricting, or senseless.
10. You feel emotions and appetites so strongly that you fear you cannot control them—hate, jealousy, anger, lust, hunger, fatigue.
11. You hardly ever think of the Savior; he seems irrelevant to your life, or worse, part of a confusing system that seems to work against you.
12. You get discouraged easily and wonder if life is really worth it.[15]

The differences between these two lists is striking. I think what stands out to me the most is the fact that when you feel the Spirit, you will feel "happy, calm, and clear-minded" and you will also feel a desire to pray. In 2 Nephi 32:8, we read "For if ye would hearken unto the Spirit which teacheth a man to pray, ye would know that ye must pray; for the evil spirit teacheth not a man to pray, but teacheth him that he must not pray." If you feel a desire to pray and confirm your decision, that is from the Spirit. But if you feel discouraged from praying, or if you feel anxious, confused, depressed, or unhappy, you can feel confident that the feelings or "promptings" you are receiving are from the adversary.

It is natural that AJ would feel confused about the prompting to go home, but she did not have feelings of confusion when she chose to follow it. Rather she felt at peace with the decision and confident that it was the right choice. She beat herself up later for it with hard thoughts about herself that definitely were not from God. Once she stopped doing that though, she again felt peace and even though she does not know why she felt inspired to come home early, she feels confident that someday she will know and understand and is moving forward with her life happily and peacefully.

If you felt prompted to come home early from your mission, consider the two lists above to help you discern whether what you felt was from the Lord or from Satan. Also, remember what James E. Faust said in his talk "The Great Imitator": "[The devil's] voice often sounds so reasonable and his message so easy to justify. It is an enticing, intriguing voice with dulcet tones. It is neither hard nor discordant. No one would listen to Satan's voice if it sounded harsh or mean. If the devil's voice were unpleasant, it would not entice people to listen to it."[16] While Satan can be crafty in his deceptions, he is not good at providing peace. Think back to when you've committed a sin; did you ever feel peace as you committed it? You may have felt a momentary rush or even felt momentarily good as you committed it, but after it was done, did you feel peace? I don't think you could.

Remember that an explanation about why you needed to come home may not come immediately, but like everything else in life, explanations don't always come when we want them to. A lack of explanation doesn't mean you should doubt your answer to come home though. If you have felt true peace from the Spirit about following a prompting to come home early, go forward with faith and confidence that it was right. Look back on your mission joyfully. Remember the good times and remember the struggles. Recognize your growth and take the lessons you learned from it and apply them to the rest of your life.

Inability to Continue Due to the Wickedness of Others

In chapter 2, you read about Alex, a young man who chose to come home early because he felt he could not accomplish his purposes as a missionary due to unrighteous dominion by his mission president and an unworthy companion. His story is in that chapter to help those who struggle with mental health understand the importance of forgiveness—Alex's mission president and mission president's wife said some terrible things to him that hurt him deeply and that he was never quite able to move past. His inability to move past these feelings caused him to make some other choices that led him on a path where he ultimately took his life. However, his reason for returning was actually a personal one.

It is painful to think that anyone would make circumstances so unbearable for missionaries that they would feel forced to leave because they could not do what they had been called to do. However, it does happen, although rarely. Alex's story is the only one I heard where this happened, but I sadly doubt his is the *only* story, even if this type of situation is rare. If this situation applies to you, please let your stake president know what happened so that he can contact the proper Church authorities through the proper channels. This is something the Church wants to know about and address immediately.

As you move forward, either to a new mission or on with your life, remember that what happened was not your fault and that therefore the Lord accepts your sacrifice. You have a willing heart and a desire to serve Him. That is what He sees. He doesn't see a quitter or a failure. He sees His child and He is proud of you for removing yourself from a terrible situation.

Loss of Testimony

This situation is undoubtedly heartbreaking for all involved including the missionary. For the missionary, depending on the home situation, there is undoubtedly the fear of disappointing others, the fear of a lack of support upon returning home (perhaps even of having no home to return to), and the fear of being ostracized from friends and/or family. It is also undoubtedly a time of confusion and a time of redefining oneself, especially if the missionary had been a lifelong member of the Church.

To the family members and friends that have to watch a loved one leave not only a mission, but the gospel, you are dealing with a great loss and therefore a deep sense of grief. The section on grief in chapter 4 will help you recognize and understand better what you are feeling, even if the examples are not completely in line with what you are experiencing.

Know that Heavenly Father and Jesus Christ still love your missionary, even more than you do, and that they are keenly aware of his or her struggle of faith. Do not lash out in anger at your missionary. Do not disown him or her. Do not stop being a friend (unless the relationship becomes abusive or unhealthy for whatever reason). Always extend love and kindness. Avoid pressuring him or her to come back to church, but do not cease to share spiritual experiences. Let your missionary know what is important in your life, including the gospel, but be wary of sharing these things with the sole intention of convincing him or her to come back. Your missionary will sense that and your spiritual experiences will not reach his or her heart, which may currently be closed off to such experiences.

Know that Heavenly Father and Jesus Christ also love you and are aware of your sorrow. Lean on their love. Find support through family and friends. Continue praying and reading the scriptures daily. Seek professional counseling if needed to work through difficult emotions. Attend the temple when possible. And do not let your happiness be dependent on whether your missionary comes back to the gospel.

To the missionary who has lost his or her testimony, if your family members are members of the Church, please do not also leave them. Even if they have disowned you, keep a place in your heart open for them. The only thing worse than watching a family member leave the gospel you love, is watching the family member leave you. Please continue to stay in contact with your family. Be patient with them as they share their spiritual experiences, and just as you wish for them to be open to your new worldview, be open to theirs. You can still have a wonderful relationship with your family members if you (and they) allow it.

If your family are not members, but you have friends in the Church who are sad about your leaving it, please also do not disown them. It is normal to want to separate yourself from everything that has to do with the Church when you leave (see the next chapter), but it will only cause you further isolation and pain. Even if you do not want to be a member of the Church anymore, your church friends probably still want to be your friend. They may want to know what happened and may even try to convince you that you are wrong. While this may be annoying, remember that their heart is in the right place. You can always respectfully ask that they not ask these questions anymore.

If the opposite is true—everyone disowned you—my heart goes out to you. This is not in line with what the prophets have taught, and I am sorry. They are dealing with pain in an unhealthy way. Please know that not all members of the Church will be so unkind to you. If you can, keep a place open in your heart for forgiveness. Your family and friends may come around after the hurt passes and wish to reconcile. In the meantime, try not to give in to reading anti-Mormon literature, which will only lead to more disillusionment and a greater rift between you and your loved ones. If you can, remember the good times and feelings you had with the Church and remember that the Church isn't out to hurt people. It is a good organization with a mission to help others.

If you have not left the Church, but are still struggling with a crisis of faith, chapter 6 will help you.

Final Thoughts

Clearly, there are many personal reasons for why someone might choose to come home early. As with all reasons for an early return, they can be as unique as each individual. I hope this chapter shed some light on the legitimacy and struggles of these reasons as well as clarity about the next steps to take, so that you can move forward with confidence regarding future choices.

Notes

1.   James E. Faust, "Choices," *Ensign*, May 2004.
2.   Sheri Dew, *Go Forward with Faith: The Biography of Gordon B. Hinckley* (Salt Lake City: Deseret Book, 1996), 64.
3.   Ibid.
4.   Dan Rascon, "Psychologist warns about top 10 mistakes to ruin an LDS mission," KUTV.com, May 9, 2016, http://kutv.com/news/local/psychologist-warns-about-top-10-mistakes-to-ruin-an-lds-mission.
5.   Jeffrey R. Holland, "Missionary Work and the Atonement," *Ensign*, Mar. 2001.
6.   Jeffrey R. Holland, "The Inconvenient Messiah," *Ensign*, Feb. 1984.
7.   Amy Hartfield, "Beating Homesickness: Understanding Homesickness and Learn How to Overcome It," (Alex Coffey, 2014), Audible Audiobook (no printed version).
8.   Marvin J. Ashton, "A Yearning for Home," *Ensign*, Nov. 1992.
9.   Hartfield, "Beating Homesickness."
10.   Ashton, "A Yearning for Home."
11.   Hartfield, "Beating Homesickness."
12.   Ibid.
13.   *Adjusting to Missionary Life* (Salt Lake City: The Church of Jesus Christ of Latter-day Saints, 2013), 29–30.
14.   Don Norton, "How can I know when I have the Spirit of the Lord with me? I'm a college student having a lot of new experiences, and sometimes I can't tell if I'm just feeling 'good' or if my feelings are genuinely righteous," *Ensign*, Aug. 1978.
15.   Ibid.
16.   James E. Faust, "The Great Imitator," *Ensign*, Oct. 1987.

CHAPTER 6

Coming Back to Church

I would like to share the story of my friend Tyler who served in the Philippines at the same time as me. Tyler grew up in the Church and had a strong testimony of the gospel. We were in the same district in the MTC actually, and my memories of Tyler are of a happy, confident, charismatic elder who had a great spirit about him and who was fun to be around. I really remember the Spirit just emanating from him, and it was unsurprising to me when he was called to be our district leader because he drew people to him naturally. When he spoke, people wanted to listen to what he had to say. He inspired others around him often with his good attitude and his joy in the gospel. After he left for the field (and I stayed behind with my broken wrist), I didn't see him again until more than a year later.

When I came home, my mother told me that another missionary from the Philippines had just come home. She'd found out about him from a Missionary Mom's social media page and had been chatting with his mother. "What's his name?" I asked. When she told me, I was both sorry and, admittedly, excited! I was sorry that Tyler had come home early, but excited that I had a friend to talk to about our shared struggles. I reached out to him and he replied, but it was pretty obvious he didn't want to talk about it. I respected that, but I noticed even through social media a marked change in his attitude. He seemed depressed. It is strange that I could tell just through simple messaging that he wasn't doing well, but his words had none of their usual zest for life. He was angry at his mission president for calling him a "quitter," angry that he'd gotten sick, and angry that no one at home seemed to understand him. I could relate to his feelings, but they seemed much more intense than mine.

We chatted a few more times over the summer, and a year later I had the chance to see him again in person when a group of friends and I went to his hometown for some hiking. We met up in the evening and he took me for a ride on his motorcycle, which was a blast. It was great to see him again! I asked if we could visit the nearby temple just because I'd never seen that one before, and he took me over there. Then he took me to meet his parents, who seemed glad that Tyler had gotten out to do something and also glad that they could meet the "other missionary" that came home early. I remember they were interested in how I handled the experience and also interested in why I hadn't returned to my mission. They were very nice to me, but I could tell that Tyler's father was rather disappointed that his son had not returned to the mission field because he wanted to know my opinions on elders not returning to their missions. I didn't really know what to say. Tyler seemed to have a lot of pain on his face as his father spoke. I tried to just steer the conversation to other topics and eventually we talked about what I was doing at school, which seemed to help Tyler relax.

What I remember from that evening most poignantly was my thought when I first saw Tyler again: "What happened?" Gone was the happy, confident, charismatic, spiritual young man that I had known in the MTC and in his place was a discontent and rather gloomy, angry young man. I am struggling even now to put into words just how striking the contrast was. He was still Tyler. He was still a good person and I felt perfectly safe spending time with him that night, but he was different. Though I'd only known him for nine weeks in the MTC, the change was impossible to miss.

I reflected often on that night. I wondered many times why my experience was so different from Tyler's. We'd come home for the same reason, yet I'd moved on happily with my life. I was content and at peace with my decision, and even though I didn't want to talk about my mission or even missionary work, hearing about it didn't cause me visible pain. I was not depressed. I was still working on forgiving some people, but I wasn't letting anger destroy me the way it seemed to be destroying Tyler.

Later Tyler emailed me to tell me he was disconnecting himself from social media for a time, but that I could still email him if I ever wanted to. I didn't really have a reason to email him, nor him me, so we fell out of touch. The next time I heard from him was two and a half years later when he re-emerged on social media. He seemed to have become something of a mountain man: he had a beard and talked often about camping, hunting, and nature. Then he began dating the girl who would become his wife. He married her in the temple and seemed pretty happy, although I never got the joyful, confident, spiritual vibe from his social media posts that I'd gotten from him in the MTC.

In preparing to write this book, I called Tyler to get his story. It was the first time I'd heard his voice in about six years. It sounded more at peace with life than it had that evening on his motorcycle, but still lacked the very upbeat tone it had had in the MTC. He sounded like someone who had experienced a lot of life in a short amount of time. He told me his story from beginning to end: from choosing to serve a mission to coming home, to leaving the Church (the first I'd heard about him leaving) and coming back.

In this chapter, I'd like to share the part of his story about leaving the church and coming back (you can read the first part of his story in chapter 1). I love the candor and honesty of his story. It does not have a fairytale ending; rather, it is still in progress. I hope it will help you in whatever stage you are at: thinking about leaving, thinking about coming back, on your way back, or having returned physically, but still struggling with being back mentally. For those who are completely back and fully active again, perhaps it can remind you of what it was like to return after a period of inactivity and strengthen you to speak up about your experience and draw others to you that could use your help on their journey back. For others, like me, who have never left, you can learn a lot (as I did) from Tyler's experience.

For me, the most striking thing was how his story didn't fit the cookie-cutter mold of coming back (go away, mess up, repent, come back to church, all good!); that it takes a lot more than just coming back to church physically to feel comfortable again and to re-fellowship with ward members. I thought Tyler might be a bit of an outlier in that regard, but further research showed that his experience of being back, but not being totally comfortable, even four years into his return, is actually quite normal for those who seek to return to church. How long is normal? It depends on the person and their experiences: both the experiences that caused them to leave and their experiences while they were gone. And the experiences that they have upon returning to church.

Tyler's Story

I left the Church because I felt like I didn't belong anymore—like I wasn't wanted. When I first came back from my mission, people made stupid comments: "Why are you back?" or "What did you do wrong?" When it first started, I thought that I must have done something wrong to get sick and come home. My parents were a great support initially. They told me, "No, you didn't do anything wrong. You got sick and had to come home, and that's okay." But all of the questions and negative reactions just kind of stuck with me. As the weeks passed, I became very quick in my answers to people. When someone would ask why I came home, I would just say, "I got sick" and leave it at that. I hated the pain of explaining it over and over again and was afraid of their reactions. Since I had also come home after only two months, people wondered if I'd even left yet, and when they'd ask, I'd say, "Yes, but I got sick and had to come home early." I'd hit it straight on, but I didn't really have a lot of confidence in myself as I said it, and I still felt like I was being judged or that I'd done something wrong.

A couple of months went by and the questions changed to, "When are you going back out?" Even my dad tried to guilt trip me into returning the mission field at this point. One thing he said that really hurt was, "I always dreamed that my sons would serve full-time missions" like my mission hadn't counted. I was extremely depressed at this point, and that comment and others from my father threw a whole new bender at me. After my father said that to me, I told him, "I'm not going back out." And he was just like "Okay, we'll see." I just thought, "Whatever. I'm not going to do what you want anymore."

So, all of these negative experiences at church and then with my father made me realize that the reason I was depressed was because I kept going to church and associating with these people. I decided to just stop going. I was still living at home and my parents said, "If you live with us, you have to go to church." But I would find ways to kind of sneak around and not go to church. For example, I would dress up, leave, and then go sit in a park for three hours. Or go on a drive for three hours. Or something like that. And then at end of the three hours, I would come home and make up some story about how church was and who I talked to or whatever and let that be that. But my parents were really smart. They had a little spy they would check up with to make sure I was going to church. One time I was at a park and my mom pulled up next to me, and asked, "What are you doing?" I felt terrible. I thought, "I can't tell my parents the truth because it will break their hearts." I can't remember what I told her. So, I just kept feeling like I had to go to church, but it wasn't my choice at all anymore.

So I moved away and went to college. I probably went to church maybe once a month just because I had really good roommates. They'd say, "Hey, man, come to church with us!" But, eventually, I stopped being around on Sundays. I'd go hiking or camping or something just to be away for the weekend. I also began avoiding any church-related activities at all costs, even praying or reading my scriptures. In hindsight, the way I kind of look at it is similar to shock therapy: if you have an animal, and offer the animal something, and the animal goes to take it, and then you shock the animal, they're going to be very wary the next time they go anywhere near that thing because it is associated with pain. Anything Church-related became associated with pain for me.

So I thought, "I'm not going to do those church things anymore. I'm just going to do my own thing." And I felt good about it. I didn't have depression in my life anymore.

Now, through it all, I still felt like the Church was true. I mean, there were times when I was like, "Is it really true?" But I always came to the conclusion, "Yeah, the Church is true, but the people aren't. So, I'm going to avoid the people." And I did. I didn't hang out with anyone LDS, including my family. I made new friends who weren't LDS, or who had fallen away from the Church, because they were more understanding and accepting of me. I'd tell them about my mission and coming home early, and they'd say, "Ah, man, that sucks. I'm sorry. You want to go play some soccer or something?" And that was really nice. No judgment, no questions. Just an "I'm sorry" and a "Hey, you want to go get this off your mind?" And after a while, I just kind of got into the habit of not ever going to church or being with LDS people, and it was just like "Oh, this is fine. I don't have to deal with this at all anymore. I can hang out with other people and I don't have to associate with people that could potentially cause me pain."

I also started finding the lifestyle I had outside of the church to be a lot more fun. You can go to parties. You can drink, you can smoke, you can do whatever. And everyone is accepting of you. I felt like I could be who I was rather than having to try to conform to what people thought I should be in the church. I feel like people in the church think, "You have to be this returned missionary and then go to college and get married within a couple years. I was like, "No, I kind of want to find out who I am and what my values are. I want to figure out own moral compass." So that's what I did. I made plenty of mistakes along the way. I didn't do anything illegal, but I did get caught up in that stuff for a while, and it was a lot of fun for a while.

While I was gone, I also started looking into some other religions a little bit. But I'd always just think, "Ah, they don't seem like they're cool," and also "I still know the Church is still kind of true. So, I don't want to pursue other religions that much, other than just having spiritual experiences in the mountains." I'd just hang out in the mountains all day. That was my church for a while, just getting up and away from people and being in nature.

Eventually, I ended up moving home again. And, if I lived at home, I had to go to church. I really didn't want to, but I would show up every now and then. The singles ward I went to was really nice and supportive. I also knew a lot of people from high school and that probably helped a bit too. Two other buddies and I would always go every Sunday and just kind of shoot the breeze. We wouldn't necessarily be involved in lessons and things like that. We'd just go hang out.

So I just kept going. Then I would go smoke or drink or something like that. But eventually I started thinking, "I don't feel so good about this anymore." So I would go back to church and think, "Maybe I need to clean up my act a little bit. And maybe I should get on that bandwagon of dating Mormon girls again, you know, try to find someone of higher caliber." Because most of the non-LDS girls I'd dated, I'd just think, "Yeah, you're all a bunch of hippies" or "You're kind of weird. It wouldn't work out with us." But when I dated Mormon girls, I was like "Yeah, I could see things working out because we have similar values, even if I'm not strong in the Church." I always just felt like the Mormon girls' values were similar to mine—what I really wanted anyways.

Then as I kept going to church, I'd also think, "I should probably get worthy again to go to the temple," because I had family members that were going to go to the temple for endowments and to get married. So, eventually, I met with my bishop and he was a really nice guy. Just really down to earth, and I think that's because he joined the church at a later age. He was really able to relate to me, and just like, "Yeah, I know what you're talking about." So, I could connect with him really easily. Also, the way he explained the Atonement was so much better than anything I'd ever heard before up until that point—and I can't remember exactly how he explained it—but it just rang true to me a bit more. And I realized, "Yeah, I'm going to mess up a lot in my life and that's okay because that's what the Atonement was for." Anyways, I started working with him and then, eventually, was temple-worthy again. It was really nice to experience that and be at a point in my life where I was like, "Yeah, this is nice." It was nice to feel that way again.

And then I was like, "I'm getting older. Maybe I should look for someone to marry or just date more seriously than I have been." Eventually, I met the woman who is now my wife and I was like, "Okay, I really need to get my act together a little bit more, because she would never want to marry somebody who isn't a really good guy and healthy and all that stuff."

So I started to get in shape and cleaning up my act even more. We started dating. And the whole time I was like, "Why would she even want to marry me? I'm not even worth it." And I was just getting down on myself because I'd done so many stupid things in my life. Depression kind of crept back in a little bit, but eventually it got better and I was just like, "Depression, go away. You're a negative influence in my life. I just need to be happy." So I kind of faked it until I made it.

But I always had a roller coaster of highs and lows and still do today. I go between "Yeah, I like the Church" and "No, I don't like the Church today. I don't want to go to church" often. It's been like that ever since my mission. The main reason I've stayed in the church is because of my wife. I don't want to let her down. But, I mean, even now I still have days where I don't want to go or even have a time frame of several months where I don't want to be at church at all. I feel like it's a waste of my time, and I'm not learning anything new, and it's all the same. Whereas I'll go up in the mountains and just feel peace and calm.

My wife is a good influence on me. When I get in one of my low periods, she'll say, "Okay, well, let's at least go to sacrament meeting and see how you feel after that." She's very understanding, but she doesn't enable me. She's good like that.

It's still hard for me to go to Sunday School classes or elders quorum. Even sacrament meeting is hard for me. One hour feels like how three hours used to feel. I don't really participate in classes and I don't have any callings. I've been asked, but I just say no. That was something I learned I could do when I first stopped going to church: I could say no to a calling or to speaking in sacrament meeting, and I admittedly really liked that it kind of caught people off-guard. So, I still have some of that left in me where I don't like having a calling or being more involved. It brings back some negative memories.

It's hard and frustrating to hear people talk about their missions all the time, especially in elders quorum, and I just wish they would talk about some other life experiences—there's more to life than your mission! Maybe that's just me judging a bit, but that's what I think. Also, people are judging people for doing bad things like smoking, drinking, or whatever. All I can think is, "Yeah, but you don't know those people. They're good people. I knew people that would still go to church, and they smoked a pack of cigarettes a week. They were trying to be better. They were good people." I'm honestly more drawn toward the members that have had a different life. If I see someone with like a full-sleeve tattoo in church, I think, "I want to be friends with that guy! He seems cool." Whereas the guy that went on a mission, went to BYU, and married while he was still there, and now has three kids, I'm not interested in being friends with him. I feel like I kind of have an idea of who he is, which is me judging. But, at the same time, I've had experiences with people who fit that cookie-cutter mold that have made me not want to be friends with people like that anymore.

All this being said, I do see myself getting to the point where I participate again in church, whether it's in class or over the pulpit. Either calling people out a bit or saying, "You know, everybody has these cookie-cutter experiences. This is my experience and it is totally different. This is what happened. So, you know, take it with a grain of salt." I think it would touch people in a way. I'm just not at that level where I feel like I can share it without having issues or not wanting to be at church because it is still too soon. Even though the mission was eight years ago. Which is saying something. It's been that long and I still haven't recovered. And I'm not sure how long it will take. But I do think I'll get there.

Returning home early from a mission is often a time of great distress and pain. The adversary works hard to intensify feelings of failure, and these feelings are often exacerbated at church by well-meaning ward members, family, and even Church leaders. Sometimes, they are exacerbated in lessons such as those about missionary work or staying true to commitments. Church can become a source of great pain to someone who came home early from a mission, even though the teachings of the Church provide exactly the healing that the person needs. Therefore, it is unsurprising that according to a study conducted by

Dr. Kristine Doty-Yells and several colleagues that "34% of ERMs had a period of inactivity, and of those, 33% have never returned. Nearly half of the survey respondents (47%) reported they are not as active in the Church as they were before they went on their mission."[1]

What causes these feelings of pain, distress, and failure? How do they get to the point that someone would leave the church? Doty-Yells and her team narrowed the reasons down to two through their study: (1) reception of ward members and (2) the amount of spiritual experiences on a mission. They found that "ERMs who felt their ward members received them well upon their early return were less likely to experience a period of inactivity. . . . Similarly, missionaries who had strong spiritual experiences while on their missions were also less likely to experience a period of inactivity, compared to ERMs who did not have strong spiritual experiences. . . . However, the reception of ward members was a slightly more powerful predictor, indicating that powerful spiritual experiences on the mission may not fully compensate for a cold reception from ward members after returning home early from a mission."[2]

People leave the church or go inactive for a period of time for other reasons: family issues, doubts and unanswered questions, a desire to find out what life is like without the Church, and so on. From talking to those who left the Church in direct relation to coming home early, however, I have found the two reasons Doty-Yells cited for early-returned missionaries leaving the Church to be accurate.

Tyler had some good spiritual experiences on his mission, but they were largely overshadowed by rudeness from his trainer and negative comments from his mission president (see chapter 1). He did not have a supportive ward when he came home, or at least he perceived them to be unsupportive. Although he did receive some support and encouragement, he was already beaten down from his experiences on the mission and took the negative comments much more to heart than the positive comments. In the end, he felt unwelcome at church and left. It was really as simple as that. He found friends outside of the Church that were accepting of him, and he decided to try a different lifestyle. In all of this, Tyler was searching for goodness and a way to live happily. He found happiness for a time in socializing with people who didn't live Church standards and even in participating in some of the activities. He enjoyed the freedom of less expectations on his conduct. For a while, it was a good life.

I think what drew Tyler back to the Church was the idea of something more to experience than just what this world has to offer: more truth, more goodness, and more experiences that lead to *lasting* peace and happiness. He is still on a roller coaster with regards to the Church, but he is staying because he has seen the other side of life. He admitted that there are things about that other life that he misses, mainly the freedom of living your life however you want rather than having to always live up to a certain standard. But, when he goes to church and when he's feeling good about it and can see where he is in life now, he's happy he came back. He's especially grateful for his wife and knows that without the Church he wouldn't have this amazing woman in his life.

Obviously, Tyler's life isn't perfect now that he's back nor is he gung-ho about the Church again. He is still struggling with some left-over negative emotions from coming home early and is still grappling with seeing things from a different perspective since he left the Church for a while. He gets annoyed with people more easily and isn't yet ready to accept a calling or speak up in church yet. He is rather judgmental too, which is ironic since he sees much more clearly the way that people who have never left the Church are judgmental and gets upset by it. But he still goes. He's excited to see others who have led less-than-perfect lives at church. I think he really understands what Joseph B. Wirthlin meant when he said, "The Church is not a place where perfect people gather to say perfect things, or have perfect thoughts, or have perfect feelings. The Church is a place where imperfect people gather to provide encouragement, support, and service to each other as we press on in our journey to return to our Heavenly Father."[3] I think he wishes more people in the Church realized this so that he could feel comfortable speaking up and sharing his experiences. I encouraged him in our conversation not to wait for that, because that won't happen until those who have different experiences start speaking up and offering their perspectives. Wards who are critical of those who aren't "cookie-cutter Mormons" will continue to be echo chambers until those among them who aren't cookie-cutter Mormons speak up.

For those wondering if they should stay in the Church or leave, or if they should return to Church activity or stay away, Tyler offers this piece of advice,

> Ask yourself why you are going to church. Do you actually want to be there or is it just something you are supposed to be doing? And if it's because it is something you are supposed to be doing, do a test. For one month, don't go to church and write down in a journal how you are feeling. Write at least once a week about what has felt good and what has felt bad. Then, the next month, go to church and all of the meetings, and write down in your journal again how you are feeling— what felt good and what felt bad, and compare how you are feeling. Then choose the happiest path. If you choose that you'd be happier away from church, then okay, but at least repeat this test every six months and try again. See how you feel. Because I think sometimes we get so set in what we're not going to do, that we can become stubborn and not change even if we kind of want to because people will question us and we'll get defensive. So, we need to personally revisit what our plans are. Maybe some people can fake it till they make it and go to church anyways, but for some people, especially myself, I needed the introspection and awareness that trying it without offered. But keep that journal and notice how you're feeling. By doing that, you might be able to avoid some of the pitfalls that I did.

I read recently a story on lds.org's blog titled "Why Don't I Feel Like I Fit in at Church?" that echoes the advice Tyler just gave. The author, Katie Steed, said, "While my time away from church had some extremely dark moments, I honestly consider it as one of the most important times of my life. Never had I prayed so hard, examined myself and my beliefs so thoroughly, or faced my uncertainties so head-on as I did then. Once I came to terms with my struggles and questions, I realized how much I wanted to believe in the things I had been taught in the Church and decided to go back."[4]

If you haven't left the Church, I am not going to encourage you to do so. If you can stick it out and hold on to your faith and get through the storm of unfair questions and judgment, I say do it because from what I've read and heard, it sounds like the time away and the path back is fraught with even more misery. Ask those who are giving you encouragement to stand up for you to those who are being judgmental and unfair. Lean on others for support and remember that you don't have to go through this alone.

However, if you really feel like you can't stick it out and you are going to church only because it is expected, but you hate every moment of it, and you feel like your testimony is on the brink because of it, perhaps taking a break from church *attendance* for a *short* time is warranted. Commit to returning in a month though, and journal how you are feeling. Stay as close to the Lord as you can—Tyler gave up everything Church-related and that led him into some addictive behaviors and other things that he later regretted. You don't need more pain in your life. Don't give up everything. Let this time away be a time of introspection and even a way for you to draw closer to God. Think about why the negative comments affect you so deeply. What do you really believe about yourself now that you have come home early from a mission? Is what you believe true?

Also, ask yourself, who is the source of peace? Can you lean on Him? Do you really feel like Jesus Christ has given up on you? It can absolutely be tempting to think "Yes, He has!" or "I failed Him. He wants nothing to do with me now. He's mad at me," but those are *lies* from the adversary. Do not fall for them! Jesus Christ loves you unfailingly and even if you have some repenting to do, no one wants you to partake in the Atonement and feel peace again in your life more than He does.

In fact, if I could tell you one thing, no matter where on the path of faith you are, it is this: God loves you. No matter what you've done, no matter how far you've strayed, no matter how hopeless your situation may feel, no matter how mistreated you've been, and no matter how tempted you are to sin, God *loves* you.

If you've gone away, you absolutely can come back! We read in the scriptures about the prodigal son who was welcomed back home in resplendent fashion by his father: "But when he was yet a great way off, his father saw him, and had compassion, and ran, and fell on his neck, and kissed him . . . [and] the father said to his servants, Bring forth the best robe, and put it on him; and put a ring on his hand, and shoes on his feet: And bring hither the fatted calf, and kill it; and let us eat, and be merry: For this my son was dead, and is alive again; he was lost, and is found. And they began to be merry" (Luke 15:20–24).

No matter what your reception by the ward members (we read too in Luke 15 that the prodigal son's brother did not feel that he deserved a wonderful welcome home), Heavenly Father is so happy to have you back. Hold onto His love during this time of uncertainty and discomfort. The stronger you hold onto His love, the better you will be able to ride any potential storms from coming back—whether those storms look like inquiring questions, judgmental looks or comments, giving up habits you picked up while away from Church, or a lack of friends because you've been gone so long that you no longer know anyone at church. You will be okay. Just hold on and keep going. You're where you need to be.

And it will get better. Katie Steed said,

> As I felt better at church, I started to wonder if, like me, others felt afraid to share their questions and experiences. . . . It was difficult, but I began speaking up and was honest about my uncertainties and experiences. . . . My fear of being different began to disappear completely, and, without fail, any time I talked about my trials, questions, or thoughts, another person always came forward with similar worries and expressed relief that the subject had been brought up. I was amazed to find that I had more in common than different with my peers. I found some of the best friends I've ever had, and I have never felt closer to the Savior.

She also added,

> To anyone who feels they don't fit in at church—you truly do. We all have imperfections, and we all need each other's support. Your experiences and faith are a needed part of the Church. Our questions help us find out what we truly believe, and sharing them in church can help us find answers. Our trials and experiences help us relate to one another and make connections that enrich our lives, especially in a ward family. . . . None of us is perfect, and none of us should expect anyone else to be perfect. Life is hard enough without setting too high of expectations on ourselves or others. If we support, accept, and love each other in spite of some differences, we will be more like the Savior. We are all on the same path with the same goals of happiness and returning to our Heavenly Father.[5]

And may I also add, on behalf of those of us who have never left the Church, and so may sometimes make comments that are insensitive or judgmental, be patient with us. You're right, we don't know. Everything that I wrote in this chapter, I wrote based on other people's experiences. I *don't* know what you are going through. I can guess and I can even empathize in some ways, but I don't really know and I need you to speak up in church and tell me. I need to hear your thoughts and opinions and experiences. My favorite comments in church are from those who have different perspectives. Those comments help me stay strong in the gospel, and they make me a better Latter-day Saint because they push me to think deeper about the way I approach certain topics and quite often give me the push I need to become better.

Also, keep in mind that even though we appear to be "cookie-cutter," none of us actually are. We *all* have baggage. We all have things in our history. My dad appears to be that cookie-cutter returned missionary, who went to BYU and got married while he was there, had children immediately, got a great job, and now lives a great life. But he has had experiences in his life that would blow your mind. You'd think, "*Him?* He knows what it's like to struggle with *that*? He knows what it's like to experience *that* kind of pain?" I'm the girl who went to BYU, married before she graduated, and is a stay-at-home mom who writes on the side. Yet I returned early from a mission and have had other experiences in my life that relate to you more than you'd think. You just never know. So listen to us too. Even if our life experience is through another darn missionary story! We learned something through that experience that will perhaps deepen your understanding of your own life experiences.

Finally, one last thing: we've already established that the Church isn't for perfect people. Therefore, please don't wait until you are perfect to start participating in church again, by attending, speaking, or accepting a calling. These things may be hard right now because of negative memories, but eventually, you will need to face those memories head-on, work through them, and put them in their proper perspective. By facing those memories, you will be able to find a new level of freedom in your church attendance because you will feel empowered to speak up and share your perspective and help others do the same. You will invite light and goodness into your life, and others will be drawn to you. You will feel happy. You will be able to forgive yourself for past mistakes, and you will know that the Lord forgives you too. You will benefit those of us who need you and your perspective most.

Do not let your imperfections control your happiness any longer. Do not let the fact that you came home early from your mission rob you of peace any longer. So often we get so hung up on the events of our lives, that we miss the point of those events. What were you supposed to learn? What can you learn now?

The way forward may not be smooth or easy, but *keep moving forward*. It may feel at times that you are standing still, or even moving backward, but if you keep trying and keep doing your best to stay close to Heavenly Father and Jesus Christ, you will keep progressing. Consider keeping a journal about coming back to church so that when things get hard and you don't feel like you are making any progress, you can read your journal and see how far you have already come. Whatever you do, don't give up on yourself. You are worth all of the peace, joy, and love that can be found in the gospel. You may not always feel like you're worth it, but you are. Prayerfully ask God to help you feel that.

While I have never experienced leaving the church, I have at times experienced crises of faith that have left me wondering if the Church is really true. Such crises generally come at times when my life is not going the way I expected it to or the way I feel I deserve. I've tried to live a good life, and I get frustrated when things do not go my way. I have blamed God or the Church for my problems. I think such reactions are normal, but unacceptable. They're normal because I'm human with an imperfect understanding of things, but unacceptable because I'm placing blame where it does not belong. I've always been able to work through my frustration, anger, or pain without leaving the Church, but not without doubting my faith. Doubts are a natural part of conversion and growth. As Elder Uchtdorf said,

> It's natural to have questions—the acorn of honest inquiry has often sprouted and matured into a great oak of understanding. . . . One of the purposes of the Church is to nurture and cultivate the seed of faith— even in the sometimes sandy soil of doubt and uncertainty. Faith is to hope for things which are not seen but which are true. Therefore, my dear brothers and sisters—my dear friends—please, first doubt your doubts before you doubt your faith. We must never allow doubt to hold

us prisoner and keep us from the divine love, peace, and gifts that come through faith in the Lord Jesus Christ.[6]

Because I have always chosen faith over doubt, I've always come out of my crises stronger. I clung closely to the Lord during them—even when I was mad at Him. The Atonement is real and it can heal. "All that is unfair about life can be made right through the Atonement of Jesus Christ."[7] You may have read that line in *Preach My Gospel*. I testify that that is true. The Atonement exists to enable repentance, but more than that, it exists to enable healing. I testify that coming closer to Christ and putting our sorrows, frustrations, and sins on Him does create healing, happiness, and ultimately peace in our lives.

So come back. Or stay. We need you. We are imperfect, judgmental, "cookie-cutter" Latter-day Saints who need you! Seriously, you have what we need. Come back and forgive our mistakes and stupid comments. Speak up and let us know who you are. And stay. You are welcome more than you think.

Notes

1. Kristine J. Doty-Yells, S. Zachary Bullock, Harmony Packer, Russell T. Warner, James Westwood, Thomas Ash, and Heather Hirsch, "Return with Trauma: Understanding the Experiences of Early Returned Missionaries," *Issues in Religion and Psychotherapy*, vol. 37, no. 1 (2015): 42. Available at http://scholarsarchive.byu.edu/irp/vol37/iss1/9.
2. Ibid., 42–43.
3. Joseph B. Wirthlin, "The Virtue of Kindness," *Ensign*, May 2005.
4. Katie Steed, "Why Don't I Feel Like I Fit In at Church?", February 6, 2018, https://www.lds.org/blog/why-dont-i-feel-like-i-fit-in-at-church?cid=HP_FR_9-2-2018_dOCS_fBLOG_xLIDyL2_&ab_enabled.
5. Ibid.
6. Dieter F. Uchtdorf, "Come, Join with Us," *Ensign*, Nov. 2013.
7. "Lesson 2: The Plan of Salvation," *Preach My Gospel: A Guide to Missionary Service* (2004).

CHAPTER 7

For Church Leaders

Some of my fondest memories of growing up in the Church include talking to my Church leaders as a youth and as a young adult. I was fortunate to always have Church leaders who loved the Lord and respected the office of their calling. I always had the impression that they sought to do the will of the Lord and to receive inspiration and revelation. I will forever be grateful to my stake president who helped me so willingly and openly when I came home early from my mission. He made coming home early such a positive experience for me and helped me move forward with my life with the reassurance that the Lord approved of my decision and that I was loved by Him.

After speaking with several leaders in preparation for writing this book, I came to the understanding that leadership callings are both extremely difficult and extremely rewarding. They can feel heavy at times; there seems to always be the stress of juggling the demands of a job, a family, and the ward, stake, or mission, and personal needs. Many spoke about how the office of the calling was bigger than themselves, and the struggle (at least initially) to feel comfortable with the title of "Bishop" or "President." Several also spoke of a great desire to accomplish and communicate what the Lord wants for that ward, stake, mission, or individual, and how it can be difficult at times to discern between what the Lord wants to have said or done and what the leader thinks should be done. Even those with years of experience in the calling expressed how this remained the most difficult part of their calling, although they also added that they eventually learned how to trust the inspiration they receive and their life experience.

One bishop of five years described the difficulty with discernment this way:

I was ward clerk for a while, and, as a ward clerk I knew when I was succeeding. I knew when the books were balanced and all the data was entered and the records were correct. It was hard and fast. Being a bishop is more difficult because it's harder to know when I'm succeeding. It's harder to know when counseling people, for example, that I'm counseling them the way the Lord would have me counsel them. Now, I definitely feel the Spirit. I definitely receive revelation. But, rarely does it come in big brackets that say "start revelation, end revelation." It takes a little work sometimes to figure out. And it doesn't necessarily all come in the middle of a counseling session. Sometimes it takes a little bit of time and a little bit of praying and effort and thinking to really figure out what the Lord would have me do.

He followed up his statement with a story about some of his first nights of interviews as a bishop. He told me,

Those first nights of interviews, I remember thinking, "What am I supposed to say to these people? I don't know what to do." But I went, and as soon as I sat down and started talking, ideas and thoughts just came into my mind. And I learned not to worry when I don't know how to solve the problem right now, or if I don't know what to say to somebody right now because the Lord will let me know. It's comforting to realize that I'm just the guy in the chair, and that it is really our Heavenly Father working through me to help people we both love.

In response to his story, I said, "Sometimes the Lord just trusts you. You've been prepared, you know? And He allows us to go on our own experiences," to which he replied, "That's true."

This bishop gained a testimony early on that the Lord trusted him to lean on Him when needed but to also trust that the Lord had prepared him for the calling. He recalled later in the interview several life experiences that had helped him greatly in his calling as a bishop to relate to others and to understand their concerns and needs. While he finds the resources and trainings available to bishops invaluable, he found that the best resources he had to draw from were his own life experiences, which he felt in many ways, looking back, were the Lord preparing him to be able to succeed in the calling. Other leaders that I spoke to expressed similar sentiments about how the Lord qualifies and helps, and how they gained a testimony that the Lord would help them fill the office of the calling, even if they felt inadequate.

With regards to early-returned missionaries, all of the leaders I spoke to had varying levels of experience with these individuals, but all expressed their deepest sympathies for what the missionaries go through and their great desire to help them. They expressed to me that the most difficult part of helping an early-returned missionary is helping him or her decide what to do next, and to try to help the missionary discern the will of the Lord. Or, if the will of the Lord is that the individual stays home, how to help him or her be okay with that, and to move forward with life and stay a faithful member of the Church, and not let this experience haunt the missionary the rest of his or her life. Stake presidents and bishops in particular also expressed to me their desire to rid their ward, stake, or the individual of the effects of our Mormon culture, which *all* asserted has improved greatly in recent years, but there is still work to be done.

These leaders, particularly stake presidents and bishops, also spoke to me about how they have tried to make sure individuals are truly physically, spiritually, and especially emotionally ready to serve a mission. They spoke of what they have done in their ward or stake to help these individuals and their parents know how to best prepare for a mission and what a mission entails. They also expressed their desire to learn from others about what worked in their wards or stakes, or what they did or said that really helped an individual.

I will share these leaders' strategies for helping early-returned missionaries to accept themselves and their mission experience and to know what the next step is. I will also share some thoughts from these leaders about things you can do to help rid your ward, stake, mission, or an individual of false stereotypes or stigmas based solely on cultural notions. Finally, I will share and discuss strategies from these leaders about how to best ensure that an individual is truly ready to serve a mission, and share some of my own thoughts on the subject based again on my experience, as well as what I have learned from talking to many returned missionaries (both those who came home early and who completed the intended amount of time). Toward the end of this chapter, there is a special section for mission presidents where I discuss some of the unique challenges they face with this phenomenon due to the nature of their calling, but I do believe that they will find the rest of this chapter to be helpful as well.

In addition to reading this chapter, as you read the rest of this book pay particular attention to the differences in what early-returned missionaries go through based on the reason(s) they come home, particularly in regard to their interactions with priesthood leaders. Also, pay attention to what the parents may be going through upon their child's early return (discussed in the next chapter) and how their reactions may impact their child. Each person is an individual and will experience things differently, but the more you understand things in general terms, the better you will be able to receive inspiration and revelation for the individual.

How the Missionary Sees You

Before we move forward with the strategies, let's pause for a moment and talk about how the missionary (in whatever stage he or she is in: pre, current, or returned) sees you. As you are probably aware, especially if you grew up in the Church, and if you held other callings of leadership, the missionary sees you both as an authority figure and even as a type of father figure. This is especially true of mission presidents who have the responsibility of overseeing large amounts of young adults who are at an especially vulnerable transition time in their life. When on a mission, young adults are given independence, but, as Dr. Kristine Doty-Yells says in her article "Return with Trauma," "The mission president is a source of adult authority and guidance, but his influence is distant on a daily basis. This provides missionaries with a large degree of autonomy as they practice adult responsibilities and progress in the identity development of emerging adulthood."[1] Missionaries often feel like they can call their mission president for advice or assistance at any time (in problems large or small), much the same way they would one of their parents. However, they also see the mission president as a man called of God, entitled to revelation for the mission, and even the missionary's personal mission. Many times missionaries feel like whatever comes out of their mission president's mouths can come directly from Heavenly Father, and often act in faith on what their mission president tells them.

The same is true of stake presidents and bishops. Bishops are sometimes called "the father of the ward,"[2] in fact. They are also seen as individuals who can help in problems large or small and offer advice and counsel, much the same way a parent might. However, they too have been called of God and have certain keys and rights to revelation regarding their stewardship and regarding the individual whom they are counseling with.

Therefore, because of these realities, there can at times be a perception that a leader should act in a particular way: he should be at all times spiritual and should *never* let the natural man come out. He should always be kind, loving, and understanding. If he is frustrated, upset, or even short with someone, it can be perceived as the Lord working through him and that it is in fact the Lord being frustrated, upset, or short with the individual. That is the *perception*. Therefore, if an early-returned missionary is ever treated unkindly or in a way that they perceive to be unfair by their leader, this has a much bigger impact on them than even if his or her parents were to do or say the same thing. From a Church leader, it seems to come from God himself, and this can be damaging. Or it is perceived as the natural man coming out, and the person grows to disrespect his or her leader, or even the office of the calling.

Whether these reactions are the fault of the leader, the missionary, or both depends upon the circumstance. I merely bring them up because I have been told stories from early-returned missionaries about bishops refusing to shake their hands, stake presidents who were unkind or not understanding about the nuances of situations, and even mission presidents who called missionaries "quitters." Please see chapters 1 and 2 for examples of this. In addition to these examples, one young woman told me about her experience with telling her mission president that she was struggling with depression. She said,

> I just felt like my mission president didn't understand what I was saying. He would just stare at me. I know you have to experience depression to truly empathize with someone, but it felt like he didn't even make an effort to understand. He just stared and eventually just said, "Well, maybe just go home. That's probably what's best." And I was expecting him to be overjoyed to try to help me. I expected him to want me to be there because I told him so many times, "I have such a strong testimony and I have valuable things to say. I want to be here so bad. And I worked so hard to be here." He had no idea how hard I had worked to

get myself on a mission. But he just kind of dismissed it. I kept saying to him, "This isn't me. But I don't know how to get back to being me again." And he just said, "Well, then just go home." And then we both stood up to get my trainer again. And as he walked out he said, "You're fine, Sister." I was not fine. I was NOT fine.

He called us the next day and he just seemed really annoyed, as though it was a burden for him to try and find flight plans to send me home. He wouldn't let my parents call me, but eventually my mom called me the night before I came home. She was very mad and she basically just said, "I have been bugging your mission president and the stake president to get your phone number. I just want to know if you're okay. I'm not going to be okay with this until I know that it was your decision to come home, because I don't want you come home if you don't want to come home." And I was so torn because I didn't want to come home. But I knew that it would not be fair for anybody—or for me—to be there because I just was a zombie and I wasn't doing much. I felt like I couldn't contribute anything. And I knew it just wasn't going to be healthy for me to be there. And so I just said, "He made a good call. I know I need to go home." But I was still struggling.

After that phone call, I was driving around with my trainer, crying so hard. I told her, "I wanted to change lives. I wanted to teach everybody and I wanted to work really hard." She said, "Sister, you think you didn't change lives but I know we were supposed to be together. You can go home and tell everybody that you did what you were called do—you came on a mission. You were called to serve me and change my life. That's all you needed to do." So after that I felt a lot of peace and I knew after that it was the right decision. I had served faithfully and knew that the Lord was pleased with my work. And so I was able to go home feeling good about what I had done.

Dr. Doty-Yells reported that "[out of 348 survey participants] almost half felt they were treated indifferently or poorly by their ward leaders."[3] Certainly, there are two sides to every story, and the Lord knows each side. There are certainly going to be misunderstandings on both sides at times, and this is to be expected. I would just strongly caution anyone in a leadership position from saying or doing things that may be perceived as unkind. Individuals do not recover quickly from such statements and do leave the Church over them sometimes.

Of course the responsibility to leave the Church or to not forgive a leader rests squarely on the shoulders of the individual. Furthermore, there are times when a Church leader does need to speak boldly, honestly, and frankly—when it absolutely would be a disservice to a missionary to let him or her stay on a mission (or return to a mission) if certain issues are unresolved regarding health or worthiness. The Savior often spoke with boldness during His ministry. To the woman taken in adultery, He said, "Neither do I condemn thee. Go and sin no more." He did not excuse her from her sin, but also set her on the path of repentance with love and the promise of forgiveness (see John 8:2–11). Also, remember always the words in Doctrine and Covenants 121:41–44:

> No power or influence can or ought to be maintained by virtue of the priesthood, only by persuasion, by long-suffering, by gentleness and meekness, and by love unfeigned; by kindness, and pure knowledge, which shall greatly enlarge the soul without hypocrisy, and without guile—Reproving betimes with sharpness, when moved upon by the Holy Ghost; and then showing forth afterwards an increase of love toward him whom thou hast reproved, lest he esteem thee to be his enemy; that he may know that thy faithfulness is stronger than the cords of death.

All of the missionaries I spoke with who felt unfairly treated by a leader never experienced an increase of love from the leader after the sharpness. They felt that the leader had simply walked away, leaving them to feel the weight and sting of what that leader had just said or done. Those who were spoken to boldly, or even sharply, but felt that the treatment was fair, always felt an increase of love from the leader afterward. For effective examples of boldly, yet lovingly, ministering, please see chapter 3.

The way the mission president treated the sister in the previous story seemed to be that of someone who could not be bothered with a missionary who was less than perfect. According to the sister, no attempt was made at finding her a good therapist, or even any attempt at saying some encouraging words other than "You're fine," which wasn't encouraging. He left that work to her trainer. It is the responsibility of leaders to treat those under their stewardship the way the Lord Himself would treat them. So, please, shake the hands of those who come home early (no matter what the reason) and offer words of encouragement and understanding to those who are confused or dealing with feelings of failure. Understand that even if you feel they could muscle it out, they may need a break that only a reprieve at home can offer them.

One former mission president said to me, "I would hope that it never comes to a point where the natural man overcomes the calling...at a training, President Nelson told us, 'Presidents, you're not just responsible for those missionaries, you're responsible for their children and their children's children.'" Remember, your role as a Church leader extends far beyond the individual's mission experience. This quote from President Nelson tells you the magnitude of your office. Please be careful in what you say. And as this mission president said, "I know when you have 400-something missionaries out there, there are going to be times when things just don't go right. There will be things that you will say in a moment that you wish you didn't say, and I would hope in those cases that mission presidents and individuals say 'I'm sorry' and move on."

Again, what is done with the offense rests squarely with the individual. However, remember that how you are perceived does give what you say and do greater weight and therefore has a greater impact on the individuals that you meet with and serve. This will be the foundation of the rest of this chapter.

Helping the Individual Who Returned Early

When a missionary returns early, he or she will be dealing with feelings of loss and failure. The missionary had expected to serve for the full eighteen months or two years and, for whatever reason, is no longer able to do that, at least not the way he or she had planned. Some will handle these feelings better than others and take care of whatever they need to take care of and get back out there or will move on with their lives smoothly. The majority though will struggle. According to Doty-Yells, "Of the [348 survey respondents] 73% said they had feelings of failure . . . regardless of the reason they returned, regardless of whether their early return was related to personal conduct."[4] These missionaries will be looking to you, as their priesthood leader, to help them.

First Things First

The most important thing you can do is to reassure the missionary of the Lord's love for him or her, and that if the reasons for the early return are medical, mental, or emotional, that the Lord knows that the missionary has done the best he or she can, and that his or her offering is accepted by the Lord. To back this up, you might quote Elder Holland when he said in a preview of a face-to-face event with early-returned missionaries,

> I don't know that in all eternity, every mission was outlined to be two years or, for the young women, eighteen months. That's kind of a modern invention. . . . So I want you to be proud. Appropriately proud. I want you to take the dignity and the strength and the faith that came from your [time] and cherish that forever. I don't want you to apologize for coming home. When someone asks you if you've served a mission, you say yes. You do not need to follow that up with "But it was only [however long]." Just forget that part and say, yes, you served a mission.[5]

This will especially help young men who know that it is a priesthood duty to serve a mission and feel that they failed the Lord by returning early. As you counsel with early-returned missionaries, try to also "forget" that "early" part and treat them as a returned missionary.

If a missionary comes home due to worthiness issues, this can be more nuanced, especially if they have the opportunity to return to the field once everything is worked out. However, even these individuals deserve respect for recognizing their need to go through the repentance process; they need love and support. They also need to recognize that they served a mission and to learn the appropriate lessons from that service and have the appropriate credit for those moments where they did serve the Lord and let the Lord work through them. Obviously, if the worthiness issues were due to unresolved transgression, they were on a mission illegitimately. However, in Michael's story in chapter 3, the Lord still worked through Michael to accomplish His purposes. However, Michael did not receive the full benefit of those purposes until he repented fully of his sins.

And if the worthiness issues are related to transgressions committed on the mission, the missionary still had experiences and still served a mission. It was unfortunately cut short and more work could not be done due to the sin. We all fall short at times: sometimes it is our body, sometimes it is our mind, sometimes it is our family, and sometimes it is our own lack of faith or selfishness. But we all need help and support from our leaders at times to know that the Lord still loves us and that we *can* get back on track.

However, what about those missionaries who chose to come home for reasons of homesickness, lack of desire, loss of desire, or loss of testimony? They did not keep their commitment to the Lord, and that shouldn't be given a "free pass," right? For those missionaries, be wary of coming down too hard on them. What they especially need is to feel the love of the Lord and help working through the feelings that caused them to end their mission willingly. They do not need condemnation. They need time and help to work through their fear or lack of faith, and also to, yes, possibly repent for not fulfilling their commitment and forfeiting the opportunity to help others, depending on their state of mind when they made the decision. Please see chapter 5 for more information.

One stake president recognizes that he is not a therapist, but sees the benefit many early-returned missionaries may have by speaking to a professional counselor, and utilizes regularly LDS Family Services's six free counseling sessions for early-returned missionaries. These counselors are professionally trained to ask questions that can get to the heart of any issue, and help the missionary understand what happened physically, emotionally, and spiritually, and help missionaries understand what they want and what the Lord also wants for them. This is a wonderful resource available to you, especially if you struggle to know what to say.

Stay Home or Go Back Out?

The first thing that may be tempting to talk about is whether the missionary will go back to his or her mission. Please avoid this temptation. As one stake president put it,

> Especially for mental health. . . . When these young men and women come home because of mental health issues—or maybe physical problems due to mental health issues—even the thought of going back

163

on their mission just gives them great anxiety. They get nervous and they get scared again, because they just left an environment that was not fun. It was hard and they couldn't do it. They tried, they prayed, they cried, they weren't sleeping, they were losing weight, and they were getting sick. That's not a fun environment. . . . And the thought of going back to that, boy, it just haunts them. So when the missionary first comes home, the last thing I talk about is whether or not they will go back out. I first say, "Let's get you home. Let's get you healthy. Let's get you happy. And then we'll see what happens." Let's be honest, they really shouldn't think about going back out until some things are resolved.

The Church also discourages leaders from pressuring the missionary to go back to the mission field in *Ministering Resources: Missionaries Who Return Early,* which is available online to Church leaders, stake, and ward council members. Eventually, he or she will want to talk to you about that. Just probably not right away, especially if the early homecoming was due to mental health.

Once an individual is settled in his or her mind regarding the reason he or she came home, he or she will often move to the next step which is the decision to return to the mission or to go back out. This question can weigh heavily on an early-returned missionary's mind, and the answer is as individual as the individuals themselves. Everyone has a unique purpose in this life, and the ways to accomplish those purposes are vast, yet specific to each person. As a priesthood leader, you can help the early-returned missionary make this decision by being available to be counseled with (my stake president even let me call him on his cell phone as I needed to, which wasn't too often), and by encouraging the ward or stake to give the missionary space to make the decision on his or her own.

Also, encourage the parents to give the missionary space to make this decision (see chapter 8). Encourage the missionary to be prayerful, to read the scriptures, and to make a decision and then take it to the Lord at the temple, trusting that the Lord will provide an answer (even if that answer is that either decision is okay, as it was for me). Let the missionary tell you about the answer or inspiration that he or she received. If the answer was that either direction is okay, ask the missionary what he or she really wants, and then encourage him or her to make a decision and stick to it, not looking back. As I mentioned earlier in the book, my stake president told me, "Kristen, you're the kind of girl where if things don't work out the way you want them to, six months down the road, you're going to beat yourself up and tell yourself that you should have gone back. That you're being punished or something. And I have to tell you that that is not the case! You will be blessed either way according to the Lord's timing and you have to let yourself move on and not look back." Those words helped me to have confidence in my decision to move forward with life and to not look back and wonder if I'd truly made the right decision.

If, of course, you feel inspired to tell the missionary that he or she has not felt the Spirit correctly, or that you are receiving a different answer, do speak up and say so. Again, you are seen as an authority figure and even as a mouthpiece for the Lord at times, and your words will impact the missionary, and perhaps even help him or her feel the Spirit as he or she should. You do also have the final say about whether or not a missionary is ready to return to the field. Be prayerful and open to the Spirit so that you can feel confident that if the missionary returns to the field and comes home early again, that it was what the Lord wanted. Or, if the missionary falls away, it is not due to a lack of good counseling on your part. Trust the Lord to help you help the missionary. Know that the Lord loves this individual, just as He loves you, and wants success for this individual in life, and He will make sure the right people, resources, and opportunities enter this person's life exactly when he or she needs it.

Staying Home and Moving Forward

If the missionary decides to stay home, treat him or her like a returned missionary and as an asset to the ward. One bishop told me that he sees all returned missionaries, early-returned or not, as "a huge asset to the ward in helping strengthen individuals." He said too that one thing he has seen help these missionaries is a calling. He extends callings as soon as possible because they need a purpose. He said, "A lot of times people fall away because they feel like they don't have a purpose. When someone comes home early, you may feel that he or she should be given some time to think and come to terms with things, and that may be appropriate, but I would not give him or her too much time."

Also, in addition to being given a calling, they should be treated like any other returned missionary with regards to being invited to give a homecoming talk and to present to the high council. Even if the individual refuses either, or both, it is always nice to have the option than to feel even more like a failure or different because the option was never given. For my part, I did not present for the high council because I did not want to talk about my mission. I was told that I'd be asked to talk about my mission and what I'd learned from it. I wanted to do neither at the time. I wanted to forget I'd ever gone on a mission. However, I did choose to give a homecoming talk because I could focus on the topic I'd been assigned and incorporate what I wanted from my mission into the talk. I felt much less intimidated giving a talk to a silent ward than presenting for a group of men who I feared would ask pointed questions and make me recall things I did not want to recall.

Of course, I likely had a great misunderstanding about what happens when a missionary presents to the high council, and if I had gone I likely would have found it to be a warm and loving experience. But I did not know anything about presenting for the high council before serving a mission, and this "tradition" surprised me when I returned. I knew of homecoming talks though, and having heard many of them by growing up in the church, I knew what to expect. I was also comfortable giving talks (again having grown up in the Church) and just due to my own personal enjoyment of public speaking. However, several early-returned missionaries I spoke with expressed their desire at the time to *not* give a homecoming talk because they wished to forget their mission entirely and because of their fear of judgment from the ward. They simply wished to go back to life as usual and to blend in. However, the invitation was still appreciated.

Helping Them Overcome Their Fears

Many stake presidents and bishops find that the most challenging aspects of supporting early-returned missionaries is helping them overcome the fear of what everyone will say behind their backs, and how to not let coming home early "be a thorn in their sides" (as one stake president put it) for the rest of their lives (how to not let words like "missionary" or "homecoming talk" trigger feelings of failure or inappropriate regret in them). These are two separate issues and I will address them one at a time.

First, helping someone overcome the fear of what everyone else will say behind his or her back is once again a case-by-case issue. Some people take things more personally than others. Some people were more entrenched in Church cultural notions than they realized—the notions that only missionaries who did something wrong come home early, that they are "bad," and even that they should be shunned. There is also the notion that early-returned missionaries will become inactive, that it's inevitable. The first thing you must do is work with the missionary to dispel these myths from their mind by reassuring them of God's love for them and that they are not a "bad person," or a "quitter," or a "failure" or whatever else they are telling themselves.

Of special note, if the individual came home for worthiness issues, tell them that they made the right call and are home for the right reasons: to get things sorted out and to get life back on track. It is unfortunate that the fact that he or she sinned is more public and that the nature of it was such to get him or her sent home, but it is what it is, and the best thing to do is to hit the problem straight on within himself or herself, and then with the ward, family, and friends. They too are not "bad," or "quitters," or "failures."

One mission president said,

When missionaries were getting ready to go home [early], they'd sometimes come to me and say, "President, what am I going to say when I face my ward?" Let's say the reason was belated confession. I'd say, "Without telling anybody anything, just say you needed to come home to take care of some stuff. Hit it straight on; people are going to wonder. Then tell them that you are going to work through it, and your plan is to go back out as soon as you can. You expect that to be in a year [or however long]. If you hit it like that—straight on—people actually respect the situation and will support helping you get back." And if it was a medical or emotional reason, I'd tell them to just hit that straight on too. I'd say, "Tell them what happened [in as much detail as you feel comfortable]. Tell them that you need to recover and that you plan to go back or unfortunately you're not going to be able to go back out, but that's okay, you're moving forward and the Lord accepts your sacrifice and offering." It's how to hit it straight on that the missionaries coming home early need to be coached on—that's what I found anyways.

Yes. The early-returned missionaries who address the reason for why they came home "straight on" with their ward members, family, friends, and themselves were the ones who moved forward with life the easiest, fastest, and happiest. Those who hid the issue or tried to blend in actually struggled the most because they felt deep down that they had something to hide and worried about someone discovering their secret.

So how do you coach early-returned missionaries to hit it straight on? You tell them to take a deep breath, to look people in the eye, to smile kindly, and tell them what happened. Details aren't necessary. "I got sick," "I'm struggling mentally," "I messed up," "My family needs me," or even "I'm still figuring things out myself" will do just fine. You tell them that the first time might be nerve-wracking and the second and third and maybe even fourth time will be too, because they will not know how the person will react. Reassure them that that feeling is normal, and also that they do not need to worry about controlling the person's reaction. The person is going to have the reaction he or she will have, and that the missionary did his or her part by hitting it straight on. Also, the missionary's worth is not determined by the person's reaction. With time, telling people will get easier, and the missionary will likely find that most people's reactions will be kind and uplifting.

Of course, there may be some people who are rude or awkward toward the missionary. This is wrong, but it is not the missionary's responsibility. Sometimes people are awkward because they simply don't know what to say, even if they do want to help. Help the missionary to forgive these individuals and to not internalize what may be said to them. Other times the comments will be culturally related. Overcoming cultural notions is difficult, because culture is really what shapes our thoughts and our actions. It can be more entrenched than we realize. Everyone is on his or her own journey toward perfection, and unfortunately, some individuals are further behind than others and say hurtful things. Tell the missionary to not halt his or her own journey toward perfection by internalizing the negative comments, or by becoming resentful or bitter toward the individual. Furthermore, it may be helpful to point out that these conversations will be similar to many other interactions in life. No matter what the subject, sometimes people are just awkward or unkind socially, and the missionaries should apply the same social lessons they learned elsewhere (including on missions) to these types of interactions.

Finally, how to help individuals not let this experience be "a thorn in their side" is simply helping them hit the issues straight on in themselves. What cultural notions need to be addressed within the individuals? What feelings need to be worked through? By following the advice already given in this chapter and the advice that will follow as we turn now to ward and stake cultures, you will see clearly how to help individuals move forward with their lives and look back on their missions fondly or at least as learning experiences that propelled them toward God rather than away from Him. For more about culture, please see chapter 9.

Changing the Culture

As I discussed the topic of coming home early with leaders, one bishop said to me,

> There's a cultural stigma of coming home early from your mission that the Lord doesn't care anything about. I think He sees us all as individuals, and, as a bishop, I've had a lot of situations where *culturally* in the Church something is weird, not normal, not expected, or whatever. The Lord doesn't care about that. The Lord sees people as individuals, and [as leaders] we work hard to apply the gospel principles that are general to specific individual situations.

While it is a responsibility of each individual to rid himself or herself of ideas that are untrue or condemning of others, there is a responsibility that falls on Church leaders to guide or *lead* their wards or stakes to a higher way of living and thinking. Changing cultural attitudes is not an easy task, but with help from the Lord, it is possible to help members open their hearts and minds to change.

One stake president in 2012 (his second year of presiding) noticed that there were a lot more missionaries coming home for reasons related to anxiety and depression, more so than worthiness issues, and he noticed that a cultural change needed to happen in his stake in the attitudes toward these missionaries. And so, he spent the year during the second hour of each ward's ward conference discussing with the adults the need for this cultural change. He said,

> With every ward that year, I put together my own little PowerPoint and trained the adults in the second hour after sacrament meeting. I talked to them about missionaries coming home early and how it used to be that if a missionary came home early, it was because he or she did something wrong; he or she committed some major sin. Now that is not the case. They're coming home because of health issues or coming home from anxiety and depression, more than the other way. I told the ward members and parents that we need to not treat these people like we did when I went on a mission in the '80s. If you were a missionary and you got sent home, you were in big trouble and you were treated like you were in trouble. I told them that that image has got to go, and we need to love and embrace these people and not ask why they came home. We need to just tell them, "Hey, I love you. I'm glad you're home. What can I do for you?" We also talked about what we can do to prepare missionaries better to resolve their anxieties and depressions and prepare them better for serving on missions.

This stake president noticed a cultural change in his stake after that year and hasn't felt the need to address it since. One bishop in that stake (who became bishop in 2013) told me regarding his ward's treatment of those who come home early or others who don't necessarily fit the mold,

> I think we do a pretty good job of that. I don't think we're perfect. I don't imagine there is a perfect ward. And there are, I think, members who are better at it than others. And it's different for different situations. . . . The best experiences I think I've had with early-returned missionaries are the ones where members said, "Hey, we're glad to see you. No matter what." I remember one in particular who came home, and you could tell he was a little sheepish coming into church. I saw several people wrap their arms around him and give him a big hug, and say, "We're glad to have you here." And people didn't care why he was home or what the situation was. There wasn't a lot of talk about, 'When are you going back out?' or that kind of thing. It was just "Man, we're glad to have you, and I know it's a hard time and I feel for you."

No doubt this ward's positive reaction to that missionary was a result of some of the training done by the stake president earlier. It was also likely the result of other good teachings going on in the ward on Sundays, good activities throughout the year, and personal and family scripture study at home. As we continue to teach others and ourselves correct gospel principles, we naturally want to adopt such principles and become better people. Other ideas that a couple bishops shared with me for talking about the culture with their wards was fifth Sunday lessons and sacrament meeting talks. One bishop told me about how he has already suggested "How We Can Help Early-Returned Missionaries as a Ward and as Individuals" to be a topic of first Sunday counsels in Priesthood and Relief Society.

Also, Relief Society presidents should be especially aware of sisters that come home early. One sister told me a story about how no one in her Relief Society would sit by her after she returned early due to physical health issues. They would literally get up and walk away from her. Please be aware of these sisters, and please do speak up if you notice any such treatment. It may not be appropriate to call out the actions as they happen, as this could embarrass the missionary and the unkind individuals unnecessarily, but do talk to the individuals about it and reassure the missionary that she is welcome.

Asking missionaries who complete the intended amount of time to be more open about their trials in their homecoming talks is another way to help soften the culture surrounding missionary work. One person told me,

> In missionary homecoming talks, you don't hear about those first few months where you think "All I want to do is go home. This is hard. This is a hardest thing I've ever done." You hear people say that it is the hardest thing they've ever done, but they speak in general terms about it. I certainly wasn't prepared to go . . . based on missionary homecoming talks I'd heard. I mean, I'm not saying we should be gloom and doom in our homecoming talks. But I think it'd be good perhaps in priest quorum or at activities to talk about the fact that they're going to have some hard times too, and those hard times are normal to need to adjust to. [These changes] would be good so that we don't set expectations so high that people get out and say, "Why am I not having the kind of experience that I heard about in that missionary homecoming talk? Why am I so weird? Why am I not normal?"

I think if missionaries who have completed the intended amount of time were more open about their struggles, and exactly what those struggles entailed, the culture surrounding missionary work would change faster. Instead, they often talk about how much they grew and learned by being on a mission, and how much closer they came to Christ as a result of the experiences they had on their missions. This is good and appropriate, but without the details of the experiences and *what* exactly stretched them and made them grow, there becomes a notion in our culture that a *mission* is simply a place where one goes to feel the Spirit all the time, and that an individual grows simply by getting the chance to study the gospel all the time and teach it. How did these returned missionaries deal with challenges? How did they stay positive? How did they find the inner strength to keep going? How did they wrestle with the Lord for that strength? How did they overcome the natural man and not turn back and go home? Did they ever cry? Did they ever think, "This is too hard"? What happened to make them rely on the Savior so much? These returned missionaries absolutely should share their good experiences, but not at the expense of the details of the experiences that made them grow and learn. Certainly details that are sacred or too personal should not be shared over the pulpit, but those details that are appropriate to share should be encouraged for the betterment of the ward and prospective missionaries (and those who came home early who are under the impression that they simply couldn't cut it).

Of course, this is not meant to undercut anyone who truly loved his or her mission, despite the challenges. That's the end goal: to love the service you are rendering, no matter what. Just encourage them to not gloss over the challenging parts. Ask them to emphasize how they used those challenges to bring themselves closer to Christ and to enjoy their missions. This idea is discussed further in chapter 9.

I hope these ideas give you a starting place for your own inspiration about how to begin to change the cultural attitudes in your ward or stake surrounding missionaries who come home early (and perhaps other issues as well). I hope that you'll study these things out in your mind and perhaps adopt some of the strategies shared or come up with your own.

Preparing to Serve

It is not always easy to tell when someone is ready to serve a mission. One stake president admitted to being surprised by some individuals who completed the intended amount of time and by others who struggled and returned early. Additionally, it is also not always easy to tell who is worthy to serve a mission—many missionaries do go on missions unworthily, much to the amazement of Church members, including myself at times, who wonder why the Lord didn't inspire the leaders that this individual was unworthy. Perhaps this can be explained by the fact that the Lord uses imperfect individuals all the time, and He can use imperfect individuals to further His work. He can also use the situations on a mission to teach His children about the importance of being clean and worthy, and missions can propel people to repentance. For an example of this, see Michael's story in the chapter 3.

While it can be difficult to discern whether someone is prepared or worthy to serve a mission, you can do several things in your ward or stake to better help individuals be ready for missions, and more importantly, for the temple covenants they will make before they embark on a mission.

Temple Preparation vs. Mission Preparation

So many times, I found myself talking to an individual on the phone who came home early due to reasons of belated confession, and as they told me their story, I asked them to pause and tell me about their temple experience. They would often tell me something to the effect of, "Yeah, I went to the temple, and I knew I had some things to work on, but I got through it and it was okay." There was such a lack of understanding and a lack of seriousness (at least at the time the covenants were made) about the saving ordinances they had just taken part in. They seemed to have treated the temple as a speed bump on their way to the mission.

Because this attitude toward the temple bothered me, I asked leaders if they felt more emphasis ought to be placed on Mission Preparation or Temple Preparation, two common classes held at either ward or stake levels. One bishop gave this interesting response:

We've actually had this discussion in bishopric training meeting. . . . The counsel we've been given (from the stake president and the Brethren) is that the temple shouldn't be a side project just because you're going on a mission. I mean, often those two are fairly coincident, but we're encouraged to have separate interviews for missionary recommendation and for a temple recommend. And I think that [our stake president] put it really eloquently when he said, "A mission is full-time and it's a very visible thing. A person leaves on a mission for two years and we don't really hear from him or her. Then the individual comes back and he or she is a whole different person. But it's only a two-year time span. Receiving your endowments has implications into the eternities. And I think it should be given that kind of treatment and that it shouldn't be a secondary thing."

He's right. A mission, while it also can have implications into the eternities regarding bringing others to the gospel, is only a two-year time span for the missionary, whereas the covenants made in the temple are solely for the missionary's benefit and eternal salvation. He continued,

That said, I think there's something worthwhile preparing people for [missions]. Because you go away; you leave home. When you go to the temple and receive your endowment, that takes a few hours and then you kind of go back to a normal life. I think there's something that's worthwhile about a big goal (a mission), but I don't think we should be teaching that to the exclusion of why the temple is so important. I think we should give them equal treatment. And I don't think we have done as good a job in the Church as perhaps we could have. I remember before I went on my mission, I spent my whole time as a youth thinking about missions and talking about missions, and it wasn't until I was actually getting ready to go on a mission that I thought, "Oh, I guess I get to receive my endowments as well! I haven't really thought about that." I think we ought to probably do a better job of teaching that.

Elder David A. Bednar in his talk "Called to the Work" echoed this bishop's thoughts. He said,

I now want to discuss briefly a fundamental but frequently overlooked aspect of preparing for a call to the work.

Three interrelated words define a pattern of preparation and progression for sons of God: *priesthood, temple, mission*. Sometimes as parents, friends, and Church members, we focus so extensively upon missionary preparation for young men that we may neglect to a degree the other vital steps along the covenant pathway that must be fulfilled before beginning full-time missionary service. Working as a missionary certainly is one but not the only important building block in the process of creating a strong foundation for a lifetime of spiritual growth and service. Priesthood and temple blessings, both of which precede arriving in an assigned field of labor, also are necessary to fortify and strengthen us spiritually throughout our entire lives. . . . In our homes and at church, we should give balanced emphasis to all three elements of the Lord's pattern of preparation and progression for faithful sons of God: *priesthood, temple, mission.* All three require us to love being and remaining worthy. Be worthy. Stay worthy.[6]

I think so often young people, especially young men, can get so caught up in the adventure and work of a mission, that they forget the importance of the temple. It is also much easier to endure the guilty feelings of being in the temple unworthily (only a few hours) than to be on a mission unworthily and endure that guilt for months on end, especially if one does not understand the significance and importance of temple covenants.

So, again, as the bishop that I interviewed said, preparation for a mission and preparation for making temple covenants are both important, and equal emphasis should be placed on taking Temple Prep and Mission Prep. If anything, I personally would lean a bit more heavily on Temple Prep. Those covenants have implications into the eternities, whereas a mission is only two years of someone's life (although, again, the events of a mission can also certainly have implications into the eternities as well). Of course, how you handle these two important preparations in your ward or stake is up to the direction and inspiration that you receive from the Lord.

Mission Preparation for Young Women

On the other hand, Young Women's lessons and activities often focus on the temple, particularly in regards to the sealing of families together (especially marriage). Many young women are prepared spiritually for a mission, but many are also surprised at how difficult missions are mentally and physically. Missions are not talked about as often as marriage is for young women, which in the past may have been appropriate. However, since the age change in 2012, "the number of sister missionaries has nearly tripled."[7] More young women now feel like they will have the opportunity to serve a mission and look forward to doing so. Perhaps more activities can be centered around the realities of a mission and preparing to serve one. These activities should not overshadow the temple or even the importance of marriage, of course, but they should become more frequent as more young women express interest in serving a mission.

Furthermore, while there are certainly many young women who dream about serving a mission while growing up, there are also many young women who choose to serve a mission, really, on a whim. The whim can happen for many reasons: not sure what to do next in life, sounds like a good idea, the Spirit prompted them to go, and so on. None of these reasons are necessarily bad, but Church leaders should be aware that these whims occur often. They ought to be sure that young women are physically and mentally prepared to serve, and if they are not, leaders should encourage them to prepare physically and mentally several months to a year before they submit their papers.

I chose to go on a mission due to a prompting. I thought about a mission for six months. I'd never considered going on a mission before in my life, yet in six months after weighing the pros and cons that I knew of about a mission versus finishing school, I decided to go on a mission. I was spiritually prepared, but the physical demands of a mission were surprising to me. I would have been fine had I not gotten sick, I'm sure, but a regular exercise routine would have helped me greatly. Mentally, I was unprepared for the trepidation I would feel about talking to people, unprepared for the culture shock, and unprepared for how *tired* I would be every day and how this fatigue would wear on me mentally. I think if my leaders had asked me to exercise regularly for six months, had me practice falling asleep quickly and getting up early, and had me take a mission preparation course that really *talked* about some of these mental and physical challenges, and didn't just go over the spiritual things in *Preach My Gospel*, I would have had a much different experience. I still would have gotten sick, but I likely would have been more willing to go back out after I'd recovered from the parasites. Instead, when considering going back to the field, I felt a lot of fear.

I wanted to serve and teach people the gospel, but I didn't want to go back to a mission. It had not been what I'd expected.

Decrease the Pressure to Serve Right Away

Some young men and women will be ready to serve a mission the moment they turn eighteen or nineteen, but many could use a little more time to mentally prepare being away from home, living with someone they don't know, and talking to strangers all day. During interviews, when I asked, "Why did you serve a mission?" almost every young man answered, "Because it was expected of me." Some followed up with, "I had a testimony and I wanted to share the gospel, but really, when you get down to it, it was expected of me to go. I didn't want to disappoint anyone and I didn't want anyone looking at me weird at church."

There is some cultural pressure to have young men serve a mission as soon as they are able to, even though the age range is eighteen to twenty-five. Many of the Church leaders I spoke to seemed to understand that eighteen is great for some, but too young for others, and were actually grateful for the age change because it seemed to allow more room for making sure a young man is ready to leave. One bishop said,

> I felt like when the age was nineteen it was, "Well, you're nineteen!" And if you weren't in the MTC two weeks after your nineteenth birthday, what were you doing? But with eighteen, it made it so that you go more when you're ready. I mean, you can't go right at eighteen if your birthday is in November and you're still in high school. So, I felt like that [age change] helped with making sure they're ready. And there are some eighteen-year-olds who are ready and the right thing to do is to leave right away. There are others who, I think, a year away from home perhaps at college would be good to help them really get comfortable living on their own.

The stake president who did the year-long ward conferences focusing on early-returned missionaries, did that training right around the time of the age change announcement. He said that as part of his training he told the ward members, "Eighteen is the minimum age. That's not a hard number. It used to be that nineteen was a pretty hard

177

number. When you turned nineteen you were gone, and if you didn't go, why? But today, eighteen is a minimum age. It is not a hard, fast number. These missionaries go when they're ready, and if they're not ready until twenty or twenty-one, then so be it."

As a result, this stake president's stake has had great success with sending missionaries out when they are ready to go, and they often are able to complete the full-term of expected service. The stake members are often understanding and supportive of young men, and young women, who take the time needed to prepare properly for a mission.

Adding to this point, when I asked one mission president what his older male missionaries were like he said, "They had more life experiences." And then he added,

> And, I think part of your question is, "Why do some elders feel pressure to serve right at eighteen?" To answer that, I think just because when they lowered the age to eighteen, many young men just felt like, "Wow! I can go at eighteen and my buddies are going at eighteen, and so I'm going to go right after high school." The wisdom behind that is—at least I know from a Church perspective—it doesn't allow them to get into trouble that some might get into. Also, there is obviously a great maturing that takes place on a mission. And so, to get out at eighteen and have that mission experience to build upon for the rest of your life—holy cow! And in college, returned missionaries are better students. They have priorities, hopefully, more set in their lives that are in line with the Church. So I can see some wisdom in that. If you have desires, can work hard, and have a testimony obviously, you're actually going to do well whether you're eighteen or you're twenty-five. But I will say that some eighteen-year-old missionaries would benefit from being away from home and having experiences either in a university setting or something to help them mature. So eighteen is the age at which you *can* serve but it's not necessarily when you *should* serve. I think that's the best way to say it. Everyone needs to look at their own circumstances and decide.

And deciding that can be difficult for some. One bishop said that his philosophy has been to really try to encourage young men and women to serve missions. In fact, he tries really hard to walk the line between encouraging young people to serve missions and pushing them to go on missions. But he absolutely recognizes that some young people who have that desire to go just aren't quite ready. To those young people he says, "I'd love to see you go on a mission, but you're not ready. However, I'd love to see you get ready. I also don't think me pushing you out on a mission right now is going to do anything for you." One resource that this bishop utilizes is a free pre-mission evaluation offered by LDS Family Services for "candidates who experience social and emotional issues that may impede mission success."[8] He said that this does two things for him as a bishop and for the prospective missionary:

> One it says, "Yeah, you're not ready. Let's work on some other things first." The other thing it could do is give [me and the prospective missionary] a lot of confidence. . . . The counselor will say, "They're ready; they're in good shape." That's done a lot for my confidence in submitting a recommendation, but also the [prospective missionary] is going to say, "Yeah, I've worked through all those issues. I'm ready to go, and I'm going to be a great missionary." And I think that just the confidence that comes from that seal of approval does a lot for that missionary. It doesn't mean that things won't be hard, but I think you have to remember that these professionals at LDS Family Services see a lot of people and probably have a better feel than just about anybody, for who's ready to go and who's not from a mental health standpoint. And having that stamp of approval can really boost somebody's confidence.

He also added, "I'm not a mental health professional and no one expects me to be. I've always appreciated that about the Church—that they've always said, 'You have ecclesiastical authority, but you're not a professional [counselor] and don't be afraid to send somebody off to a professional.'"

I hope you have some ideas now for making sure a young man or young woman is ready to serve a mission. Having desires to serve God is essential to being able to serve a mission, but it is not always enough, and sometimes other things ought to be considered. You will still need to use the spirit of discernment to decide if certain young people are truly ready, but the resources also available to you are amazing. And if you send someone on a mission and he or she returns home early, trust that God still has a plan for that person and that you can now be instrumental in helping that person stay faithful to the gospel and either return to his or her mission or move forward with life.

For Mission Presidents

The calling of a mission president is unique and I would like to touch on some of those unique aspects of the calling now and offer the wisdom of other mission presidents for how to handle certain situations that may come up with regards to early-returned missionaries and their families. I will also add my own commentary and that of others as appropriate.

Sending a Missionary Home Early

The decision to send a missionary home early or to help them stay on a mission can be difficult, but also rather straightforward. One mission president said that with regards to worthiness issues, things are generally pretty straight forward. Sometimes they can get help or repent while in the field, but other times they really need to go home and get things resolved there. In those cases, most mission presidents reassured the missionary of the Lord's love for him or her, and in the cases of worthiness, how happy the Lord was that the missionary was finally working to get things resolved (or that the missionary had confessed a transgression in the field instead of continuing unworthily), which helped the missionary a lot. One mission president asked his missionaries who went home early, particularly for worthiness issues, to continue writing him a weekly letter or email. "I asked them to tell me about their prayers, scripture study and other things they were doing to help prepare them to come back out. I think this one thing was very helpful for those who had to go home for a period of time before they could come back out. It kept them moving forward and focused on getting back out as soon as possible." This is wonderful advice and can be applied to missionaries who need to go home early for any reason, but still desire to return to a mission.

Regarding those who had physical or mental health issues, things were not always straightforward. Another mission president said the difficulty with those issues was determining whether or not the issue was chronic and what could be overcome. For mental health issues, sitting down with the missionary and really listening to his or her concerns was especially helpful, and involving a therapist if the missionary was willing was also useful. Physical health issues were a little more

180

cut-and-dry: if the missionary improved quickly, there was no need to send him or her home, but if it became apparent that he or she could not recover in the field, he or she needed to be sent home.

Regarding those who wanted to go home due to family troubles or personal reasons, the mission presidents I knew of or spoke to treated each case individually and really strived to understand what was bothering the missionary. They really tried to resolve the root concern and sometimes even called the parents of the missionary to see if they could help. One mission president told me,

> I would first assess the reasons for wanting to go home and if we could overcome those reasons then they would stay. I would meet with the missionary as soon as possible and try and understand why they wanted to go home. I would seek to find a solution that they were willing to agree to in having them stay on the mission longer. Sometimes this would include a change in area or companion. Always, it would include a commitment to give it more time and more frequent interaction with me, whether it be daily calls or texts or some other frequency of interaction. I was always a cheerleader for them by trying to help them see that they could accomplish the original goal of completing a mission. I never used guilt or shaming, but only encouragement. Sometimes it would involve them speaking to parents back home. Normally, I would have already called the parents, letting them know the situation, and coaching them on some things they could say that would help the missionary stay out. In almost every situation if I could get a missionary to commit to stay for a certain period of time and then work on some other things, they would stay and complete their mission. If, however, I couldn't get them to try to keep certain commitments, then they would almost always go home within a couple of weeks of me first meeting with them.

He told me that by doing these things, he never felt like he failed as a mission president. He also reminded himself that despite his best efforts, the missionaries still had their agency.

For more information on the nuances of each reason for why a missionary may want to go home early, please see the first five chapters of this book.

Cultural Differences

I found most often that early-returned missionaries who were offended by something their mission president said to them were from a different cultural background than their mission president. I also found that some mission presidents had a much harder time understanding or sympathizing with missionaries from other cultures. One mission president told me one way he overcame these challenges:

> Thankfully, in the Church, the doctrine and principles are the same despite different backgrounds and cultures that we all come from. I guess the best way I can describe it is that I believed in what Joseph Smith said, "I teach the correct principles and let them govern themselves." All missionaries were taught the same lessons and principles from the scriptures and *Preach My Gospel*. Through all of these when I had a missionary who was from another [culture] I could ask him or her (if there was an issue) what was the right thing to do, and I never had an issue needing to persuade them of what is right or wrong.

Instead of relying on his own background and potentially saying something that would not work on a missionary who didn't grow up in the same culture he did, this mission president relied on the doctrine to communicate with missionaries with whom he didn't share a cultural background. By doing this, he was able to avoid a lot of accidental offenses and also was able to keep the natural man at bay when he felt especially frustrated.

My own mission president was Filipino, and thus from a different cultural background than me, and I remember feeling the Spirit strongly when he advised me using doctrine. A couple weeks into my mission, he visited my area, and briefly interviewed me. I told him that things were going well, but that I was admittedly struggling seeing all of the poverty and couldn't understand how people could live this way and why they hadn't sought to make their lives better yet. He smiled and told me that Christ had been born in a stable. He didn't seek to be born in a palace, although he certainly could have. Instead, he humbled himself and began his life in very humble circumstances, and then humbled himself more and ministered among the poor of the Earth. This spoke volumes to me and went over much better than anything he might have said regarding the politics of his country or any lecture he may have given me based on any offense he may have taken from my innocent comments about his country.

"Adjusting to Missionary Life" Booklet

"Adjusting to Missionary Life" is a booklet published by the Church in 2013. This booklet is an invaluable resource for missionaries who are struggling with the physical, emotional, social, intellectual, and spiritual demands of a mission and has excellent advice for missionaries who are struggling. It is a resource that both you and your missionaries can draw from as needed to get the help needed to stay in the field.

Communicate with Parents

According to "The Experience of Parents of Early-Returned Missionaries" published by Dr. Kristine Doty-Yells in September 2017, parents often struggle with feelings of loss when their child returns home early from a mission. In fact, out of 199 parents surveyed, "almost three-fourths of ERM parents reported a difficult adjustment to their missionary's early return, regardless of the reason for it."[9]

One reason for this difficult adjustment seemed to be the lack of communication from the mission: "the satisfaction level was significantly correlated with the amount of communication—so the less communication, the greater the dissatisfaction. . . . Forty-five percent of parents were dissatisfied with the amount of communication with their missionary regarding the circumstances of the early return, and just over half felt that more communication would have helped them understand and adjust to the early return."[10]

Furthermore, "forty-five percent of ERM parents had no communication with the mission president before their missionary was sent home. Almost 55% were dissatisfied with this amount of communication, . . . Almost 65% of the parents believed that more communication with the mission president would have helped them adjust to the early return. Analysis of variance indicated that parents who experienced greater amounts of communication with the mission president had less difficulty with their adjustment to the early return."[11]

Doty-Yells also found that nearly 50 percent of parents had no communication with health care professionals who treated their missionary in the field and that three-fourths of parents were dissatisfied with this amount of communication and believed that more communication with the professionals would have helped them adjust to the early return.[12]

As a mission president you have so many responsibilities and so much to think about and look after. Your stewardship is over the missionaries, and the stake president has stewardship over the parents. However, please do all you can to keep parents in the loop regarding their children or keep in touch often with the stake president and make sure he is keeping them in the loop. Parents are so anxious about the well-being of their children. Being away from them for several months is difficult, even if it is okay, and to suddenly find out that their child is struggling, especially with a physical or mental health problem, and to have little to no say in their child's treatment or return home, is scary. As Doty-Yells reported, three-fourths of parents struggle when their child returns home early, not just with helping their child cope with the loss of the mission, but with the loss of the mission themselves.[13] They question their parenting and God's plan for their family (see chapter 8). While you are not their therapist, you can help mitigate their concerns and fears upfront by communicating with them as much as possible, and by encouraging any doctors and therapists to do the same (and by encouraging the missionaries to sign whatever legal documents are necessary to allow their parents to know what is happening).

Final Thoughts

In conclusion, please remember to utilize your resources and to, of course, trust the Spirit. Be mindful of how you are perceived and be loving even if you must be bold. Reassure the missionaries (and their parents) of the Lord's love for them. Also, trust yourself and the experiences that lead you to be able to accept this calling, and to know what to say. Remember, too, that the Lord loves you and He loves His children that you have stewardship over and He will help you as you prayerfully seek to help them.

Notes

1. Kristine J. Doty-Yells, S. Zachary Bullock, Harmony Packer, Russell T. Warner, James Westwood, Thomas Ash, and Heather Hirsch, "Return with Trauma: Understanding the Experiences of Early Returned Missionaries," *Issues in Religion and Psychotherapy*, vol. 37, no. 1 (2015): 34. Available at http://scholarsarchive.byu.edu/irp/vol37/iss1/9.

2. Thomas S. Monson, "Presiding High Priest and Father of the Ward," LDS Media Library, June 2011, https://www.lds.org/media-library/video/2011-07-132-presiding-high-priest-and-father-of-the-ward?lang=eng.

3. Doty-Yells; et al, "Return with Trauma," 40.

4. Ibid., 41.

5. Jeffrey R. Holland, "Elder Holland's Counsel for Early Returned Missionaries," LDS Media Library, March 2016, https://www.lds.org/media-library/video/2016-05-012-elder-hollands-counsel-for-early-returned-missionaries.

6. David A. Bednar, "Called to the Work," *Ensign*, May 2017.

7. Alyssa Litoff, "New Wave of Mormon Missionaries is Young, Energetic and Female," ABC News, January 27, 2015, http://abcnews.go.com/US/wave-mormon-missionaries-young-energetic-female/story?id=27924269.

8. "Missionary Services," LDS Family Services, retrieved April 28, 2018, https://providentliving.lds.org/lds-family-services/missionary-services.

9. Kris J. Doty-Yells, Harmony Packer, Malisa M. Draper-Brooks, Russell T. Warne, and Cameron R. John, "The Experience of Parents of Early-Returned Missionaries," *Issues in Religion and Psychotherapy*, vol. 38, no. 1 (2017): 56. Available at http://scholarsarchive.byu.edu/irp/vol38/iss1/1056.

10. Ibid., 55.

11. Ibid.

12. Ibid., 55–56.

13. Ibid., 56.

CHAPTER 8

For Parents

D r. Kristine Doty-Yells relates,

In 2002, my world changed when my oldest son returned home from his mission after only a few months. I was stunned and bewildered, and I had no idea what I should do. This is not something I knew how to prepare for. The idea of an early return never occurred to me. My son seemed to do just fine in his adjustment. I was the one who struggled with grief and loss. I mourned the spiritual experiences he would not have and the growth he would not gain. What made it worse was that I knew only one other young man who had returned early, and his parents moved away shortly afterwards, so I felt alone. Few friends talked with me about it. My ward family said little. Some of those who ventured to say anything at all said hurtful things in the awkwardness of the situation. In the absence of knowing how to handle such a tender topic and trying to avoid aggravating the pain, most said nothing at all.

I struggled for years with what it meant. Meanwhile, after a brief period of inactivity, my son married in the temple, began a family, and moved away to accept a new job. In time the memories took a back seat, and I seldom even thought about it. Two more children, both daughters, completed full-time missions, and that seemed to resolve the challenges of the first. Time indeed healed the wounds.

Then in 2010 it happened a second time. My youngest son returned home from his mission after four months due to depression and anxiety. He was sad, humiliated, and subsequently fell into inactivity. Reeling from the shock, I found that this time it hurt on a much deeper level. Memories from the first experience returned with a vengeance, and suddenly I felt as though my competence as a mother, and in-home missionary trainer, was called into question.

In both cases my sons returned early, went back out into the field, and returned early again. After four of these experiences of my sons' returning home early, I was beginning to feel like an expert—an expert in pain, embarrassment, shock, and even shame. Why did this happen to my sons? What did it mean to them? What was our family meant to learn from it?[1]

As you just read in Dr. Doty-Yells's account of her two sons coming home, her world changed and she struggled to understand the many emotions she felt. As a parent, you probably picked up this book thinking it would help you better understand your child and whatever it is he or she is going through. You probably also hoped to learn how exactly you can help him or her. I hope that you have found the book to be beneficial that way. This chapter will discuss more specific ways you, as a parent, can help your adult child. But, as in everything, if you don't first understand what is happening with you, you are not going to clearly understand what is happening with anyone else. In other words, before you can help your child, you must first help yourself.

How the Early Homecoming Affects You

Dr. Doty-Yells's personal story of experiencing four early homecomings highlights many of the emotions parents feel when their children come home early: shock, confusion, loss, grief, isolation, pain, shame, and embarrassment. She highlights at the end of her story the questions many parents ask: "Why did this happen?" and "What does this mean about my child?" She also asked questions similar to "What does this say about me as a parent?" "Am I a good parent?" "Did I prepare my child enough?" and "What do I do now?" Finally, she asked the question that is most helpful: "What was our family meant to learn from it?" *That* is the key to getting through this difficult time—through any difficult time, really. *What* are you meant to *learn* from it?

Of course, some parents do not struggle much when their child returns home early. Some even feel a sense of relief or happiness, especially if the child really struggled physically or mentally while in the field.[2] Other parents feel a great sense of loss that manifests itself as "a range of emotions such as feelings of shock and denial, confusion and uncertainty, resentment and anger, guilt and blame, sadness and depression, fear and worry, shame and alienation, and frustration and helplessness."[3] Indeed, "The most common emotions that parents reported feeling in relation to their missionary's early return were sadness (80.9%), disappointment (63.3%), and confusion (59.3%)."[4] Those who felt relief made up 28 percent of Doty-Yells's study and those who felt happiness made up 16.6 percent.[5] Finally, Doty-Yells reported that "almost three-fourths of ERM parents reported a difficult adjustment to their missionary's early return, *regardless of the reason for it.*"[6] However, I did find that in talking to other parents who adjusted well to their missionary's early return, including my own parents, that they also dealt with a sense of loss, disappointment, or lack of closure, regardless of the relief or happiness that they felt upon the early return.

It is no surprise, really, that parents of early-returned missionaries experience a sense of loss upon a child's return. There is a loss: a loss of growing opportunities, of spiritual opportunities, and even a perceived loss of blessings of having a missionary out in the field. These losses are not easy to deal with because "just as children in the LDS Church are socialized to prepare for missionary service from an early age, parents are also taught to prepare their children to serve. . . . By the time parents send their child on a mission at age eighteen or nineteen, they are often deeply invested, both emotionally and financially, in their child's missionary experience."[7]

To be so invested in something both emotionally and spiritually, to be looking forward to the growth opportunities and blessings, and to have those things suddenly taken from you would absolutely cause shock, disappointment, sadness, and even anger! All of those feelings are common to grief, which is what we experience when we experience loss (for more on grief, please see chapter 4). However, not all losses are created equally, and Doty-Yells identified two types of losses parents of early-returned missionaries go through when their son or daughter returns home early: ambiguous loss (aggravated by family boundary ambiguity) and grief and loss without death.

Ambiguous Loss

Ambiguous losses have *no clear resolution*. "Ambiguous loss is defined as a situation where a loved one is physically present, but psychologically absent, as in the case of cognitive disability, dementia or mental illness. Or, alternately, the loved one is psychologically present but physically absent, as in the case of military deployment, incarceration, missing persons, or presumed death without a body."[8] There is certainly an ambiguous loss for parents when their child leaves for a full-time mission. Your child is physically gone, but still psychologically present. You receive emails and occasionally phone calls home, and you know that your child will return someday. There is a loss, but it isn't a clear loss.

Now, your child is home and physically present, but psychologically distant or absent. They may feel out of place at home, long to be back in the mission field, or be experiencing a mental illness. Furthermore, this return happened suddenly and the mission was lost (even if only temporarily). And, if the stay-home-or-go-back-out question hasn't been resolved, you likely aren't sure how much you should get used to him or her being home. Naturally, there is a lot of uncertainty and ambiguity about helping your child moving forward with life (and about moving forward with your life too).

My father experienced this ambiguity when I returned home early. He was really uncertain about how to approach me with regards to whether I would stay home or go back out. He didn't have hopes in either direction—he just wanted to know which path I would take. There were unique circumstances surrounding my early return due to the nature of my physical illness and the trauma that came along with experiencing it in a third-world country. My sister was also getting married in a few months, and now I had the opportunity to be at the wedding. I was in a lot of limbo with my decision.

Recalling his experience during the first month of my early homecoming, he said,

> I think the hard part is you want to be supportive in either direction. So helping the missionary come to, or at least finding that the missionary has made a permanent decision, I think is the place where a new chapter can begin. That's where you can begin to move on. But until the missionary makes a decision about whether they're going to go back or stay, then you're kind of left in limbo to know how to best support them. I don't think I ever really needed to heal. But I think I needed closure to have an idea of which way to go with my thoughts and maybe with my words toward you.

Once I made the decision to stay home, my dad felt at peace and knew how to move forward with how to speak to me and approach me. Having served a mission himself, he felt like I had experienced enough to know what a mission was and he could see that I had experienced growth both mentally and spiritually. He didn't feel like he had lost anything or that I had really lost anything, except perhaps some of the experiences that come from transfers and new companionships. I had been fortunate enough to teach many people in the short three months that I was in the field, and feel the sweet success and joy that comes from seeing people accept the gospel. I felt good about moving forward with my life, and my dad felt good about it too. The ambiguity left for both of us. I became physically and psychologically present at home.

We will talk more about helping your son or daughter make the decision to stay home or go back out toward the end of this chapter. For now, let's continue on with discussing loss.

Family Boundary Ambiguity

When your child left on a mission, you expected to not see him or her for eighteen months or two years, and have relatively little contact. It is a clear-cut boundary, even if it is temporary. Your child was still considered a member of the family, of course, but his or her role in the family had changed. When your child returned early, that clear-cut boundary of his or her role in the family was no longer intact and the family boundaries and roles had to be reevaluated. Because of the ambiguity around the situation regarding *why* this happened and *what* is going to happen next, uncertainty and dysfunction are bound to be present. This is called family boundary ambiguity.

Jeff explained,

> We were not ready for him to be home. Not that we didn't want him home, but we wanted him to serve the full two years. We just knew how important it was to serve the whole thing. When he came home it was tough. There was no fanfare at the airport at all. My wife and I said from the beginning, "Let's go through this, and you need to get back out there." We had to talk through it a lot, because it had to be his decision to go back out; it wasn't our decision. We knew that we wanted him back out because we felt that when the Lord calls a missionary, He calls him for two years. Our son still had ten months to

go. We felt strongly about that. And so we just kinda kept pushing him. Something that concerned us was that we didn't see him keeping up the missionary standards—not that he was doing anything bad—but we just didn't see him on a regimen of reading the scriptures. We didn't see him continue as if he was a missionary and that concerned us.

Jeff and his wife wanted there to continue to be a "clear-cut, although temporary" exit from the family.[9] They did not want to redefine the boundaries, nor did they think in their son's particular circumstances that they should. Again, we will talk more about your role in the stay home or go back out decision later. For now, I am just using Jeff's story to illustrate an example of family boundary ambiguity.

Dr. Doty-Yells also experienced this type of ambiguity when her sons came home. She hadn't expected it. In her own words she was "stunned and bewildered" and had "no idea what [she] should do." She had expected her sons to stay in the field and was not prepared when they came home early. She even questioned her own role in the family and whether she had fulfilled her assignment to prepare her boys adequately for missions. As she went through the experience, Dr. Doty-Yells questioned what her family was meant to learn from this, because she felt these events affected the entire family.

You also likely feel some uncertainty about how to proceed with your child and what role he or she should have in the family now as they recover, repent, or reevaluate their desire to serve. Should he or she keep up the missionary schedule or should your child relax and take a break? What would be most beneficial to your child, you, and the family? These questions likely weigh heavily on your mind right now, and I will address them after I cover the second type of loss.

Grief and Loss without Death

Another type of grief that parents of early-returned missionaries may experience is grief and loss without death. This type of grief is often experienced by parents "of children who are born disabled or who develop a mental illness, parents of children who experience a change in gender identity, and parents of adult children whom they perceive are not succeeding. . . . Parents in these circumstances described a range of emotions, such as feelings of shock and denial, confusion and uncertainty, resentment and anger, guilt and blame, sadness and depression, fear and worry, shame and alienation, and frustration and helplessness. Some parents reported coming to terms with or accepting their child's situation after a period of time. However, they mourned the loss of their ideal child, or the child they thought they had, and had to adjust their expectations and their dreams for their child accordingly. . . . Parents of ERMs may experience related emotions and challenges."[10]

Dr. Doty-Yells "mourned the spiritual experiences [her son] would not have" and thus felt the loss of an ideal child—a more spiritually-mature one. She also felt alone. "Few friends talked with me about it. My ward family said little. Some of those who ventured to say anything at all said hurtful things in the awkwardness of the situation. In the absence of knowing how to handle such a tender topic, and trying to avoid aggravating the pain, most said nothing at all." She also likely mourned the loss of being able to talk to other parents of returned missionaries about the experiences her son had had on his mission and the growth he had experienced, because she likely felt like she did not fit in with them.

My mother also felt this type of loss when she realized I wasn't going to return to my mission.

> My hope was that you would come home, heal, and go back out. And I didn't necessarily want you to go back out to the Philippines, but I did hope you would go somewhere because I hadn't really even considered that your mission was actually over. I just thought you had this hiccup and I knew you would just learn from it; I really believe that everything we go through is to learn. So I just thought, 'Okay, this is just a learning experience for all of us.' And it is honest to say that some of that hope, aside from just wanting that for you, came from this whole cultural thing we've got going on in the Church, that that is the expectation, that if you don't complete the mission as prescribed, then it's a failure and there's shame there. So I think that I did kind of unfortunately get sucked into a little bit of that thinking—hoping you would go out so that that would be your story.

For Kimberly, all four of her children that she sent on missions returned home early for various reasons. She recalled feeling *a lot* of anger with circumstances surrounding the early return of her first child, both regarding the worthiness issues that led to the early return, and because she felt that the missionary department made it extremely difficult for him to return to the field. She said that they were forever keeping her son in limbo (and therefore her in limbo as well). She also felt angry at God as the situation wore on until—finally—her son returned to his mission. But, just as she sent her son back on his mission, her daughter returned early due to depression. She felt a lot of sadness for her daughter, even as she was trying to reconcile her anger from the first early return. Her anger at God stayed. "I just didn't get it," she recalled. "Why was this happening? Why would God call them on a mission and then send them home?"

Upon her third child's return, she felt a mixture of anger and sadness and also fear due to the physical and mental reasons behind her daughter's return. She still didn't understand why God was allowing this to happen to her children. She had heard all her life that "God has a plan," but her child had not suffered from depression before her mission and now she needed to be on medication (and still does several years later). She is also still recovering from the terrible parasite she contracted while on her mission. Kimberly wanted to know what the point of all this suffering was and was so angry with God. It was at this point that Kimberly sought professional help. Seeking this help allowed her to better understand her anger, especially her anger toward God, and work through it.

So, when her fourth child, another daughter, returned home early due to worthiness issues, Kimberly felt angry again, but not at God. However, she was upset with her daughter, not only because of the sin, and the lying and hiding that went into it, but because her daughter was now making her go through the early homecoming experience *again*. Kimberly had experienced this loss three times before, and now was experiencing it yet again due to the poor choices of her daughter.

All three of these mothers mourned the loss of the "ideal child" or rather, the "ideal missionary child." Each struggled to cope with the strong feelings they had about what they felt should have happened with their child(ren) and not what actually had happened. However, each of them did eventually find peace, and I am now going to discuss how.

Finding Peace

Acknowledge Your Feelings

The first thing you must do is acknowledge your feelings, no matter how negative they are. In fact, it is okay to acknowledge that this early homecoming is *not* "all right." As Kimberly said,

> Your kid has a desire to serve a mission and do what's right. Your kid is trying so hard to make good choices and do good things. And they have to come home. It's not all right. That is not right in any world. You have these dreams and aspirations—it would be like driving along and getting in a car wreck and losing your legs. Is it all right? No, it's not all right! You have no legs. So it's not all right—right now—but it will be. It will be all right. But right now, it's not all right. Just acknowledge that *in this moment* it's hard—it's really hard! It's hard for the kid coming home and it's hard for the family.

It's okay to feel hurt and upset and even angry, and it is important that you acknowledge your feelings and feel them. You have just suffered a loss and acknowledging your feelings is essential to moving through grief (which is what we experience when loss occurs). If you do not acknowledge what you are feeling, you cannot move forward with recovery and with your life. If you have a hard time acknowledging your feelings, pray for help to feel them and acknowledge them in a healthy way, or seek professional help.

Also, remember, just as Kimberly said, "It will be all right." It will be—it really will! After you acknowledge your feelings, read the rest of this chapter so that you can get to that place where it is all right.

Personal Interventions

"Personal interventions, such as prayer, scriptures study, temple worship, and forgiving or letting go, were the most effective strategies for the parents."[11]

Indeed, my mother found that personal prayer and scripture study were all she really needed to feel at peace with my decision to stay home, and many other parents reported the same thing. My mother told me she also greatly appreciated and drew a lot of strength from a talk called "But If Not" by Lance B. Wickman of the First Quorum of the Seventy. This talk addresses the question that so many parents ask: *Why* did this happen?

Elder Wickman calls this question "natural and understandable" but also a question "that usually [goes] begging in mortality."[12] Rather, "the Lord has said simply, 'My ways [are] higher than your ways, and my thoughts than your thoughts' (Isa. 55:9). As the Son's will was 'swallowed up in the will of the Father' (Mosiah 15:7), so must ours be."[13] Each early homecoming is a unique circumstance to be experienced by each individual, and there is not one overarching "why" for the phenomena.

Elder Wickman knows however that dropping the "why" question is not a simple task. To this he says,

> Still, we mortals quite naturally want to know the why. Yet, in pressing too earnestly for the answer, we may forget that mortality was designed, in a manner of speaking, as the season of unanswered questions. Mortality has a different, more narrowly defined purpose: It is a proving ground, a probationary state, a time to walk by faith, a time to prepare to meet God. It is in nurturing humility and submissiveness that we may comprehend a fulness of the intended mortal experience and put ourselves in a frame of mind and heart to receive the promptings of the Spirit. Reduced to their essence, humility and submissiveness are an expression of complete willingness to let the "why" questions go unanswered for now, or perhaps even to ask, "Why not?" It is in enduring well to the end that we achieve this life's purposes. I believe that mortality's supreme test is to face the "why" and then let it go, trusting humbly in the Lord's promise that "all things must come to pass in their time."[14]

My mother humbled herself and submitted her will for me to the Lord. She said that as she watched me pray and go through the process of deciding whether to return, she began to feel peace, and that it was okay if I decided not to return—that my mission still had value and that I could still be faithful in how I lived the rest of my life. She said, "I just came to [realize] that you served the mission that you were meant to serve. You weren't meant to be in Philippines longer than you were." And then, since I interviewed her in the midst of writing this book, she said,

And, honestly, I think right now you're fulfilling that mission. I think that the end of your mission is this. It's like you had that experience that led you to this that is going to strengthen and serve so many other people who face going home early for various reasons. I mean, our whole lives are a mission, right? But I think this is an extension of your Philippines mission: using [your early homecoming experience] and using your writing talent to bless other people. That's kind of how I look at it.

Clearly, my mom came to and has continued to feel peace in regards to my decision to stay home. Whether or not she is accurate about this book being a fulfillment of my mission to the Philippines is something she and I likely won't know until the next life.

Just pausing for a moment here, in regards to that, since I am talking about the *why* behind an individual's early return, I remember when I faced the decision to return or stay home truly feeling that the Lord would be pleased either way. It really was up to me, and there was no *right* decision. He could use me either way. Was I sent home so that I could write this book? I personally doubt it; I was sent home because I became sick. However, I have continued to seek ways in which to serve the Lord and I am happy that my experience in coming home early can be used for good. My mother may be right that this is the end of my Philippines mission, but I personally think that mission ended when my stake president released me. I'm happy to think of this book as a byproduct of my Philippines mission though!

Likewise, the Lord can make your child's situation a good one for him or her, whether he or she returns to the field or not. Once we humble ourselves and submit ourselves to the will of the Lord, the Lord can send us comfort and answers—even if the answers are not what we expect or don't come in the time frame that we expect.

How do we exercise faith in the meantime? Elder Wickman said,

> The Prophet Joseph Smith defined that first principle of the gospel as "faith *in the Lord Jesus Christ*." It is that defining phrase—"in the Lord Jesus Christ"—that we sometimes forget. Too often we offer our prayer or perform our administration and then wait nervously to see whether our request will be granted, as though approval would provide needed evidence of His existence. That is not faith! Faith is, quite simply, a

confidence in the Lord. In Mormon's words, it is "a *firm mind* in every form of godliness."[15]

We often hear from the secular world that "seeing is believing," but this supposes that faith is the conclusion rather than the premise, as Elder Wickman later suggests in his talk. The Lord's ways are best defined by a different maxim: "Believing is seeing." By applying faith first, we open ourselves to God's wisdom and allow knowledge to come in, trusting that, whether it comes in at a trickle or a downpour, it is for our ultimate benefit and gain. As you turn your heart to the Lord, submit your will to His, and exercise faith that everything will work out for your good, even if your missionary does not make the choice(s) you desire, you will receive comfort and inspiration on how to best help your child and yourself.

Social Support

It is so hard to go through something difficult and feel all alone. If you are doing all you can through personal interventions like scripture study, prayer, and attending the temple, and still find yourself struggling, it is crucial that you reach out for support. It is especially helpful to find those who have gone through your same struggles. MissionFortify.com lists support groups that are held across the Wasatch Front that meet weekly for an hour and half. These groups are open to parents and early-returned missionaries.

If you cannot attend a support group and do not know anyone else who went through this experience, talk to a trusted friend or family member. It may even be necessary to speak to a professional therapist, especially if you feel a lot of anger or resentment toward the situation, your missionary, or God. Kimberly told me,

> The peace did not come from praying and fasting and reading my scriptures. It did not. Maybe that works for some people, but I knew that I needed to talk to someone who had the skills to ask the questions necessary for me to find healing and peace. My counselor was also LDS so he could talk about our beliefs and the Atonement, and could share scriptures and stories. I also had more than one session. In fact, we had to talk several times to kind of really dig deep and get through all the baggage.

Regardless of who you talk to and how, it is important that if you are struggling, that you do find someone who you can trust. Please do not isolate yourself—that will only push you further into your grief. Instead, trust that God will guide you to the people you need to talk to and don't be afraid to put yourself out there and ask for help. Remember, humility and submission are key to receiving comfort.[16]

Reflect on Lessons Learned

So often we expect life to unfold a certain way, and all too often it does not. Those are the moments where we have opportunity for learning and growth. As Larry Richman said in a BYU Devotional address, "Spiritual growth can often be achieved more readily by trials and adversity than by comfort and tranquility. Trials can teach us that faith in God the Father and His Son Jesus Christ is the source of inner strength."[17]

Reflecting on what she learned from this trial, Sandra shared a changed perspective about the need for desire to do missionary work. She said, "My second son is going to be leaving on a mission next week, and talking about it, his choice to serve a mission . . . it has changed my whole perspective. At the beginning of the school year he said, 'I don't know if I'll serve a mission.' And I thought, 'Great, just figure it out for yourself and be honest with yourself.' and so it has very much changed the way that I look at it."[18]

Leticia became more sympathetic toward what her son and other early-returned missionaries go through. She said, "It wasn't until I was actually listening to a conversation between my son and some other early-returned missionaries that I really saw a very different side of what they're going through. It wasn't until I was able to listen to those three early-returned missionaries about what they were feeling that I really even had a little bit of an understanding of how to parent better in that situation."[19] Early-returned missionaries often feel marginalized in the Church's culture. This experience also likely opened Leticia's eyes and increased her sympathy toward other people in the Church who likewise don't "fit the mold" and feel marginalized.

Naomi realized that she needed to be less judgmental and simply love the individual. She said, "Before any of this happened to my son, if I saw someone come home early, I would think, 'Okay, why are they home? What did they do?' And I learned that it's none of my business; I just need to love that individual."[20]

Reflecting on the lessons you have learned will help you see how you have grown and how the Lord is shaping your life to be what *He* wants it to be. We are meant to pass through difficult times in this life, even if we have lived righteous lives. The Lord wants trials to strengthen us and to ultimately bless us. Too often though, we use trials to doubt and destroy ourselves. You may find it helpful to keep a journal or notebook and write down the lessons you learn as you go through this trial with your missionary.

Forgiveness

Do all you can to forgive anyone who has hurt you as you go through this experience with your child. A ward member, a Church leader, a friend, your spouse, your child's mission president, or even your child—the list is potentially endless. Forgiveness can be difficult and it can take time, but always work toward that end. A lack of forgiveness will lead you to bitterness, resentment, and even depression. Don't harbor negative feelings; they will truly destroy you. For more on forgiveness, see chapter 1.

Helping Your Child

Now that you have learned how to help yourself, you are ready to learn how to help your child. As with all articles and books filled with parenting advice, adapt each suggestion for your child. You know him or her best. Be prayerful as you read this section and open your heart and mind to the Spirit so that you can know best what your child needs from you.

Love

The most important thing you can show your missionary right now is love. Your child needs to know that you love him or her and that you do not see him or her as a failure. Even if you thought that before, and were upset with him or her for coming home early, and perhaps are even still struggling with those feelings, he or she is still a child of God and deserving of love.

One father told me,

> [My daughter] was ticked. She went to Bolivia and she was sick for the majority of her mission. She endured sixteen months of it and likely thought, "I've already endured sixteen months of this. What's two more? I can do two more." And they said, "No, you can't." And so I think she felt like, "What was the point?" . . . It was important for her to hear us say that [we accept her] and that we love her immensely and what she was able to accomplish.

But what if you are angry at your child for coming home early due to unresolved sin, transgression on the mission, or just losing that desire to serve and choosing to come home? That was not okay and you are angry with your child! You likely feel that you have a right to express your anger to your child. While it may be helpful to express your disappointment to your child, it is important that you continue to show love to him or her and offer support through the repentance process. In fact, the scriptures teach that at times it is okay to "Reprov[e] betimes with sharpness, when moved upon by the Holy Ghost" but then immediately you must, " [show] forth afterwards an increase of love toward him whom thou hast reproved, lest he esteem thee to be his enemy" (D&C 121:43). We all fail the Lord from time to time; we all sin. The important thing is that we repent, and repentance is much more easily accomplished with help from those we love.

In fact, you may halt the progress of your son or daughter's repentance if you do not show him or her the love and support mentioned in the Doctrine and Covenants. I love what Hank Smith said on his Facebook page,

> If there is someone in your life (including yourself) who is trying their best to change, let them repent. Promise them you'll help them bury their sins and mistakes deep by never bringing them up again. When it comes to mind, acknowledge it silently and then dismiss it. You cannot allow your past (or anyone's past) to hold you hostage. Refuse to allow yesterday to ruin today and tomorrow. I promise you God cares more about the future than the past. Forgiving yourself and others is the key to real peace and freedom.[21]

He said this in response to a quote from Elder Holland, "When something is over and done with, when it has been repented of as fully as it can be repented of, when life has moved on as it should and a lot of other wonderfully good things have happened since then, it is not right to go back and open some ancient wound that the Son of God Himself died to heal."[22]

Show Support

Even if you are not pleased with the decision to come home early (no matter who made the decision), you can still support your child as he or she goes through the many emotions that accompany an early homecoming. Support can come in many different forms: a listening ear, a shoulder to cry on, a chauffeur from appointment to appointment, or even space to reflect, recover, and heal. So often the Spirit works in quiet, still moments. Let your child have those quiet, still moments. In fact, encourage him or her. Consider giving your child a journal to write out his or her thoughts, or ask if he or she would like some space.

But don't give your child too much space—isolation is no one's friend but the adversary's. Check in with how his or her scripture study is going without demanding scripture study. Share what stood out to you in your own scripture study. If there are no worthiness issues, invite your child to go to the temple with you. Be a spiritual guide for him or her during this turbulent time.

Ask questions about the mission, and let your child share the good and difficult times with you. No matter how long he or she was out, you'll be amazed at how much he or she learned and grew. Your child will likely appreciate the opportunity to share his or her experiences. However, don't be too surprised if your child does not want to talk about his or her mission. Missions are difficult and what he or she went through could have been traumatic, and your child may need time and space to heal before being ready to talk about it.

Learn More about His or Her Condition

I was so grateful that my parents took the time to research and ask doctors plenty of questions about what the parasite was doing to my body.

I was so physically and emotionally spent; the fact that I did not have to do my own research added greatly to my recovery. I did not have to expend more effort than necessary to recover; I could focus on getting better, and I felt added love from my parents.

If your child came home due to worthiness issues, learn more about the repentance process so that you can help him or her down that path. You do not need to know the exact nature of the sin to help your child repent, nor should you push him or her to divulge that to you. Sharing your own experiences of repentance and forgiveness may help strengthen your child's resolve to repent and become clean again.

If your child came home due to a lack of desire or loss of testimony, seek to understand why these things happened, and prayerfully seek ways to show him or her love as he or she works through the emotions that accompany such feelings.

If the reason was homesickness, learn more about what you can do to help your child be ready to leave home someday, and learn more about what you can do to help him or her be ready to someday leave you (or how to help you someday be ready for that).

In all of this, especially with reasons related to personal choice or worthiness, be wary of personalizing the early homecoming, or thinking that it was somehow your fault. Dismiss thoughts that go something like, "If I'd just taught this principle better . . . " or "If I'd just been more like so-and-so . . . " or "If my scripture study were better or more obvious or on and on . . . " While some introspection may be worthwhile, demonizing yourself isn't. Even Lehi and Sariah had children who struggled—and there are plenty of scriptures that show what darn good parents they were!

Be Their Ally

Very likely, someone will say something, probably innocently, that will be hurtful to your child. Help your child to forgive this person (or persons). Dr. Doty-Yells found that "many choose church inactivity as a way to cope with shame and embarrassment. Help them accept that the situation may be awkward at first, and they may become offended. Remind them that taking offense is a choice (Anderson, 2010). [They] have more power over their situation than they realize."[23] If the offense was intentional, stand up for your child and let the other person know, kindly, that his or her remarks are unacceptable to you and to the Lord. If your child knows that you have his or her back, he or she will be more likely to listen to you and accept your help through the trial.

Avoid Urging Your Son or Daughter to Return to the Mission Field

The Church, in its online resource *Ministering Resources: Missionaries Who Return Home Early* for Church leaders, urges leaders to not pressure the missionary to return to the mission field. This decision must come from your son or daughter and can only come after fully recovery from the challenges that brought him or her home. Also, a true desire to serve is vital to missionary work, and if your son or daughter feels forced to return to the mission field or that he or she will be a disappointment to you if he or she does not return, your missionary will not do well upon returning to the field. He or she will be there out of duty and not a true desire to serve, and will likely fall into a depression and return home early again. There is, of course, the chance that he or she will rally and catch the vision of missionary work, and lose him or herself in the work. But it will be so much better for your missionary's spiritual and mental health if he or she is allowed to make the decision, and let it be between him or her and the Lord.

Dr. Doty-Yells said, "The ERM should be empowered to focus on resolving the reason for coming home before engaging in any discussion about returning to the field. Moving on with his or her future by securing employment or attending college or vocational training may be the path he or she prefers or feels inspired to take. Consistently showing patience, unconditional love and support for the ERMs' decisions will be the most helpful."[24]

In a similar vein, do not force your son or daughter to stay on the missionary schedule, but do encourage him or her to continue with scripture study and prayer until he or she makes a decision. Do not tell your child that he or she may not relax and watch television or read non-scriptural books, but do remind him or her that these things may not be the best use of his or her time as he or she makes the decision. Then let it go. Let the Spirit pierce your child's heart if your words are true for his or her situation. Let Heavenly Father also be his or her parent.

Of course, as a parent, you are entitled to your own inspiration about what would be best for your child. Just please be sure that if you feel inspired to encourage your child to return to his or her mission, that those feelings are truly coming from the Spirit and not from any sort of cultural notions that the only acceptable length of a mission is eighteen months for young women and two years for young men. Remember what Elder Holland said (which has been quoted extensively throughout this book) that perhaps not every mission was outlined to be eighteen-months or two-years long. Your child may yet choose to return to his or her mission. Don't deny him or her the spiritual growth that comes from making such a decision. He or she will also feel empowered upon returning to the mission field because he or she will know that this was his or her decision, and when times get hard (and they will get hard), he or she will not harbor any resentment toward you for "forcing" him or her to go through this hard thing.

I am grateful that my mother did not share her thoughts with me about returning to the mission field. If she had, I may have chosen to return, and looking back at my emotional state at the time, I can tell you that my heart was no longer in the mission field. I had been traumatized by what I'd been through in the Philippines, and I really needed more time to recover emotionally. Because she let me go to the Lord in prayer, fasting, and to the temple, I felt at peace and empowered to move forward with my life in the direction that I truly felt it needed to go.

While I have no doubt that my mother would have expressed her desires to me kindly, taking care to make sure I knew she would love me no matter what, I still would have felt guilty about disappointing her, and likely questioned my decision to move on even more, and would not have felt nearly as much peace with it. So please, as tempting as it may be, avoid urging your child to return to the field (or to stay home, if that is your desire). Let that decision be between him or her and the Lord. Encourage your missionary to counsel with priesthood leaders if necessary, but respect his or her space, and be supportive in whatever decision your child makes. Do not hold it against your child if he or she chooses to stay home. Do not push him or her toward marriage as though the whole reason he or she came home was to meet a future spouse! Let your child navigate this new, unexpected path, and continue to be a spiritual guide and support to him or her.

Consider the Young Church-Service Missionary (YCSM) Program

If your child still has a desire to serve, but cannot complete his or her proselytizing mission, consider the Young Church-Service Missionary program with your child's priesthood leaders. Dr. Doty-Yells stated that "YCSMs are called and set apart to serve in family history centers, bishops' storehouses, and in other needed areas of the Church. Such mission opportunities are based upon the talents and interests of each missionary and developed to fit his or her unique needs."[25] I have not studied this program in depth, but there are many examples of those who loved their church-service mission on lds.org and might be a great option for your missionary. Please meet with your bishop or branch president to learn more if your missionary is interested. I also think getting involved in community service is a great way to get outside of oneself and move forward with life.

Final Thoughts

I hope you found this chapter to be enlightening and encouraging, and that you now feel empowered to help yourself and your child make it through this difficult time. It is never easy when trials are suddenly thrust upon you, but it is within your power to allow the Lord to cause "all things [to] work together for [your] good" (D&C 105:40) and, I would add, your child's good. Continue to trust the Lord as you move through this trial. This too shall pass, and you and your child will come out of it stronger, and maybe even closer, for it.

Notes

1. Kristine Doty-Yells, "Stopping the Stigma: Lessons from Early Returned Missionaries," *Religious Educator*, vol. 18. no. 3 (2017), 141–42.

2. Kris J. Doty-Yells, Harmony Packer, Malisa M. Draper-Brooks, Russell T. Warne, and Cameron R. John, "The Experience of Parents of Early-Returned Missionaries," *Issues in Religion and Psychotherapy*, vol. 38, no. 1 (2017): 56. Available at http://scholarsarchive.byu.edu/irp/vol38/iss1/1056.
3. Ibid., 53.
4. Ibid., 56.
5. Ibid.
6. Ibid., emphasis added.
7. Ibid., 52.
8. Ibid.
9. Ibid., 53.
10. Ibid.
11. Ibid., 59.
12. Lance B. Wickman, "But if Not," *Ensign*, Nov., 2002.
13. Ibid.
14. Ibid.
15. Ibid.
16. Ibid.
17. Larry Richman, "Learning through Life's Trials," Ensign, March 2010.
18. Doty-Yells; et. al., "The Experience of Parents of Early-Returned Missionaries," 60.
19. Ibid.
20. Ibid.
21. Hank Smith, Facebook post, January 21, 2018, https://www.facebook.com/hanksmithcds/posts/10155124205812805.
22. Jeffrey R. Holland, "The Best Is Yet to Be," *Ensign,* Jan. 2010.
23. Kristine J. Doty-Yells, S. Zachary Bullock, Harmony Packer, Russell T. Warner, James Westwood, Thomas Ash, and Heather Hirsch, "Return with Trauma: Understanding the Experiences of Early Returned Missionaries," *Issues in Religion and Psychotherapy*, vol. 37, no. 1 (2015): 34. Available at http://scholarsarchive.byu.edu/irp/vol37/iss1/9.
24. Doty-Yells; et. al., "Return with Trauma," 44.
25. Ibid.

CHAPTER 9

Mormon Culture

In the well-known LDS comedy movie *The R.M.* (2003), Jared Phelps has completed two years of full-time missionary service. He comes home thinking that he has everything worked out, only to find out everything that can go wrong, does go wrong. This movie is a hilarious and well-done satire of the returning home experience and Mormon culture.

A particularly funny part of the movie is when Jared arrives at the airport expecting a "rockstar greeting" only to walk out of the gate to no one. When a woman at the airport strikes up a conversation, he tells her that he just finished a two-year mission and that he's sure his mom is just late "picking up balloons." Eventually, Jared realizes that his family isn't coming and takes a bus home.

Jared arrives at his house only to find that his family has moved— a far cry from the homecoming experience he expected. When things finally get sorted out and his parents come get him from a former neighbor's house, they are shocked to see him. They think he has come home early and want to know what happened. "Are you sick, pal?" his father asks him. "No!" Jared replies. Fearfully, his father asks, "Are you still worthy?" Jared, flabbergasted that his parents haven't realized that two years have passed, quickly reassures them that he has completed his two years and that today is the day he is supposed to be home. They are a little dubious until Jared's mother finds a letter with his return date from the mission office.

Later that evening, Jared goes to see his girlfriend, Molly, who waited (or so he thinks) all two years for him. Molly's father opens the door and is surprised to see him. He quickly asks, "Jared? What are you doing home? . . . This doesn't have anything to do with Molly, does it?" Then Molly comes to the door and she is equally surprised. She tells him "Jared, it's not worth it. You should have at least finished!" Jared quickly reassures her that he has finished, that he's worthy, and that he is excited to be with her again.

The movie does a good job portraying the awkwardness of the misunderstanding between Jared's family and friends, and that awkwardness is hilarious. However, underneath that awkwardness is an element of truth in our Mormon culture: the idea that it is unacceptable to come home early from a mission.

The Stigma of Returning Home Early

"There's a cultural stigma of coming home early from your mission that the Lord doesn't care anything about," one bishop told me. "I think He sees us all as individuals, and, as a bishop, I've had a lot of situations where *culturally* in the Church something is weird, not normal, not expected, or whatever. The Lord doesn't care about that. The Lord sees people as individuals, and [as leaders] we work hard to apply the gospel principles that are general to specific individual situations." Before we get into this chapter, I want this fact to be established right up front: these stigmas, or expectations, or whatever you want to call them, are not from the Lord. They are also not from the leaders of the Church. Rather, they are the result of shared beliefs in our culture.

According to research done in 2014 by T. S. Drake and M. S. Drake, 6 percent of missionaries return early.[1] As of March 2018, the LDS Church reported 70,946 missionaries in the field.[2] This means that in 2018 alone, 4,256 missionaries will return early. While this may not seem like many in comparison, the effects of the stigma of returning home early will likely produce feelings of failure in 3,106 of them (according to the reported 73 percent in Dr. Kristine Doty-Yells's article "Return with Trauma"[3]). The effects of these feelings can be devastating for the missionary and his or her family. Also, out of the 4,256 missionaries that return early, 1,477 will go through a period of inactivity, and out of these, 477 will never return to church activity.[4] This is in 2018 alone and is directly related to the feelings of failure supported in large part by the culture in the Church (and for more on this, please see chapter 6) and is therefore completely preventable. This stigma needs to go.

What Is a Stigma?

I'm going to wax academic for just a bit. Bear with me. This is good stuff.

In his article "What Causes Stigma?" Julio Arboleda-Flórez defines stigma as "a social construction whereby a distinguishing mark of social disgrace is attached to others in order to identify and to devalue them. Thus, stigma and the process of stigmatization consist of two fundamental elements, the recognition of the differentiating 'mark' and the subsequent devaluation of the person."[5] Furthermore, according to Margaret Shih, in her article "Positive Stigma: Examining Resilience and Empowerment in Overcoming Stigma," there are two kinds of stigmas: public stigma and self-stigma. "Public stigma relates to the judgments and negative stereotypes that society places on the stigmatized individual, whereas self-stigma refers to the degree to which individuals internalize these judgments and stereotypes."[6] In other words, public stigmas are the negative emotions or comments that people direct toward a stigmatized individual. Self-stigmas are the negative emotions or comments that the individual places on himself (or herself).

Breaking all that down, a stigma is something that is culturally created—it is not mandated by any one individual or by any one small group of people within a much larger culture. In a way, it is an unspoken, yet understood, belief about something or someone. A stigma causes a person to be marked as "different" in a bad way and therefore seen as less valuable. This, of course, is in direct contrast with the teachings of the General Authorities of The Church of Jesus Christ of Latter-day Saints, who have repeatedly taught that our value as sons and daughters of God can never be lessened—that our souls have infinite worth. Yet, somehow, despite these teachings, stigmas are created. How?

Arboleda-Flórez says, "The original functional impetus is an initial perception of tangible or symbolic threat. Tangible threats are those that pose a risk to material or concrete goods and symbolic ones are those that threaten beliefs, values, ideology, or the way in which a group ordains its social, political or spiritual domains."[7] In other words, a threat is perceived and a stigma is created. It is as simple as that. If something is undesirable, we decide that it must be removed from our culture. In many ways, *this makes sense and is a good thing*. Latter-day Saints want to become pure and holy like our Father in Heaven and Savior, Jesus Christ, and so we seek daily to rid ourselves of every unholy thing. In a larger sense, cultures and societies want to function well, so they seek to rid themselves of anything that may destroy good functioning (such as garbage in the streets or reckless driving). This instinct is actually really good. Unfortunately, as humans, we really aren't good at judging other humans. While we may at times need to judge between "right" and "wrong," and even whether someone is trying to uplift us or deceive us, the Lord has commanded us to "judge not" when it comes to someone's worth (see Matthew 7:1–3). Often, when we become "judgmental" we are simply not good at separating worth from worthiness.

Overcoming Stigmas

Stop Judging

So, how do we get rid of unhelpful stigmas? President Uchtdorf offered the solution in a what he called a two-word sermon: "Stop it!" He then said,

> It's that simple. We simply have to stop judging others and replace judgmental thoughts and feelings with a heart full of love for God and His children. God is our Father. We are His children. We are all brothers and sisters. . . . Haven't we all, at one time or another, meekly approached the mercy seat and pleaded for grace? Haven't we wished with all the energy of our souls for mercy—to be forgiven for the mistakes we have made and the sins we have committed? Because we all depend on the mercy of God, how can we deny to others any measure of the grace we so desperately desire for ourselves?[8]

It is so easy, of course, to read that and say, "Yes! Of course! We all need to just stop it!" What we find in the next minute though is that it is much easier to agree with than to actually do. President Uchtdorf offers the reason why:

> Of course, these words seem perfectly reasonable—when applied to someone else. We can so clearly and easily see the harmful results that come when others judge and hold grudges. And we certainly don't like it when people judge us. But when it comes to our own prejudices and grievances, we too often justify our anger as righteous and our judgment as reliable and only appropriate. Though we cannot look into another's heart, we assume that we know a bad motive or even a bad person when we see one. We make exceptions when it comes to our own bitterness because we feel that, in our case, we have all the information we need to hold someone else in contempt.[9]

Again, we want to surround ourselves with that which is pure and holy, and often we simply do not know what to say or do with someone who we have determined is impure or unholy. We also have been commanded to judge righteously and we use that judgment to determine who to surround ourselves with so that we can be uplifted and make it back to the celestial kingdom. Righteous judgment is difficult to always do perfectly, however, and too often we get it wrong. In the case of judging someone who came home early, we often incorrectly judge someone who is suffering from a physical illness, a mental illness, family troubles, personal issues, or even worthiness issues, and dismiss him or her as less than ourselves.

In his talk, "The Righteous Judge," Elder Lynn G. Robbins of the Seventy tells us that "There is only one way to judge righteous judgment, as Jesus Christ does, and that is to be as He is."[10] Christ in His ministry took joy in rescuing lost sheep and took joy in serving and forgiving sinners, and He alone had the authority to dismiss or condemn them. As a culture, as everyday sinners ourselves, we do not have the right to judge and condemn others, even though we often mistakenly think that we do. When we are called upon to help someone either as a leader, or as a parent, or even as a friend, the individual we are helping should come away from our counsel feeling the love of Christ and encouragement to overcome his or her challenges rather than shamed or condemned.

Educate Yourself and Others

Social psychologist Margaret Shih suggests empowering stigmatized individuals to become "active participants in society who seek to understand their social world and create positive outcomes."[11] In other words, stigmatized individuals (or those interested in such individuals) educate themselves and then educate others.

There are many ways to educate oneself about stigmas. Two main ways are to (1) Read about them from people who have experienced them, and (2) Associate with individuals who are stigmatized. Margaret Shih says,

> Individuals who are highly identified with their group, despite the stigmas associated with the group, are more likely to be empowered. Highly identified individuals frequently interact with others from the same group, and thus, are more aware of the positive aspects of their group membership. As a result, they are less likely to buy into the negative messages received from society about their stigmatized identity. Individuals who reject negative public images are more likely to strive to maintain social status and to function at a high level.[12]

That's right. If you came home early, own it. Or whatever stigma has been placed on you—own it. Don't run from it. Don't try to hide it. Own it and seek to understand both the reasons for why the stigma has been placed on you and why it is in fact a stigma. Then, seek to understand why the stigma needs to be removed (hint: because the Lord doesn't see it).

So, in that spirit, let's educate ourselves on the many stigmas in our culture surrounding missionary work and how they relate to the experience of early-returned missionaries.

The Stigma of Not Serving a Mission

We have been told repeatedly by prophets of God that "every able and worthy young man should serve a mission."[13] Therefore, in our culture, which seeks to follow the prophet, we desire to send every able and worthy young man on a mission. Because a stigma exists about being "unable" in society, many young men who struggle with physical or mental health apply for missions anyways because they do not want to consider themselves "unable" or have others consider them that way. Furthermore, in Mormon culture there is a stigma against being "unworthy." In fact, greater shame is placed on unworthiness than inability, so many unworthy young men also hide the fact that they are unworthy because they fear the culture's repercussions.

A priesthood duty is also associated with missionary work[14] and all young men who seek to do the Lord's will naturally want to fulfill their priesthood duties. Others simply want to avoid the cultural shaming that comes from not fulfilling priesthood duties. However, many of these male missionaries who are physically or emotionally unable, or are unworthy, end up coming home early, which has its own stigma attached to it. But would it have been better for these young men, culturally, if they had not gone at all or delayed their mission several months or years?

Because we are a culture that seeks to follow the prophet, and the prophets have said that "every able and worthy young man should serve a mission," we as a culture place value on missionaries. This is good, but I think sometimes it is taken to a level where we value the "missionary" more than we value the individual. And this often causes us to misjudge or mischaracterize individuals who choose not to serve missions, or to delay their missionary service. When we see such an individual, we are quick to convince him of the value of a mission in his life, missing the point that he is probably well-aware of the benefits of a mission. Our intentions are good, but unless we are willing to open our mind to the idea that he is not ready or unable to serve a mission, we miss the opportunity to help resolve (or just understand) the real issue. Worse yet, we may make the young man feel more ostracized, and even unwelcome, at church.

Sisters in their mid-twenties and beyond also report feeling made to feel less if they are unmarried and do not serve missions. One such woman told me, "I am grateful you are writing this book. I think it will also help those of us who feel like we are second-class in the Church because we chose not to serve missions."

In a church that teaches love and tolerance toward all, we really need to do a much better job at not judging each other's life choices, especially surrounding a decision that for everyone is personal. We need to be understanding toward those whose lives take a different path than the one we have culturally prescribed for them. We need to accept that the Lord sees us all as individuals, not as cookie-cutters, and that in His mind, there is no "mold" or "one-size-fits-all" member of the Church. We must stop casting stones. As Gordon B. Hinckley said, "Missionary work is not a right of passage in the Church. It is a call extended by the president of the Church to those who are able and worthy to accomplish it."[15]

The Stigma of Not Being a Returned Missionary or Marrying a Returned Missionary

Because as a culture we place value on missionaries, we also value returned missionaries. Young women are taught to aspire to marry a returned missionary in the temple. In fact, many young LDS women write down "returned missionary" as a quality they will seek in their future spouse! It is presumed in our culture that returned missionaries are more spiritual, more mature, and better prepared for marriage than their non-returned missionary counterparts. However, as one blogger put it, "spirituality can't be judged by a title."[16] Furthermore, in the April 2010 General Conference, Elder Lance B. Wickman said,

> [When deciding whom to marry] do not base your decisions solely on whether someone has served a full-time mission or holds a particular calling in your ward. These things can be, should be, and usually are indications of devotion, faithfulness, and integrity. But not always. That is the reason you need to get acquainted. Know someone well enough to learn his or her heart and character firsthand and not just his or her "gospel résumé."[17]

Certainly there is growth that happens on a mission, and if a missionary truly seeks to give his or her life to the Lord for however long he or she is out there, then that missionary will come back a more mature and spiritual person. *That* is what is desirable though: a mature, spiritual person. Not necessarily a returned missionary. Many spiritual giants live or have lived on this earth who did not serve a full-time mission. President Thomas S. Monson chose to serve in the navy rather than serve a mission. The expectation was not the same then as it is now, but the fact remains that a mission is not requisite for a happy marriage or a meaningful life.

As a side note, men, if you are open about the fact that you came home early, you will find that most women will actually be kind and understanding. My friend Tyler told me,

> As guys we tend to bottle everything up and say, "Ah, no, I just gotta stuff this down and make it go away," but I found that a lot of girls really liked that I was willing to be open emotionally about the experiences I had, and how it was rough, and the difficulties I had. And then they would ask me for advice on other things and I could create a good friendship and a good dating relationship from that.

Women, the same goes for you. Be open about the fact that you came home early, and you will find that most men will be kind and understanding about it. Of all the women I interviewed, none reported negative dating consequences for coming home early. That's not to say you won't run into some stigma in your dating life, but my research suggests that it will be rare.

Back to the point, in our culture, when someone says the words "returned missionary" the image that comes to mind is that of a young man or young woman who has served a full-time mission for two years (for men) or eighteen months (for women). It is an image of a triumphant, mature, spiritual individual. It is not the image of a sad, sick, and/or embarrassed individual. It is certainly not an image of someone who completed less than the expected amount of time.

Yet, someone who comes home early *did* serve a mission. Their mission was derailed either due to circumstances beyond their control, their own choice to come home early, or worthiness issues. Still, a mission was served. Don't they deserve the same title as their two-year or eighteen-month counterparts?

Elder Holland, through answering a question posed from a young man who came home after four months due to mental health issues had this to say on the matter:

> I think you could make a case that one of the most famous and surely one of the most successful missions of all time in this dispensation was the Quorum of the Twelve opening of Great Britain, led by Heber C. Kimball in 1837. . . . Well, that mission only lasted eight months. Now, apparently nobody said at that point that Brother Kimball had to go for

two years. Also, I suppose nobody said later on that other people went for four or five years. But the point is, cherish the service you rendered. Be grateful for the opportunity to have testified, to have been out in the name of the Lord, to have worn that missionary name plaque.

And because you were honorable and because you did give your very best service to the degree that you could, please, please do not relive this. Do not rehash it. Do not think you're inadequate or a failure . . . Please just consider yourself a returned missionary who served and was faithful and will continue to serve. And you'll continue to be a great Latter-day Saint."[18]

There you have it: if you came home early but were "honorable and . . . [gave] your very best service to the degree that you could," then you can consider yourself a returned missionary and ask that others consider you to be one as well. In these instances, the length of your mission is unimportant.

The Stigma of Not Returning with Honor

But where then does that leave those who feel that they did not return with honor? Elder Holland made clear in the aforementioned video that the comments he made were "spontaneous answers and they're personal. And we don't necessarily make this the law and the gospel for the Church," but he did seem to make clear that his personal opinion was that those who can consider themselves returned missionaries were those who were "honorable" in their service and "[gave their] very best service to the degree that [they] could."

In our culture, when we tell someone to "return with honor" what we are really saying is "Don't mess up. Don't give up. Stay out there until your two years or eighteen months are done." However, Elder Robert D. Hales in his talk "Return with Honor" told us that "the scriptures teach us that honor includes such things as faith and trust in the Lord, payment of tithes and offerings, fear of the Lord, humility, and obedience."[19] We cannot say as a culture that those who come home early, for whatever reason (including worthiness issues), did not serve honorable missions. This is strictly between them, the Lord, and their priesthood leaders. We might be tempted to say, "Well, they had honorable parts of their mission, at least until they messed up," or "They were good until they just quit, so yeah, it was honorable to a point," or "It was never honorable because they weren't worthy," but let's just apply Elder Uchtdorf's advice right here and "stop it." We do not know what was in the missionary's heart while they served. We do not know what they went through or what their thoughts and feelings were as they served. We simply know, that they, like us, went through something difficult whether it was inflicted by external circumstances or by themselves (something we all can certainly relate to).

As a culture, I think we most especially prescribe the "dishonorable return" to those who come home early due to worthiness issues. I think if we could remove the "beam in our own eye" (Matthew 7:1–5), we would see easily how all of us are sinners and do not need to "cast stones" (or hurtful words). Instead, we would realize that the missionary actually behaved honorably in coming home to clear up his or her sins. We would embrace the missionary. We would say that say, "Hey, I know what it's like to mess up, even to mess up severely. Good for you for coming home to get this taken care of. Is there anything I can do to help you?" Too often instead we say things like, "What did you do wrong?" or "How could you do that?" for the purpose of gossip or condemning. The truth is though that all of us are a lot closer in spiritual standing to the unworthy missionary than we are to God. If we are truly Latter-day Saints who love the Lord and love His teachings, then we need to do a better job as a culture to embrace everyone regardless of their sins and how and where they were committed. We all sin. Unfortunately, some of our sins are more public.

To those who feel that they did not return or serve honorably and have had those feelings confirmed to you by the Spirit, please take comfort in Elder Hales's words, "I ask that each one of us would go to our Heavenly Father and ask for His guidance, that we may be obedient and have His spirit to be with us. That we will remember who we are, be obedient to the commandments of the Lord, and return with honor together into the presence of our Heavenly Father is my prayer."[20] Although Elder Hales briefly mentioned in his talk how he whispered in each of his sons ears to "return with honor" before they embarked on their missions, he was really teaching the Church, and the world, to do all we can to return with honor to our heavenly home. There are absolutely times in everyone's lives where we behave dishonorably. No one is going to live a perfect life. What is important is that we do our best to correct our mistakes, with the proper priesthood authority as necessary, and return with honor to our heavenly home. And, we can do that, thanks to the Atonement.

The Stigma of Struggling on a Mission

Although culturally we know and accept that missions are hard, I don't think we fully understand what exactly is difficult about missions. Those who have served missions understand more fully what it means when someone says, "Missions are hard," but even returned missionaries can lack sympathy toward someone who struggles with something that was rather easy for them, or that they were able to overcome on their mission. We often culturally accuse those who struggle on their missions of not having enough faith or trust in the Lord. Indeed, our first response to someone who is brave enough to admit that they are struggling is, "Forget yourself and go to work," not realizing that that solution is not a one-size-fits-all.

For instance, missionaries who are struggling with physical health issues, depression, severe anxiety, or grief would generally like nothing more than to "forget themselves and go to work," and often reprimand themselves for being unable to do what they have been called to do. They often do try to push through these hard feelings, and often hide them and isolate themselves from others because they fear the "Forget yourself and go to work" reprimand. Furthermore, they often feel like they cannot write home about their struggles because they feel a sort of obligation to uplift their family members with their letters home. Also, some worry that their letters filled with struggles and pleas for help will not be received well. One young man told me, "I come from a large family and missionary letters were read around the dinner table when I was growing up. There was never any mention about struggles, even though I know that at least two of my siblings struggled a lot on their missions. I don't think letters about the struggles would have been well-received. Then again, perhaps my parents simply didn't share those letters with us." On my mission, I never really felt like I should write home about my struggles with my trainer, my struggles to adjust to the culture, or even my illness. My parents were shocked when they got the phone call from my mission president informing them that I was in the hospital.

Also, homecoming talks often focus on the victories and high points of a mission, but rarely mention the struggles and what drove the missionary to mature and become more Christ-like. We often remark on how much a young man or young woman "grew up" as a result of a mission, but growth doesn't come without trials. There is an idea that missions simply create more mature, spiritual young adults. But that is not quite true—it's the *trials* on the mission that do that. So, in a way, it *is* the mission, but not in the way that we often think of missions. In homecoming talks, artwork, and missionary stories, we tend to focus on the victories and highlights of missions because those things are uplifting. Newly returned missionaries also don't want to come off as complainers or "downers" by sharing their harder moments. I think though, that there can be a balance between sharing the wonderful moments and the harder moments, and in fact, I think that balance is needed in our culture.

What I mean by all this is that people don't know what "missions are hard" really means until they serve one, and a lot of missionaries think that there is something wrong with them when they get out to the field and struggle to adjust. They think about what they've heard about a mission being "the best two years" of one's life. They think about the miracle stories they were told, such as those about missionaries suddenly being able to understand and speak a foreign language, or finding that golden investigator after knocking on the last door. They hear about all the people returned missionaries baptized or taught and that one companion who is now their best friend, and they can't wait to get out there and study and teach the gospel all day and make new friends!

And that *does* happen. But much more often, missions are about overcoming the fear we all have of approaching strangers, opening our mouths, and inviting them to hear a message about the gospel. It is about overcoming a lot of rejection and discouragement. It is about working with ward members and trying to find ways to encourage them to bring others to church or activities, or how to better run their meetings on Sunday so that church is a place where the missionaries want to bring their investigators. There are a lot of meetings as a missionary too, and a lot of traveling depending on the area. Missionaries do a lot less teaching than they thought they would and since that is the whole reason they are on a mission—to teach!—discouragement goes up even more. Furthermore, missions are about learning to live with or take instruction from people you simply do not mesh with. They're about learning to humble yourself and get along with others. And, if a new language is involved, there is a language learning curve to overcome as well, and rarely is it overcome by a miracle of instant fluidity. These were the things that my mission was about, at least for me. Others may express different sentiments. And that is the beauty of missions—they really are individual growing experiences for each missionary.

Opportunities for growth are all around on a mission, but before the growth can happen, the struggles need to happen, and as a culture I think we can do a better job of understanding and embracing those struggles, and helping young adults work through them. They should not be shamed for struggling on a mission or made to feel like they should hide their struggles. Rather, they should be made to feel that their struggles are normal and that it is okay to talk about them. I don't think we should stop sharing the victories and highlights and miracles, or even lessen how often they are shared—rather, I think we need to start sharing the hard times too with the intention of showing growth, and maybe also a bit of the realities of the day-to-day trials of missionary work.

Of course, every now and then, there may be a missionary who needs the "forget yourself and go to work" letter, but that letter should only be sent with the inspiration of the Spirit (as it was by President Gordon B. Hinckley's father) and not as "the solution" for all missionary struggles. Sometimes a missionary needs words of encouragement, not a reprimand. Indeed, reprimands may send missionaries further into themselves and increase isolation because they feel that they cannot talk about their struggles without getting lectured.

The Stigma of Not Returning to Your Mission

Finally, while the stigma about coming home early has greatly lessened in the last several years thanks to many articles being published about the phenomenon in several magazines, newspapers, and even academic journals, as well as Elder Holland's Face-to-Face with early-returned missionaries in 2016, there seems to be a new stigma developing about not returning to a mission. In other words, it's become okay to come home early for reasons such as physical or mental health, but not okay to not return. Many early-returned missionaries (40 percent according to research by Dr. Doty-Yells[21]) wrestle with this decision and face added pressure from peers, parents, or leaders to return to the field. One young man shared this experience:

> Before I was dating my girlfriend, her roommate found out that I was home. She sat down with my girlfriend and basically said, "Now that he is home, we need to do everything possible to get him back out." [The roommate] would email her dad and ask for advice on what she could do to get me back out. It was a huge mess. Basically, what it came to, her roommate was telling me that my family wasn't strong in the gospel and that because I came home early from my mission that I didn't fulfill my missionary responsibilities. Even though I knew inside that I couldn't have gone any longer, it doesn't make me feel any better when people are like, "You're a failure."[22]

My friend Tyler felt similar pressure from his father who, upon hearing that Tyler did not want to return to the field, told him that he always dreamed that his sons would serve full-time missions, as though Tyler's sacrifice had not counted. One father told me that he and his wife made it clear to their son, who came home for physical health issues, that they wanted him to return to the field. He told me that they got nervous when their son started not living as much by the missionary schedule. Their son did return to the field, but the father had the impression that it was more so that he wouldn't disappoint his parents rather than a true desire to go back. Ward members often ask the question, "When are you going to go back?" instead of "Are you going to go back?" The "when" has an expectation attached to it that early-returned missionaries simply do not need. It'd be best to simply not approach the topic at all—if the young man or young woman is going to return to the mission, he or she will announce it; you won't have to ask.

The reason why many early-returned missionaries do not return to the field is that they either do not have the option to return due to the nature of the reason behind their early return, or they are still experiencing trauma. Throughout her article "Return with Trauma," Dr. Doty-Yells frequently uses words like "overwhelm," "stress," "shock," "inadequacy," "expectations," "failure," "crisis," and "development," to describe the experiences of missionaries who come home early. These words are associated with trauma, and no one is eager to return to a traumatic experience.

These issues often need time and space to be worked through, and sometimes that time and space is longer than the time allotted for a quick return to the field. That is okay. Some individuals are able to heal quickly, physically, mentally, and/or spiritually and then return to the field. Others need more time. We must remember that the Lord sees us as individuals and there is no "one-size-fits-all" when it comes to missionary work as much as we (culturally and as individuals) would like that to be the case.

I discuss the "stay home or go back out" question in each chapter of this book, with the exception of chapter 6. For additional information regarding the specifics of this decision, please visit the other chapters.

The Stigma against Parents

Last, I think there is a stigma against parents of early-returned missionaries (or parents of children who choose not to serve missions). This stigma may be more self-imposed than reinforced by others direct negative comments (usually the comments are more indirect, asking about the missionary, rather than the parenting techniques of the parent) but it stems from the idea that parents of early-returned missionaries were not as good "in-home missionary trainers" as those whose children completed the intended amount of time. This stigma is wrong and any such self-treatment or external treatment must not continue. There are many reasons for why an individual comes home early, or chooses not to serve a mission, and none of them are "inadequate parents." For more about the experience of parents of early-returned missionaries, please see chapter 8.

The Takeaway

Each of us is doing the best we can in this life and each of us needs grace and understanding. As President Uchtdorf said,

> In a world of accusations and unfriendliness, it is easy to gather and cast stones. But before we do so, let us remember the words of the One who is our Master and model: "He that is without sin among you, let him first cast a stone." Brothers and sisters, let us put down our stones. Let us be kind. Let us forgive. Let us talk peacefully with each other. Let the love of God fill our hearts. "Let us do good unto all men." The Savior promised: "Give, and it shall be given unto you; good measure, pressed down, and shaken together, and running over. . . . For with the same measure that [you use] it shall be measured to you again." Shouldn't this promise be enough to always focus our efforts on acts of kindness, forgiveness, and charity instead of on any negative behavior?[23]

And, these things also apply to the way we speak to and act toward ourselves. Too often, we are our own worst judge.

So, what should we as individuals do or say to someone who comes home early? Or to the parent of someone who comes home early? Or to anyone who feels stigmatized in anyway in the Church? I don't wish to make an exhaustive list of dos and don'ts, nor do I think I really need to make one. Simply ask yourself, before you say or do something, "Is this coming from a place of love or a place of curiosity? Or a place of condemnation? Do my actions or words tell the person how much I love or care for him or her? Do they communicate to the person that his or her time was valued by the Lord and therefore it is valued by me?" I think that if you ask yourself these questions before you speak or act, whatever you say or do, even if it is clumsy, will effectively communicate the love and concern you have for the individual. And, if you accidentally do offend, apologize. Reassure the person that you are grateful for his or her service and ask if there is anything you can do to help. More often than not, the missionary will reply, "Thank you. I'm okay though." In that case, just continue being his or her friend.

And, to the returned missionary (who came home early—I actually can't stand the terms ERM or early-returned missionary, but they do come with the territory of writing about the subject), remember that many times people say clumsy things or nothing at all because they simply do not know what to say or what to do. You have a choice in that moment to be offended and retreat deeper into yourself, or to forgive the error and perhaps gently educate the person a little more about your experience (and the experiences of others). Be patient with those around you, including your parents who are grappling with their own sense of bewilderment and loss (whether they realize it or not).

This stigma may not go away completely anytime soon, but we can always work toward that end. And, even if it never goes away completely, to my fellow early-returned missionaries, we can rest assured that our Father in Heaven loves us and that He doesn't see or care about the stigmas placed on us. You, and I, can do as Gordon B. Hinckley said and, "Go forward in life with a twinkle in your eye and a smile on your face, but with great and strong purpose in your heart. Love life and look for its opportunities, and forever and always be loyal to the Church. Never forget that you came to earth as a child of the divine Father, with something of divinity in your very makeup."[24]

Also, remember these words from President Monson:

> Now, a word for those elders, sisters, and couples who, for whatever reason, may not be able to finish their assigned time in the mission field: The Lord loves you. He appreciates your sacrifice. He is aware of your disappointment. Know that He still has a work for you to do. Don't let Satan tell you otherwise. Don't get down; don't become discouraged; don't despair.
>
> As I observed in general conference shortly after I was called to lead the Church: "Fear not. Be of good cheer. The future is as bright as your faith." That promise still holds true for you. So don't lose your faith, because the Lord has not lost faith in you. Keep your covenants and move forward.
>
> The world needs the gospel of Jesus Christ. May the Lord bless all of His Saints—regardless of where we serve—with a missionary heart.[25]

Closing Thoughts

When I came home early from my mission, all I wanted was to read a book by someone who had gone through this experience, felt the terrible feelings of failure that I felt, and had made it through and could tell me that I would be okay. I never got to read that book. In an interesting twist in my life, I got to write it instead.

So, as that person who has been where you have been, let me tell you something: You will be okay. You are going to make it through this. You have great purpose in this life, and nothing on this Earth can halt that purpose unless you let it. Continue to stay close to the Lord and invite His spirit and His healing into your life. You can go on to live an extraordinary, happy life. Choose it.

Notes

1. Doty-Yells, Kristine J.; Bullock, S. Zachary; Packer, Harmony; Warner, Russell T.; Westwood, James; Ash, Thomas; and Hirsch, Heather (2015), "Return with Trauma: Understanding the Experiences of Early Returned Missionaries," *Issues in Religion and Psychotherapy*, vol. 37, No. 1, 37. Available at http://scholarsarchive .byu.edu/irp/vol37/iss1/9.
2. "Worldwide Statistics," mormonnewsroom.com, accessed June 8, 2018, https:// www.mormonnewsroom.org/facts-and-statistics.
3. Doty-Yells, et al., "Return with Trauma," 41.
4. Ibid., 42.
5. Julio Arboleda-Flórez, "What Causes Stigma?", *World Psychiatry*, vol. 1 (Feb. 2002): 25–26, https://www.ncbi.nlm.nih.gov/pmc/articles/PMC1489829/.
6. Margaret Shih, "Positive Stigma: Examining Resilience and Empowerment in Overcoming Stigma," *The Annals of the American Academy of Political and Social Science,* vol. 591 (Jan. 2004): 177, http://www.jstor.org/stable/4127642.
7. Arboleda-Flórez, "What Causes Stigma?" 25–26, https://www.ncbi.nlm.nih.gov /pmc/articles/PMC1489829/.
8. Dieter F. Uchtdorf, "The Merciful Obtain Mercy," *Ensign*, May 2012.
9. Ibid.
10. Lynn G. Robbins, "The Righteous Judge," *Ensign*, Nov. 2016.
11. Shih, "Positive Stigma," 181, http://www.jstor.org/stable/4127642.
12. Ibid.
13. Spencer W. Kimball, "It Becometh Every Man," *Ensign,* Oct. 1977; M. Russell Ballard, "One More," *Ensign,* May 2005; Thomas S. Monson, "Willing and Worthy to Serve," *Ensign*, May 2012.
14. Ibid.

15. Gordon B. Hinckley, "Mission Preparation Track 20-1," [worldwide leadership training meeting, Jan. 2003], https://www.lds.org/media-library/video/2012-12 -1230-mission-preparation-track-20-1-gordon-b-hinckley.

16. Jeremy Goff, "The Worst Dating Advice Mormons Get: 'Only Marry a Returned Missionary'" March 6, 2017, *LDS Living,* http://www.ldsliving.com/The-Worst-Dating-Advice-Mormons-Get-Only-Marry-a-Returned-Missionary/s/84747.

17. Lance B. Wickman, "Confidence Tests," *Ensign*, Apr. 2010.

18. Jeffrey R. Holland, "Elder Holland's Counsel for Early Returned Missionaries," LDS Media Library, March 2016, https://www.lds.org/media-library/video/2016 -05-012-elder-hollands-counsel-for-early-returned-missionaries.

19. Robert D. Hales, "Return with Honor," *Ensign*, June 1999.

20. Ibid.

21. Doty-Yells, "Return with Trauma," 41.

22. Ibid.

23. Dieter F. Uchtdorf, "The Merciful Obtain Mercy," *Ensign*, May 2012.

24. Gordon B. Hinckley, "How Can I Become the Woman of Whom I Dream?" *New Era*, Nov. 2001.

25. Thomas S. Monson, "Called to the Work," *Ensign*, June 2017.

ACKNOWLEDGMENTS

Words cannot express my gratitude to each person who took the time to share his or her story with me. Each story—even if it was not included in this book—increased my understanding of the early homecoming phenomena. This book would not have happened without these individuals. I am also incredibly grateful to the many people who reviewed chapters of this book and provided valuable feedback at various stages in my own revision process before submitting the manuscript to Cedar Fort Publishing and Media. Their frank, yet encouraging, feedback helped me make this book a true resource.

I am also very grateful for the team at Cedar Fort who believed in this idea from the moment I pitched it to Lorraine Gaufin at LDS Publishing and Media Association's 2017 conference and made it into a beautiful finished product. I am especially grateful to Esther Raty and Jessica Pettit for answering so politely my steady stream of questions; Jeff Harvey and his team for their amazing work on the cover; Vikki Downs for her enthusiasm and marketing advice; and Kaitlin Barwick, Justin Greer, and Melissa Caldwell for their superb editing.

I am also grateful to Dr. Kristine Doty-Yells for her interest and belief in this project, for emailing me her published works pertaining to early homecomings, and for making herself available for questions as they came up. I also appreciate her kindness in reading the manuscript in one of its earlier stages and still writing the foreword!

I am thankful to my family and friends for their encouragement and support in all its forms: from a kind text of encouragement to letting me talk a certain idea out with them. I am especially grateful to my husband, James, for being my main cheerleader even as my evenings and Saturdays became consumed with this project.

Finally, I am indebted to my Heavenly Father and Jesus Christ who provided miracles and opened doors for me every step of the way with this book. They didn't make it easy, and there was a time when I nearly gave up, but there was always something or someone they put into my path to make this book possible. I felt the Spirit guiding me during every writing and editing session. Truly, without Them, this book would not have happened.

ABOUT THE AUTHOR

Kristen Danner Reber served a mission in the Philippines from October 2010 to April 2011. Two parasites derailed her plans to serve the expected eighteen months, and she struggled for years with feelings of failure. She graduated from Brigham Young University in April 2014 with a bachelor's degree in English and minors in editing and psychology. She has since become the operations manager for LDS Publishing and Media Association (LDSPMA) where she enjoys working closely with many professionals in publishing and media fields. Kristen also enjoys doing freelance writing and editing work, and most notably has published two articles with the *Ensign*. When she's not writing or editing, you'll likely find Kristen playing her harp or engrossed in a book. Kristen married James Reber in 2013 in the Manti Utah Temple. They live in Washington state with their two children.

Scan to visit

earlyhomecoming.com

Scan to visit

kristenreber.com